POPERINGHE
YPRES
COURTRAI
AUDENARDE
CASSEL
MENIN
HALLUIN
ST OMER
BAILLEUL
HAZEBROUCK
TOURCOING
ROUBAIX
ARMENTIERES
AIRE
LILLE
ATH
TOURNAI
Lillers
BETHUNE
LA BASSEE
CARVIN
LENS
CONDE
ST POL
DOUAI
VALENCIENNES
ARRAS
LE QUESNOY
DOULLENS
CAMBRAI
SOLESMES
BAPAUME
LE CATEAU
ALBERT
LE CATELET
AMIENS
PÉRONNE
ST QUENTIN

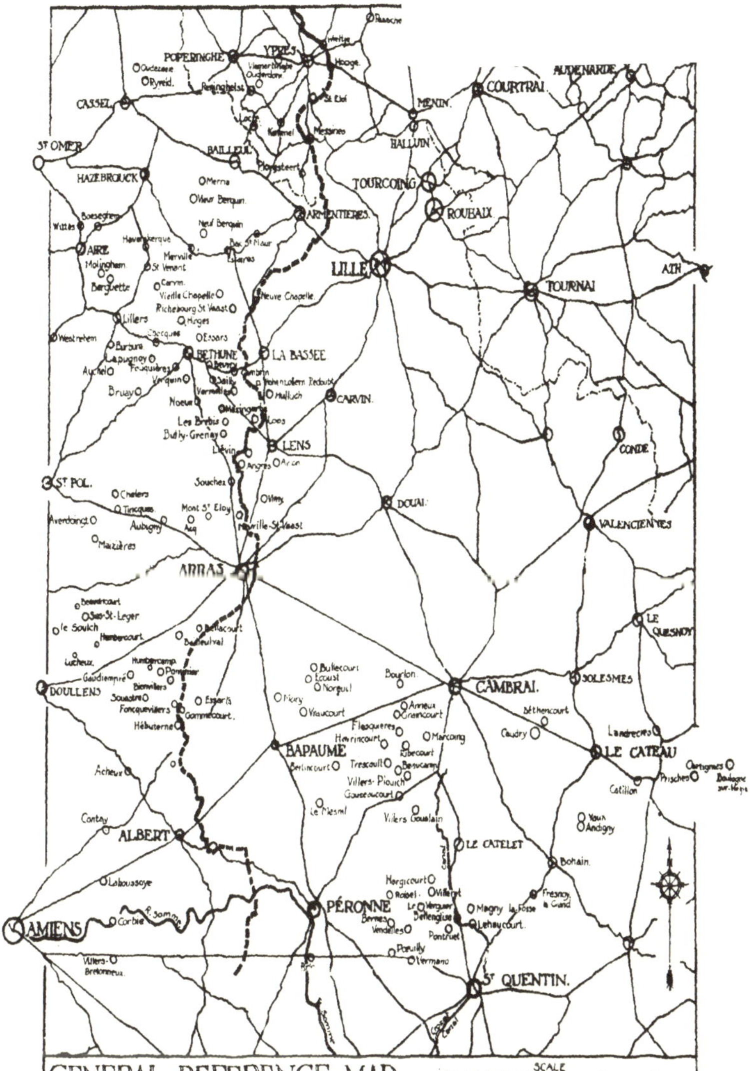

GENERAL REFERENCE MAP.

SCALE
Miles

59th DIVISION

1915 - 1918.

CHESTERFIELD.

Wilfred Edmunds, Limited, Printers

1928.

Printed and bound by Antony Rowe Ltd, Eastbourne

FOREWORD.

By Lieut.-Genl. Sir Cecil F. Romer, K.B.E., C.B., C.M.G.

This book is not intended to be a history of the 59th Division. It is something much more modest, being a collection of reminiscences and descriptions by various individuals. Such as it is, I feel sure it will interest former members of the Division and help to bring back to their memory the stirring scenes of 1915—18 and the figures of many an old comrade.

In any case, our thanks are due to Colonel E. U. Bradbridge, without whose perseverance and energy the book would never have been born; and to Captain G. J. Edmunds, formerly captain of "A" Company, 2/6th Bn. Sherwood Foresters, without whose good will the book would never have been printed.

C. F. Romer.

Aldershot, 1927. Lt.-Genl.

INDEX.

ILLUSTRATIONS.

FIFTY-NINTH DIVISION,

1915—1918.

By LT.-COL. E. U. BRADBRIDGE.

It may be of interest if I state how these accounts of some of the doings of the 59th North Midland Division came to be compiled.

I was invalided towards the end of the War, and I had time to worry various likely people to write some records of the Division. I have been worrying them from 1919 until 1926, and now I am sure I may express the thanks of all of us to the Authors of the following reminiscences.

Some phases of the life of the Division which came particularly under my own observation are:

1. The Beginning of the Division.

In January, 1915, three people assembled at the Crown Hotel, Luton, Brig.-Gen. H. McCall, C.B., Lt.-Col. Heyworth Savage (G.S.O.I.) and Major E. U. Bradbridge (D.A.A.G.). A telegram arrived from the War Office—" Are you prepared to receive troops?" We replied to the effect that we awaited them. 10,000 all ranks were sent to us from their counties in ten days. It was the Civil Police of Luton who enabled the Division to be received and billeted.

2. The Equipment of the Division.

There was absolute lack of all kinds of military equipment, and all available stores were, naturally, issued to the troops at the front; therefore, we had to improvise and requisition from civilian sources. Fortunately, we were near London, and I was constantly at the War Office persuading my old friends of the Army Ordnance Department to part with their rare articles of Ordnance Stores and Clothing. We had taken over the requisitioned civilian transport vehicles and harness left behind by our 1st Line, 46th Division. Within our own Division were many men who came from the leather works and boot factories in Leicester. We assembled them and organised a harness factory and boot repairing shops; by this means we were able to improvise transport and gun team harness.

It was vital to organise an efficient Divisional Ordnance Staff. I begged for some ranks of the Regular Army Ordnance Department, and was fortunate to get Capt. Webster, who had been with me (as an N.C.O.) in the South African War.

In the autumn of 1915 the "Q" side of the Division was put to a severe test by the searching inspection (over four days) of Major-Gen. Landon, of the War Office. He reported the Division as organised for War. We were, therefore, the first of the Second Line Divisions to be ready for service. We were detailed as the Mobile Division for Defence of the Coast.

3. The Trials of the Division.

During the last months of 1915 and the first of 1916 we were subjected to various (true) rumours of our embarkation for service overseas, but, unfortunately, our state of readiness was the cause of the Division being sent to quell the rebellion in Dublin at Easter, 1916. The Division moved to embark at Liverpool at a few hours' notice (by telephone).

Our duties in Ireland were the most unpleasant that soldiers can be called upon to perform. The chief trial at Divisional Headquarters was that we maintained, against the local Military Authorities, that we were a Division training for War, whereas they (the Command) considered us as reinforcements for their provincial district commands. In spite of the vigorous protests of General Sandbach, our Brigades were put under the local district commands throughout Ireland for command and training. The Divisional General had not even the power of confirmation of Courts Martial within his own Division.

At this time we were again called upon to supply large drafts for the 1st Line Division. The consequence of all this was that when we were at last embarked for France we were not really so good a Division as when we landed in Ireland.

Although we were " the Army of Occupation in Ireland," there was no reason why we should not have been allowed to train for war as a Division.

As a result of this policy in Ireland, we landed in France never having been trained for a single day as a complete War Division. (See General Romer's Account.)

Immediately on landing we were thrust straight into the front line and within a week were carrying out mobile operations in pursuit of the Germans in their retirement to the Hindenburg Line. No praise is sufficient for the Brigade and Unit Commanders who did not fail under this unprecedented trial.

I should like here to express the thanks that I always feel for the help and advice that Major-Gen. Sir P. Hambro, the D.Q.M.G. of III. Corps, gave me at this time. He detailed the Ammunition Column and the Divisional Train of the 1st (Regular) Division to help us supply our units. Our first severe engagements were in assault of what proved to be outposts of the Hindenburg Line; we did not capture them, and they were never overrun until the final advance in 1918.

After this trial we were taken out of the Line, and at last trained as a Division for War.

4. Personalities of the Division.

In the improvisation of Armies in Britain in 1914-18, is the right value given to the services performed by the OLD Officers and N.C.O.'s—so-called " dug-outs?" In the 59th Division, during its first vital nine months of existence, there were not more than 10 or 12 ex-Regular Officers, and no " serving " Regular Officers at all amongst 25,000 all ranks.

Of all the other officers, about half were civilians of no military training, and the other half had served, or were serving, various periods in the Territorial Army. There must have been real soundness in the martial spirit and military training of the old Regular and Territorial Army for the leaven of these few officers to have formed the efficiency of the new Division.

Brig.-Gen. H. McCall, for instance (since deceased), was 72 when he took command, yet his idea of military discipline and his administration of it guided the first steps of the Division; or Brig.-Gen. L. R. Carleton, who had been brought up in, and commanded one of the best Line Regiments—the Essex Regiment—he would not allow the Division to run before he had taught it to walk in the right way; or Brig.-Gen. A. H. C. Phillpotts and Col. the Hon. G. A. Anson, who reproduced that wonderful Battery spirit and organisation, in spite of museum guns and home-made harness; or Major-Gen. R. R. Reade, who typified the forcefulness of the Regular Army in matters of training; or Brig.-Gen. G. M. Jackson and Brig.-Gen. H. Chandos-Pole-Gell, whose Territorial training, added to their fine British personalities, made Brigades; and Brig.-Gen. T. W. Stansfeld, who showed a Brigade how it should act in war.

Then the many civilians—distinguished in their civil occupations, like Major E. Parker-Jervis, who would not believe that his business training was just what made him so excellent a Staff Captain R.A.; or the other Staff Captains, Langley, Lee, Staniforth and Hart-Davis, who soon showed that military matters would yield to correct civil methods.

Major-Gen. A. E. Sandbach, whose correct military instincts made him fight for the Division against the greater military heirarchy; and Lieut.-Gen. Sir C. F. Romer, who by experience, with calm assurance and certainty, finally perfected and used the Division, passing that unfailing test, "the satisfaction of all ranks."

Maj.-Gen. Sir Nevill M. Smyth, V.C., K.C.B.,

Commanded the Division from August, 1918, to July, 1919

Lieut.-Colonel E. U. Bradbridge,

D.A.A. & Q.M.G., afterwards A.A. & Q.M.G. of the Division from January, 1915, to June, 1917, subsequently A.Q.M.G. 4th Army Corps.

By MAJOR-GENERAL A. E. SANDBACH, C.B., D.S.O.,

On Easter Monday, April 24th, 1916, the 59th Division lay in its billets in and around St. Albans, Watford, Hemel Hempstead, Luton, Wheathampstead, and other towns and hamlets in Hertfordshire. It was training in preparation for being sent overseas.

But on the afternoon of that Monday strange things were happening in Dublin. The Fairy House Races of the Meath Hunt took place as usual, on Easter Monday, and on their return from the races, motor cars were held up and shots were fired in the air, and there was an angry appearance of disturbance. In fact, the Irish Rebellion of 1916 had begun.

As soon as the news reached London, the G.O.C. 59th Division was warned by telephone to send first one Infantry Brigade with some details, and afterwards the whole Division, to serve under the orders of General Sir John Maxwell in quelling the rising.

Sir John Maxwell had lately returned to England from Egypt, and was promptly sent over to command the forces in Ireland by the Secretary of State for War, Lord Kitchener, as soon as the rebellion broke out.

It was a curious coincidence that the 59th Division at that time was the "mobile Division" of the Home Army, detailed to repel a possible German invasion on the East Coast, and railway trains required to convey the troops to the coast at short notice were held in readiness in the sidings at Watford and at other stations, and could, of course, be diverted quickly to any other destination.

The Sherwood Foresters (178th) Brigade, commanded by Brigadier-General E. W. S. K. Maconchy, C.B., C.I.E., D.S.O., was selected as the first Brigade to proceed to Ireland. They were railed to Liverpool, where they embarked, and landed at Kingstown on Tuesday, 25th April. They met with stubborn opposition on their march from Kingstown to Dublin, especially in Northumberland Road, where a house covering the bridge over the Grand Canal was occupied by the rebels. The total casualties of this advanced Brigade were approximately five officers and 150 other ranks. The Brigade eventually occupied quarters at the Royal Hospital, Kilmainham.

Meanwhile during the night of 25/26th April the Staffordshire (176th) Brigade, under Brigadier-General L. R. Carleton, D.S.O., left St. Albans for Ireland.

The Headquarters of the Division moved with the Lincoln and Leicester (177th) Brigade, under Brigadier-General C. G. Blackader, C.B., D.S.O., and the Divisional Artillery, under Brigadier-General E. J. R. Peel, and landed at Kingstown on Friday, April 28th.

The Divisional Commander took over command of the defences of Kingstown, and reported to Sir John Maxwell at Irish Command Headquarters in Dublin.

On 29th April Headquarters occupied an empty Girls' School at Ballsbridge, near the grounds where the world-famous Dublin Horse Show is held yearly in August. There was some opposition still in this area, but rebel houses were soon cleared out.

Divisional Headquarters were soon established in the house of the Chief Secretary in the Phœnix Park, opposite to Vice Regal Lodge, with offices for the staff in North Circular Road. Later on the troops went under canvas in the Phœnix Park.

A battalion of the North Staffords had some trouble with rebels in King Street in North Dublin, and were afterwards accused of looting a jeweller's shop. The good name of the Division was, however, cleared, as it was proved that the looting was done by the Irish populace.

One incident occurred soon after our arrival in Dublin which might have had serious consequences. The Commander of the Forces ordered the Division to furnish a double line of sentries from Northumberland Road right up to the entrance to Dublin Castle. No one was to be allowed to cross this line without a permit signed by the Command Headquarters. One of our young sentries in the Merrion Square area saw a motor car approaching with two occupants at full speed. He challenged and ordered the motor car to stop. As it continued to approach the line of sentries, he fired and smashed the wind screen. Then the car stopped, and it turned out that it contained Sir H . . . . P . . . . and Mr. P . . . . on their way to Dublin Castle to organise food arrangements for the civil population. At a subsequent Court of Inquiry the sentry was acquitted of all blame, because he had simply obeyed the orders of the Commander of the Forces.

Flying Columns were sent out from Dublin to the North and West and South, in case of further risings in the country. But all was reported quiet after a few weeks of marching hither and thither. In fact, it is my opinion that conscription in Ireland could have been put into force at any time during the summer of 1916, with good results; because the Irishmen as a whole were ashamed of the rebellion, and because, as they dearly love fighting, they would have made good soldiers when they had been once enlisted and dressed in khaki uniform.

Later, in May, the 177th Infantry Brigade was sent to Fermoy; the 178th Infantry Brigade and Artillery were sent to the Curragh; two battalions of the 176th Brigade were left in Dublin, the other two battalions being sent to the Belfast district.

Divisional Headquarters were established at the Curragh, and the Divisional Commander occupied Ballyfair House, and took over command of all the troops, including Cavalry details, at the Curragh, from Brigadier-General Lowe.

Sir John French, as C.-in-C. Home Forces, made a tour of inspection of the Military establishments in Ireland. He reviewed the Division on the great open area on the Curragh. We managed to collect, from their outstations, two Brigades of Infantry, most of the Divisional Artillery, the Divisional Cavalry Squadron (Northumberland Hussars), the Field Companies R.E. and the Train. It was a real old-fashioned review and march past, carried out by the young soldiers in fine style. The horses,* which had been in our charge for nearly two years, were a splendid type and in

* *Unfortunately the horses were ordered to be left behind when we embarked for France—we were given much inferior animals just before embarkation; this had an almost disastrous effect in our first operations against the Germans during their retreat to the Hindenburg Line.*

perfect condition. The praise of the veteran Field Marshal was unstinted and well earned.

Drafts of officers and men were sent away to France during the summer. We sent of our best, and the Division was drained of the men we had hoped to take to France with us.

Recruits were received in their place, with the result that when we finally proceeded to France we were not so good a Division as when we landed in Ireland. We had been diverted from the immediate prospect of facing the Germans, to face our own countrymen.

Training progressed in the smaller formations. The circumstances were, however, most difficult with the Brigades spread over Ireland. The Artillery made use of that splendid practice ground at Glen Imaal. But we never had any chance of training, as a complete Division, for the war then being fought out in France. At length, in January, 1917, orders arrived for the Division to move to Salisbury Plain and train for overseas. We occupied quarters at Fovant, but never trained as a Division. On 13th February, 1917, His Majesty the King inspected the Division, and on 23rd February, 1917, we proceeded overseas to France.

PLAN No 1
FIGHTING IN DUBLIN
ON APRIL 26TH 1916.

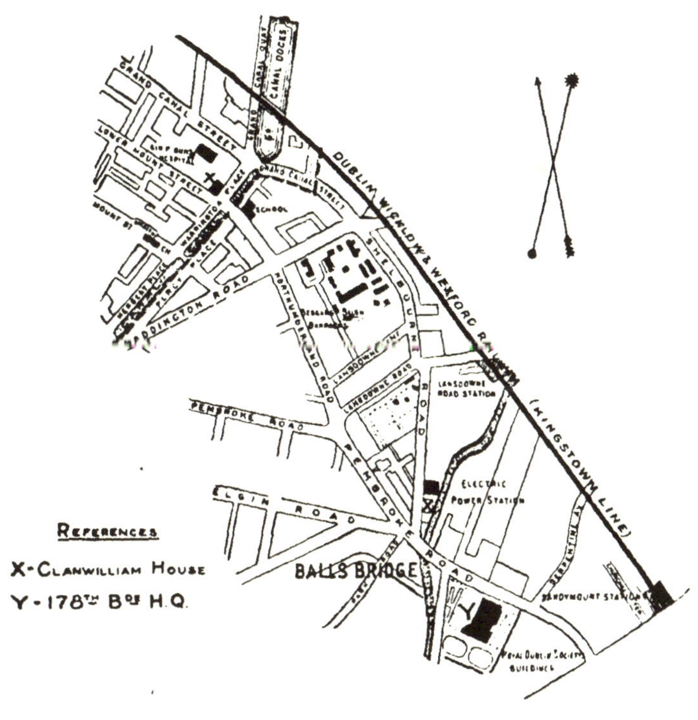

SCALE 6" 1MILE.

880' 440' 220' 0

By courtesy of Lieut.-Col. Oates, D.S.O., from the History of the 2/8th Battalion Sherwood Foresters.

By LIEUT.-GEN. SIR C. F. ROMER, K.B.E., C.B., C.M.G.

Owing to various circumstances, the Division had been given no opportunity of completing its training before being sent out to France in the early part of 1917. Before its departure from England it had been inspected, and the report of the Inspecting Officer was to the effect that the Division could be considered as only partially trained. Unluckily, on its arrival in France, it was not possible to give it time to train in one of the rest areas, but it was sent straight up to the front and put in the line South of the Somme, near Estrees, where it experienced its initiation into the mysteries of trench warfare, and gained lessons concerning mud, gas, crumps, and such like evils.

Major-General Sandbach was commanding the Division at this time, and he was fortunate in having as his G.S.O.I. Lt.-Colonel R. St. G. Gorton, to whose knowledge and devotion the 59th Division owes much of its success. Lt.-Colonel E. U. Bradbridge was the A.Q.M.G., and, aided by his two subordinates, Major Stanton and Captain Chapman, looked after the well-being and comfort of all ranks. The above officers were all Regulars, but it is interesting that several important appointments were held by officers who had had no previous experience of the intricacies of military administration. The Principal Medical Officer, Colonel Dent, was before the war a much-visited doctor in the Midlands; the Veterinary Officer, Lt.-Col. Coe, was well-known in the Leicestershire hunting fields; while the D.A.D.O.S., Major Dodds, was a business man, although after a very short residence in France there were few articles he could not screw out of the Base. It was sometimes a little difficult to reconcile the military and civilian methods. The O.C. a Field Ambulance, on being told by the Divisional Commander that he must improve the discipline of his unit, apologised by pointing out, " It is not easy to be very strict when all the N.C.O.'s and half the men are my patients at home."

The Division had not been long in the line when the Germans suddenly retired across the Somme (March, 1917), and, of course, the British troops at once pushed forward in pursuit. The Division now felt its lack of training, for it was engaged in very difficult operations, necessitating ceaseless and bold patrolling, constant initiative on the part of subordinates and accurate judgment on the part of Brigade and Battalion Commanders. The tactical situation was difficult enough, but units had, in addition, to contend with the utter absence of communications, for the Germans had destroyed the railways, roads, bridges, houses and wells. The transport of food, ammunition and stores threw a great strain on the administrative services, and also on the horses. The casualties among the latter were severe, and it took months before the survivors were restored to condition. However, the difficulties, both technical and administrative, were triumphantly surmounted, thanks to the gallantry of the troops and the ceaseless labour of the staff—not that success was gained without mistakes being made and losses suffered. Jeancourt was captured by a fine attack, but then came a repulse at Le Verguier, which the 178th Brigade assaulted at night before the wire protecting the German trenches had been cut.

Divisional Headquarters were moved to the ruined village of St. Cren, where somewhat indifferent accommodation was found in cellars, tumbled-down houses and huts. In the second week of April, Headquarters were moved to a large farm outside Bouvincourt; but the fact that this was the only building left intact by the Germans gave rise to suspicion of it being mined. There had been several instances of dug-outs and buildings being blown up by means of delay-action fuzes—a form of humour that must have appealed to the German mind—and, accordingly, it was thought safer to move away from the building into tents and huts. Captain Whitehead, the Camp Commandant, soon had a comfortable camp; his energy was wonderful, both on this and other occasions he was to be seen busy mending roads, burning manure heaps (with which the country was cursed), filling in trenches, etc. He had several valuable qualities which endeared him to his Divisional Commander and his colleagues, but one of the most useful was his "flair" for discovering asparagus beds in the most unlikely places. It was evident that with such abilities he could not be allowed to remain a captain, and later on he was given command of a Labour Group with the rank of Lieutenant-Colonel.

During April and May there were many changes in the higher ranks of the Division. Major-General Romer became, on April 8th, the Divisional Commander; Brigadier-Generals Currie and Stansfeld took over command of the 176th and 178th Brigades respectively; and Brigadier-General Stirling came as C.R.A. General Currie was soon claimed for another appointment, although during the few months he was with the 176th Brigade he did much for the training of the battalions under him. Generals Stansfeld and Stirling, however, stayed with the Division until the end, and it would be difficult to over-estimate what the Division owed to them, for there can never have been more popular and efficient commanders.

Meanwhile, there had been constant skirmishes and minor attacks. A proposed attack on Le Verguier had been arranged, but the Germans interfered with the operations by retiring. Our line was pushed beyond the village, and local advances in this neighbourhood gave us further ground, although it was clear that the Germans were now fronting us in a strong trench system—the famous Hindenburg line. Further to the North a well executed night operation gave the 176th Brigade possession of Villeret, and this success was followed by an attack on the Hargicourt quarries. This attack, carried out by the 178th Brigade, was on a larger scale. Well supported by the artillery, it took place shortly before dawn and was successful, the 8th Sherwood Foresters, commanded by that fine veteran, Colonel Oates, playing a prominent part. Unluckily, an attempt to take a portion of the hostile trenches to the North of the quarries was not successful, for, although the attacking troops gained this objective, they were subsequently driven back by a counter-attack.

Arrangements were being made to advance our line closer to the main German trenches, when the Division was relieved by the cavalry, although the Divisional artillery and some of the infantry remained behind for a few days to help the cavalry. After a very short rest, Divisional Headquarters moved to Equancourt, where they were installed in Nissen huts and the Division took over the line opposite Havrincourt and Flesquieres. Although there was scope for active patrolling, the main task of the Division was to improve its trenches, and the infantry was busy in gradually pushing forward the line, digging new communication trenches and making defensive positions in the rear. All ranks worked hard, and had the satisfaction of being complimented by the Corps Commander for the improvements they had effected.

The Division, while still holding this part of the line, was transferred from the 3rd to the 4th Corps. On July 10th, however, it was relieved and marched to the Barastre area, where it was promised at last a month's stay for training. The unfortunate artillery was not allowed to accompany the rest of the Division, but had to stay in the line—a fate which almost invariably befell it.

Full advantage was taken of the rest. Barastre lay in the centre of the Somme battlefield, and was an ideal area for training. All around it was a desert, so that field firing and machine gun practice could take place without interference. There were innumerable trenches, and the whole Division could practise a trench-to-trench attack on the largest scale, while the bombing and Stokes-Mortar experts could blaze away to their hearts' content. But due attention was also paid to the lighter side of the soldiers' life, and football, boxing, sports, horse shows, and rifle meetings offered a varied enough fare to suit all tastes.

The horse shows were very popular, especially when a few races formed part of them. It is true that most of the races were won by the Transport Officer of the 178th Brigade, Capt. "Bill" Wright; but his rivals always lived in hope of "doing him down,' 'and anyhow there was always the fun of trying to pump the innocent-looking "Bill" as to his chances. On one historic occasion General Stansfeld and his Brigade-Major, Major Hodgson (familiarly known as "By-gum-and-by-crike"—a M.F.H., no less!) drove on to the course in a "four-in-hand"—at least there were four horses in front of a "G.S. wagon, mark VI.," and on the latter a retainer dressed in a red coat and top hat, obtained Heaven knows where.

Then, too, there were tours to the battlefields of 1916, usually conducted by General James, who, in return for his trouble, justly claimed all " trophies " found on the ground. What wonderful salvage work he did perform! For months afterwards no officer of the 177th Brigade left for England without conveying a more or less bulky parcel for his Brigadier.

It was at Barastre that Brigadier-General Cope took over command of the 176th Brigade from Brigadier-General Currie, who was appointed Commandant of the Staff College at Cambridge. Under General Currie's guidance the 176th Brigade had made great progress in military efficiency and, we must not omit to add, in bugling, for the Brigadier had done his best to introduce proper "Light Infantry" methods. Who that were at Barastre in July, 1917, will forget those Staffordshire buglers' heroic efforts to blow in a " smart and soldier-like manner?" The air resounded with the din. As for the Divisional Commander, whenever he approached the 176th Brigade Camp he was confronted by the problem whether it was necessary to encourage the buglers by allowing four " quarter-guards " to blow one after the other a General Salute, while he, in the words of the poet, " suffered and was strong," or better to put spurs to his horse and flee.

About this period Major Jasper Ridley attached himself to the Division. He applied in the usual official way to be sent as a " learner," and the G.O.C., not knowing him, refused. But he showed that he possessed wonderful perseverance and initiative (very valuable qualities in a staff officer) by turning up one day and calmly assuming the duties of D.A.Q.M.G. Not only did he insist on joining the Division, but he also managed to include himself in the G.O.C.'s mess, where for many weeks he laid down the law on politics, strategy, and other subjects, until the arrival of Lt.-Colonel R. B. Airey brought him a rival with an even greater fluency of speech and equally decided opinions.

The Division had long known that the training at Barastre was for a definite purpose; that it was, in fact, to use the soldiers' phrase, being " fattened up " for the purpose of taking part in the big offensive at Ypres. It was not, however, until towards the end of August that the orders for the transfer to the 5th Army came, and the Division moved by 'bus and train, via Acheux to Flanders, where it went, on September 1st, into billets around Winnezeele. Here it continued to train, but with the added advantage of the supervision of the Army Commander (General Sir Hubert Gough) and his staff, thus obtaining the latest experience gained from the recent fighting. The Divisional Artillery now came up to the Ypres salient, and the infantry had the satisfaction of knowing that their attack would be prepared and supported by their own gunners. The Divisional Commander especially felt relieved to have in the coming battle General Stirling as his artillery adviser.

Orders for a big attack on September 20th were issued, and the Division was told to be prepared to relieve after the battle the 55th Division, which was in the centre opposite Gravenstafel. The attack of September 20th was most successful, and the 55th Division gained practically all its objectives. Immediately after the battle the 59th Division was ordered to relieve the 55th, and the infantry brigades at once began to move up. While the battalions were marching towards Ypres, the Divisional Staff was busy with the orders for the impending attack to take place on the 26th, and in planning objectives, distribution of the troops, the artillery barrage, and the many other matters which have to be settled before a "set" attack. It was arranged that the 177th Brigade should be on the right, the 178th on the left, and the 176th in reserve. Nor must we forget to mention the good work done by the administrative staffs of the Division and brigades and by the train. In the accounts of battles it is usually only the fighting troops whose exploits are recorded, but it is not they alone who are called upon to face death. None of those who remember the shell-swept road to Wieltje will withhold praise from the drivers and working parties, who night after night toiled to bring up to their comrades in the line the ammunition, food and stores.

On the afternoon of the 23rd the Division was concentrated round the "Gold Fish Chateau," and as soon as night fell the infantry filed off through Ypres. The relief of the 55th Division was accomplished without any hitch; but during the 24th it became clear, from the aeroplane reconnaissance and the reports of Company Commanders that the line taken over from the 55th Division was not so far forward as had been supposed, and that, in particular, a group of concrete "pill-boxes" was still in the hands of the enemy. This necessitated an alteration, at very short notice, in the artillery barrage.

Divisional Headquarters occupied on the afternoon of the 25th dug-outs on the Eastern bank of the Ypres canal. They formed very good battle headquarters, being almost immune from shell or bomb, but they had the disadvantage of being only 200 yards in front of two 6-inch guns. The latter maintained a dignified, slow, but constant bombardment; and every time one of them fired the dug-outs shook to their foundations, all articles of glass or crockery were hurled to the ground, and candles were snuffed out. Luckily, no one wanted to sleep, for there was too much to do. In the early hours of the 26th reports were received from the three Brigades that the troops were in position. Then the preliminary bombardment burst out, to be followed by an even more intensive fire at zero hour. There ensued an anxious period of waiting for reports from the front to say whether the attack had been successful. Captain Bowen, the G.S.O. 3, had been sent out to a point of vantage, from where he could see the field of operations, but he was unluckily wounded at an early hour. Soon, however, reliable news reached Divisional Headquarters, and it was ascertained that the 177th and 178th Brigades had reached all their objectives. This was most satisfactory, but it still remained to hold the captured positions and resist the inevitable German counter-attack. There was an anxious period for the Divisional Staff when, during the afternoon, the enemy put down a heavy barrage on our line, and alarming rumours came in to the effect that our first line had been driven back. For some time it was impossible to find out what had happened, and it was not until after nightfall that definite reports removed our cause for alarm. It was then ascertained that the positions captured in the early morning had been maintained, with the exception of a small advanced post, and the German counter-attack had been repulsed. What had happened was that during this hostile barrage some of the troops in the rear positions had wavered, although those in the front and support lines stood firm, and started to retire, but thanks to the energy of Generals James and Stansfeld and their staffs, order was re-established.

As the situation gradually became quiet, save for considerable shelling, the G.O.C. decided, on September 30th, to leave his battle headquarters and go back to a quieter spot in a wood behind Ypres called Mersey Camp. But, alas! the new quarters were just as unfavourable to sleep as the old ones, for it being bright moonlight the enemy's aeroplanes were busy all night dropping bombs round the wood. The same thing happened the next night, and altogether the Divisional Staff had no very pleasant recollections of Mersey Camp Wood.

It was decided that the Division, which had suffered over 2,000 casualties, should not take part in the next attack, and accordingly it was relieved on the 29th September by the New Zealanders. At first there was some idea of the Division being transferred to the 14th Corps for operations against Houthulst Forest, but finally the unlucky artillery alone was sent while the rest of the Division moved by slow stages to the Lens area.

Here it relieved the 1st Canadian Division in the trenches and settled down to a comparatively quiet existence. There was, naturally, plenty of work to do in getting the trenches ready for the winter, but the enemy was not aggressive, and with the exception of a few minor raids on our part and an occasional outburst of artillery activity, nothing worth recording took place. Divisional Headquarters were at Chateau-de-la-Haie, a comfortable house well concealed among woods, and the Brigade in reserve was also at the same place.

Early in November the G.O.C. was confidentially informed by General Fanshawe, commanding the 5th Corps, that the Division was to move to Bapaume in order to help exploit the success which it was expected would be gained by the 3rd Army's attack of November 20th towards Cambrai. General Fanshawe explained the course which the operations might take and the part the Division would probably play, and as a result of this interview the G.O.C. carried out with each Brigade a series of tactical exercises in order to make battalion commanders understand the difference between "open warfare" and trench to trench attacks such as they had carried out recently.

The Canadians again took over the Lens front, and on November 17th the Division began its march towards Bapaume. The movement was carried out by night in order to avoid the observation of the German aeroplanes. On November 20th Divisional Headquarters were at Basseux, where they spent the day trying to hear of the result of the 3rd Army's attack and anxiously expecting orders to march to the battlefield. But the turn of the Division had not yet come and it only moved that night to Achiet-le-Petit. From here it proceeded, on the 23rd, to Etricourt, when it came under the orders of the 3rd Corps, which was fighting on the far side of Gouzeaucourt and Gonnelieu. After spending two or three days reconnoitring the 3rd Corps' front, the Division was suddenly transferred to the 4th Corps and ordered to relieve the Guards in Bourlon Wood. The relief was completed by the morning of the 29th November, and Divisional Headquarters were established in a camp of "Armstrong" huts on the slope South of Trescault.

The Germans had by now recovered from the surprise of the 20th and there was a considerable amount of shelling, but nothing important happened until the morning of 1st December, when the enemy began a heavy bombardment of the British front line and back areas—a sure sign of a hostile counter-attack. Bourlon Wood, which formed a salient in the British line, was deluged with gas shells, and Lt.-Colonel Stuart-Wortley's South Staffords had many casualties, but our artillery had promptly put down a barrage on the enemy's front and the 176th Brigade, in spite of the German bombardment, easily repulsed a rather half-hearted counter-attack. This news had just reached the Divisional Headquarters, who were congratulating themselves on such a satisfactory result, when the astounding report came in that the Germans had captured Gouzeaucourt and Gonnelieu and were advancing Westwards. This created a very critical situation, because the enemy was now threatening the rear of the 59th Divison, which was facing North. Unluckily, the German bombardment had destroyed most of the telegraph lines. It was impossible to communicate with the 4th Corps or with the neighbouring Divisions except by motor car. Staff officers were despatched to obtain information and the G.O.C.'s two A.D.C.'s went towards Villers-Plouich in order to prevent Divisional Headquarters being surprised. Baggage waggons were packed and ordered to proceed through Metz and park off the road to await events. The village of Metz, which was the sole line of retreat, was being shelled and was moreover blocked by stragglers and transport. The A.P.M. of the 59th Division, Captain de Crespigny, did invaluable work throughout the day in Metz; kept the stream of transport moving, collected the stragglers and maintained order in spite of the constant shelling. Later on in the day the Guards' Division counter-attacked with marked success, and although unable to regain all the ground lost in the morning, they effectually removed the danger of a further German advance. It should be mentioned that in the morning of December 1st a Field Company of the 59th Division greatly distinguished itself. It was marching to rejoin the Division, without any idea of trouble, when, on reaching Gouzeaucourt it suddenly found that the German infantry was within a few hundred yards of the village. Although weak in numbers and with few available rifles, it gallantly helped to defend the village and, when driven back, successfully prevented the Germans from advancing further. Major Conlon, the Divisional Supply Officer, who also happened to arrive at Gouzeaucourt, performed meritorious service by bringing up ammunition to the Field Company in his motor car in the face of heavy fire. The Division, having repulsed the German counter-attack on its own front, was able to help the general cause by sending the 178th Brigade to strengthen the Division on the right.

The night of December 1st passed quietly except that a German gun disturbed the rest of the Divisional Staff by dropping a few shells every hour within 200 yards of the camp. This annoying habit was continued throughout the stay of the Headquarters at Trescault.

Although the enemy could make no further counter-attacks, it was not found possible to regain from him all the ground he had won on December 1st, and the situation of the British salient at Bourlon Wood remained undesirably dangerous. The 3rd Army therefore decided to adjust the line and make it safer by withdrawing from Bourlon Wood and the vicinity. The retirement, always a very delicate operation, was most successfully carried out by the 59th Division, which fell back to a position in front of Flesquieres. The Germans followed up our troops closely and even attempted to attack near Flesquieres, but they received a severe set back and suffered many casualties. After this rebuff they made no offensive of any sort, beyond artillery bombardments, and the next two or three weeks were spent by the Division in consolidating the new position. But although there was a good deal of digging to be done, the opportunities for bold patrolling were taken full advantage of. There were constant little skirmishes at night, and the Division was very successful in supplying the Corps Headquarters with prisoners.

As soon as the situation settled down, Divisional Headquarters had moved, on December 5th, from Trescault to a more comfortable hutted camp in "Little Wood," near Ytres. They did not stay here very long, but by order of the Corps moved, on the 16th, to the village of Ytres, in which good Divisional Headquarters had been rigged up among the ruined houses.

Towards the middle of December the weather turned very cold. There was a long, severe frost and snow covered the whole country. It made work on the new trenches a slow process and encouraged the German aeroplanes to visit our back areas during the hours of moonlight. They did little damage, but were the cause of a great deal of noise and consequent interruption to sleep. The Division, however, was cheered up by the news that Christmas was not to be spent in the trenches, but in a rest area far removed from the sound of shells.

The relief was carried out by the 23rd December, and the Division moved to Le Cauroy district. On this occasion the Divisional artillery came too, and enjoyed a well-earned rest after their hardships in the Ypres salient and vicinity of Cambrai. The snow was still thick upon the ground and it was difficult to do much training, but battalions and batteries began at once to "polish up." The Divisional Commander held a series of tactical exercises, and as soon as the snow went football competitions, team-races, etc., were started. The 178th Brigade Headquarters organised a scratch pack of hounds and shewed a real fox hunt. Amiens was not too far off, and the cooking of the Restaurant de la Cathedrale, or was it the presence of Marguerite, attracted many members of the Division.

But it was well that everybody should have a good time while possible, because it did not require very great acumen to see the danger clouds on the horizon.

The Division spent the whole of January in Le Cauroy area. On February 11th it took over the trenches on either side of Bullecourt, Divisional Headquarters being installed at Behagnies. It formed part of the 6th Corps of the 3rd Army and had the 6th Division on its right and the 3rd Division on its left.

The Division had not been long in this section of the line before signs of a German offensive on a large scale became evident in the shape of new roads, dumps, additional artillery positions and the testimony of prisoners. On our part, strenuous work was carried on in order to improve our defences, work which was carefully supervised by the Corps and Army Commanders. New lines were dug, additional communication trenches completed, strong posts created and guns withdrawn to "silent" positions. Raids were made on various parts of the German line in order to obtain prisoners, and valuable evidence was obtained. It became clear that the attack would take place before the end of March.

The German aeroplanes became very active, and on moonlight nights dropped bombs all over the district, on one occasion hitting the Divisional Headquarters camp, just before a very elaborate dug-out, the pride of the C.R.E., was completed. Our artillery was meanwhile enjoying itself by shelling German dumps, trying to smash the enemy's new roads, and putting down barrages at odd moments. The German artillery remained silent except for a most methodical registration on our trenches, which enabled our sound-ranging experts to discover every day additional hostile gun-positions. By the middle of March they informed the Divisional Commander that nearly 700 guns and howitzers of various calibres had registered our trenches, a fact which showed that when the storm did burst it would be serious.

On March 20th the 178th Brigade was holding the right sector of the Divisional line and the 176th Brigade the left sector, each having two battalions in the forward zone and one battalion in reserve. The actual front trenches were very lightly held and battalions were distributed in depth. The 177th Brigade formed the Divisional reserve and was in huts round Mory.

Soon after 4 a.m. on March 21st, a terrific bombardment broke out and our area was deluged with gas and shells of every calibre, including those of heavy trench-mortars. The effect of this artillery and mortar fire was to destroy our front systems. Between 8 and 9 a.m. the German infantry advanced, and by means of its superior numbers, helped by the overwhelming artillery fire, succeeded in breaking through our lines. Their principal effort was directed against the Noreuil Valley, the point where the 59th and 6th Divisions met, and they swept up the valley and then outflanked our defences. But the 178th and 176th Brigades and our forward artillery fought with the greatest heroism. Outnumbered, outflanked, and even surrounded, they fought on, regardless of self, delaying the German advance and thus giving priceless time for the arrival of reinforcements. Of the men of the two Brigades holding the trenches in front of Brigade Headquarters, less than 100 came back. The day of March 21st, 1918, will always be a glorious memory for the 59th Division. Among the many officers who were killed were Lt.-Col. Stuart-Wortley, of the 5th South Staffords, Lt.-Col. Thorne, of the 6th North Staffords, and Major Trench, of the Sherwood Foresters.

Meanwhile, the 177th Brigade had been ordered to counter-attack towards Noreuil. But the counter-attacking troops were themselves outflanked, and in view of the German superiority, it was decided to hold on to the second battle positions facing Ecoust. Here the three battalions of the 177th Brigade, reinforced by the Pioneer Battalion and the remnants of the machine-gun companies and aided effectually by the artillery, had to resist for many hours successive attacks carried out by masses of German infantry. Thanks to their steadfastness they repulsed these attacks, capturing prisoners belonging to three German Divisions and preventing a hostile "break-through." The critical nature of the situation can be judged from the fact that our artillery, even the heavies, were firing over open sights.

Late in the afternoon the leading troops of the 40th Division, which was in Corps reserve, came into the firing line and made the position almost secure. At 7 p.m. Major-General Ponsonby took over command and the 59th Division was officially relieved. But the 177th Brigade stayed in the line for a few more days and defended with great tenacity on the 22nd and 23rd the village of Mory, while the remnants of the 59th Divisional artillery, under that gallant veteran, Brig.-General Stirling, also remained, and, in fact, fought till the final exhaustion of the German attack.

For the next ten days Divisional Headquarters, accompanied by the remnants of the 176th and 178th Brigades, went through a period of wandering. On March 22nd they left Behagnies and fell back to huts near Bucquoy, but on the 23rd, for some unknown reason, they were ordered to Bouzincourt, just outside Albert. Here was witnessed the unusual spectacle of a panic in a Heavy Battery. About 9 p.m.—in the bright moonlight—some half-dozen "caterpillars" drawing 9.2 howitzers or 6-inch guns came thundering down the road, without their officers, under the impression that the Germans were close behind them. Luckily, the energetic Captain de Crespigny was on the spot and the panic was easily stopped by drawing the leading "caterpillar" across the road.

Late the next day Headquarters moved to Contay, whence they marched on the 26th to Fienvillers, a quiet village west of the St. Pol—Amiens Road. It was naturally expected that they had been ordered here to rest, refit, and receive reinforcements. But on the 28th they were directed to Labeuvrière, and having arrived there were told that there had been a mistake and the place allotted to the Division was Villers-Châtel. So on they proceeded to the latter place which provided comfortable quarters and where a few drafts joined. But the authorities again changed their minds and on the 1st the Division, joined now by the 177th Brigade, was railed up to the 2nd Army and put into huts and billets North of Poperinghe, the Headquarters being in Conthove Chateau.

Drafts were now able to reach the Division, which once more had fairly strong battalions, but the great majority of the men did not come from the Midlands and were strangers to each other and to their officers and N.C.O.'s. Unfortunately, the situation did not allow any time to train or make the Division an efficient unit, and on the 5th it took over a sector of the front line on the Passchendaele ridge. Divisional Headquarters were installed in the Ypres Ramparts, secure quarters and comfortable enough had there been any method of getting rid of the smoke from the fires.

The sector was a quiet one, although life was not very pleasant, as owing to the severe fighting of the previous autumn the ground was an awful wilderness of water-filled shell holes, but the very fact of being in the line made training impossible. Meanwhile, the Germans had captured Armentieres and were making a big push against Neuve-Eglise and Bailleul. The situation became so critical that it was found necessary to take the 59th Division from the Passchendaele sector and, in spite of its need for re-organisation, to send it into the fighting line.

By April 12th the Division, less the artillery, which was still with the 3rd Army, was concentrated round Brand-hoek, and on the 13th it moved towards the battle front. At this moment the Division suffered a great loss from the departure of Colonel R. St. G. Gorton, whose ability and loyalty had been of such value. He was replaced by Lieut.-Colonel G. Crossman. While the Division was actually moving, orders were received to send a Brigade to the 19th Division, which was fighting gallantly North of Neuve-Eglise, and the 178th Brigade was selected. On the 14th

Divisional Headquarters reached Westoutre, and the 176th and 177th Brigades moved into position of readiness behind Locre, where they spent the day under shell fire. Late in the afternoon the 9th Corps, to which the Division now belonged, issued orders for it to relieve at once the 34th Division. The latter was holding a position immediately in front of Bailleul, facing South, and had been attacked during the day. Scarcely any reconnaissance was possible, and moreover, owing to the day's fighting, it was hard to find out the exact line held by the 34th Division. But the relief was carried out, although daylight had come before the last units were in position.

The line held by the 176th and 177th Brigades was over 6,000 yards in extent, and the difficulty of taking over unreconnoitred positions in the dark had necessitated the use of all available men of both Brigades. The only reserve, Divisional or Brigade, was the Pioneer Battalion. In order to remedy such an unsatisfactory state of affairs it was hoped to thin out the front line and thus build up, at any rate, Brigade reserves; but the enemy interfered with this solution, for in the middle of the day a violent bombardment broke out, followed by an attack.

At first the battalions of the 176th and 177th Brigades successfully resisted the enemy's onslaught, and even when a small hill to the East of Bailleul was captured by the Germans, it was speedily regained by a smart counter-attack. But the attacks continued, and later in the afternoon the enemy succeeded in breaking through on the left of the line. He then moved along the ridge towards Bailleul, and gradually the whole of our line crumbled. Bailleul was lost and the two Brigades fell back in some confusion on the Division, which was holding trenches between Bailleul and Mont Noir. Darkness increased the confusion, and it was difficult for Divisional Headquarters to find out for some time what had happened. But it soon became evident that our losses were fairly heavy, and the Corps Commander ordered the 34th Division to take over the defences. During the battle Lieut.-Colonel Roffey was killed; a serious loss to the 177th Brigade, as he was an excellent battalion commander.

Lieut.-Gen. Sir Cecil F. Romer, K.B.E., C.B., C.M.G.

Commanded the Division from April, 1917, to June, 1918.

Major-Gen. A. E. Sandbach, C.B., D.S.O.

Commanded the Division from February, 1916, to April, 1917.

Mont Noir Chateau, where Divisional Headquarters were installed, was now being shelled by the enemy, and accordingly Headquarters moved to Westoutre. As the latter place in its turn became, on the 17th, the object of the enemy's artillery, the Staff took shelter in a small farm outside.

The Division was soon afterwards rejoined by the 178th Brigade, which had done excellent work with the 19th Division, and was attached to Lieut.-General Hunter-Weston's reserve corps. Divisional Headquarters proceeded on April 26th to Vogelje Convent, North of Poperinghe, and the Division was for the next fortnight engaged in digging new lines of defence. It had, however, been decided by the supreme authorities, that the wastage in the nation's man power necessitated the breaking up of some of the divisions, and the 59th was one of the victims. It was not to disappear, but was ordered to send away its existing battalions, which were to be replaced by B.1. units.

With this fate hanging over it, the Division moved back on May 6th to St. Omer, where the dreaded break up was accomplished. The battalions, North and South Staffords, Lincolns and Leicesters, and Sherwood Foresters, were bidden farewell by a sorrowing Divisional Staff, and were sent off by train to the base.

The 59th Division, it is true, remained, but it ceased to be the North Midlands.

THE 178th BRIGADE, 59th DIVISION.

By BRIG.-GEN. E. W. S. K. MACONCHY, C.B., C.M.G., C.I.E., D.S.O.

The 178th Brigade was formed from the 2nd line of the Notts. and Derby Territorials, and was first commanded by Col. Bemrose, who was succeeded in July, 1915, by Col. E. W. S. K. Maconchy, C.B., C.I.E., D.S.O., when the units were in camp at Dunstable. It was then officially designated the "2nd First Notts. and Derby Brigade," and was composed of the 5th, 6th, 7th and 8th Battalions of the second line and styled the 2nd Sherwood Foresters Brigade. The 2nd North Midland Division, of which it formed a part, was then under the command of Brig.-Gen. H. McCall, C.B., with Headquarters at St. Albans.

The Commanders of the Battalions at this time were:—

5th Battalion, Major Aitchison;
6th Battalion, Major Clayton;
7th Battalion, Capt. Payne;
8th Battalion, Lieut.-Col. Coape-Oates;

of whom only the last-named was an officer of the Regular Army (retired).

A strenuous system of training was instituted at Dunstable, and all ranks responded with the greatest zeal and energy.

Between the 9th and 11th August, 1915, the Brigade marched (in two detachments owing to shortage of transport) to camp at Watford, in Cassiobury Park; and from thence on August 15th a draft of 260 men from the Brigade was sent to reinforce the 1st line in France. They were an exceptionally fine lot of men, and went off in high spirits.

At Watford four large parks in the neighbourhood were placed at the disposal of the Brigade. These afforded excellent training grounds, and full opportunity was taken of the facilities thus provided.

At a very early stage instruction in bombing was started, and here the composition of the Territorials proved very valuable owing to the number of officers and men who were accustomed to handling explosives in mines and other professions in civil life. The bombs were made out of jam and other tins at first, and no precautions were taken. In spite of this no accidents occurred, although bits of tin flew freely about, and more than once the Brigadier and the bombing officer received clods of earth in their faces. A spectacular display of an attack and defence between opposing lines of trenches in Moor Park with bombs and mines was given before a distinguished party of visitors—fortunately without any mishap. This instruction in bombing stood the Brigade in good stead afterwards in Ireland, and the casual manner in which the men had been accustomed to treat bombs did much to prevent any nervousness in throwing the Mills bombs afterwards.

Troop trains were provided in sidings at Watford, Berkhampstead and Boxmoor for instruction in entraining, and the Brigade was very carefully practised in these duties.

In September the zeppelin raids began, and as Watford lay on the route of the raiders to London special arrangements had to be made and alarm stations allotted to each battalion. Arrangements were also made with the municipal authorities for the organisation of hospital centres and fire brigades. No bombs were, however, ever dropped on Watford, although many nights were spent by the troops at their alarm stations.

On September 15th the whole Division was reviewed by General McCall in Gorhambury Park, near St. Albans, and it was again inspected at the same place on October 1st by General Sir H. M. Leslie Rundle, G.C.B., G.C.M.G., G.C.V.O., D.S.O.

Throughout the autumn field days between the different Brigades of the Division were organised by the Divisional Staff, and provided very useful exercises.

On October 18th the Brigade evacuated the Camp in Cassiobury Park and went into billets in Watford for the winter. On the 31st the Bishop of Southwell, the Diocese in which the Brigade was recruited, held a very impressive service in the Central Hall, Watford.

Major-General Reade now took over command of the Division, and inspected the Brigade on the 16th November.

Battalion, Brigade and Divisional training continued unabated up to Christmas, 1915, when the Brigadier accompanied General Reade and other officers of the Division to France on what was generally known as a "Cook's Tour." The Brigadier was attached to a Warwickshire Territorial Brigade at La Haie Farm, opposite Gommiecourt, commanded by Brig.-Gen. James, who subsequently came home to command the Leicester Brigade in the Division. To complete the coincidence, General James was the brother of the Vicar of a parish in Watford, and a son of the old Rector of Watford Parish Church.

The whole party returned on January 4th, 1916, after a very interesting and instructive experience.

Parties of Commanding and other Officers from the Brigade, including the Brigade Major, Capt. Lee, went to France later for similar "Cook's Tours," and all lectured on their experiences on their return.

The Winter and Spring were very wet and stormy, which interfered a good deal with the training, not to mention the zeppelin raids, as on the occasions when these occurred the men and staff had to stand to most of the night.

On the 14th February Major-General A. E. Sandbach, C.B., D.S.O., took over command of the Division from Major-General Reade and inspected the Brigade on the 15th.

On the 17th Major Cecil Fane, 12th Lancers, took over the command of the 7th Battalion from Major Payne, and in April Major Hodgkin (Cheshire Regt.) took over command of the 6th Battalion from Lieut.-Col. Clayton, owing to the ill-health of these two officers. Both the new commanders were "Regulars," and had seen much service already during the war.

Up to this time, April, every kind of training had been taught except musketry, which could only be taught on the miniature ranges owing to lack of ammunition and proper rifle ranges. A small amount of ammunition was supplied at this time, and a small proportion of the men were put through a short course. It will therefore be evident that at the time when the Brigade was called on to fight in

Ireland in this month only a very small proportion of the men had ever fired a service bullet out of their rifles.

With the exception of training in musketry, the Brigade was now in a very efficient condition, thanks to the untiring energy and loyal zeal displayed by the Battalion officers and the keenness and ready response of the rank and file. Discipline was excellent and crime practically non-existent.

In the training of these new Armies during the Great War there was a curious point which struck officers of an older generation. Any young officer of 18 or 19 years of age would get up and lecture fluently and without a trace of embarrassment before a large assembly of his men, and would not be in any way disconcerted by the appearance on the scene of a group of senior officers. In the older generation the result would inevitably have been a fiasco.

On the 21st April preparations were begun for the battalions of the Brigade to go into camp in turns at North Minns, to carry out a course of musketry, and the camping grounds were selected. Orders were also received that the Brigade had been detailed for "Home Defence" only, which was taken to mean that it was not to be sent abroad. As the 23rd was Easter Day, the usual large proportion of all ranks were allowed to go on leave until midnight on Monday, the 24th. The Brigade was therefore totally unprepared for any sudden move.

The Brigadier himself returned from leave on the evening of the 24th, and at 6.30 p.m. sudden orders were received to get ready for a move. At 9.30 p.m. orders to move were received, the Headquarters to go in the first train at 4 a.m. At this time warning of a zeppelin raid was received, so that no lights could be used, and all arrangements for the move and the actual entraining had to be carried out with the town and railway station in complete darkness. Thanks, however, to the frequent practices in entraining, all went off without a hitch, and the first train started at 4 a.m. punctually. No intimation was given of the destination of the Brigade.

The leave men all turned up with a few exceptions, due to delay in the train service on account of the zeppelin raid. The move was not without its humorous side. The Easter holiday was a favourable opportunity for getting married, and had been freely taken advantage of in the Brigade. One of the grooms at Brigade Headquarters was married on the Monday afternoon in Watford, and his honeymoon was rudely interrupted at midnight.

Liverpool was reached at 10 a.m. on the 25th, and there it was learned from the dock authorities that the destination of the Brigade was Dublin, where a rising had occurred and heavy fighting was reported to be taking place in the streets.

As the Brigade had very little ammunition—perhaps fifty rounds per man—and no bombs, the Brigadier rang up the Director of Operations at the War Office from the quay, and explained the state of affairs. An agitated voice said: "Good God! how much do you want?" Four hundred rounds per man and ten thousand bombs were asked for, to be at Kingstown the next morning.

The ammunition and bombs arrived at Kingstown the next morning, but could not be unloaded off the ships before the advance on Dublin began.

Officers were sent into the town at Liverpool to search hotels and shops for maps of Dublin, but only a few copies could be found there, these being torn out of guide books in hotels.

The Headquarters of the Brigade and one and a half battalions embarked on the "Ulster," one of the fast Irish mail boats which had been diverted from Holyhead, at 3.30 p.m., and sailed for Kingstown escorted by a destroyer. During the crossing the Commander of the destroyer came on board and informed the Brigadier that he had had news by wireless that Kingstown had been taken by the Sinn Feiners and that the landing would be opposed. This, fortunately, proved to be inaccurate, and disembarkation took place peacefully at Kingstown at 10.15 p.m.

Here an officer from the Irish Command met Headquarters, gave the Brigadier orders, and informed him of the general situation. It appeared to be very serious. The

Irish Command Headquarters had moved into the Royal Hospital, Kilmainham, and the few Regular troops in Dublin and those brought up from the Curragh were having severe fighting. The route from Balls Bridge into Dublin was reported to be strongly held. The houses and points held were detailed, as they were well known to all, the Sinn Feiners having been allowed to practise occupying their positions some days previously.

This disposes of the statement in the newspapers of that time that the Sherwood Foresters were "ambushed" and surprised. The Brigade was called upon to attack known positions composed of stone-built houses three and four stories high, occupied by concealed riflemen, and this, with no Artillery and no bombs. Fortunately the latter, bombs, were obtained, as will be seen later.

The orders were for 300 men to be sent at once to occupy the arsenal and munition factory at Arklow, in Co. Wicklow, two battalions to march to Kilmainham by a roundabout route inland via the Stillorgan Road, and the remaining two battalions to advance direct on Dublin via Balls Bridge, Northumberland Road and Merrion Square.

Headquarters was established in the Yacht Club at Kingstown after the troops that had arrived in the first two ships had been marched out two miles and bivouacked in a field. By this time it was the early hours of the morning.

The detachment for Arklow was detailed from the 2/5th Battalion, under the command of Capt. Rickman.

By 7 a.m. the remainder of the Brigade had arrived and disembarked, and dispositions were then made as follows:—

The 2/5th, less the Arklow detachment, and the 2/6th to march by the Stillorgan Road to Kilmainham.

The 2/7th and 2/8th to advance direct on Dublin, the 2/7th leading.

Headquarters accompanied the latter.

A start was made at 10 a.m.

The 2/5th and 2/6th Battalions had an uneventful march to Kilmainham, and arrived there without meeting with any opposition.

Between Kingstown and Balls Bridge it was learned that there was a bombing school of instruction close to the road. This was indeed a find, and on reaching it the chief instructor was sent for. He and some of his officers accompanied the force and behaved with great gallantry. They also placed their resources at the disposal of the Brigadier, and by the end of the day had supplied over 500 bombs.

Various officers in uniform on leave from units in France met the Headquarters en route and asked to be allowed to join the Brigade. They were attached to the 2/7th and 2/8th, and one, Lieut. Roche, was attached to the Headquarters as Orderly Officer.

The Staff Captain, Capt. Staniforth, had been left at Kingstown to superintend the unloading of stores, etc., and only Capt. Lee (the Brigade Major) and the Signalling Officer were left, which rendered the staff very short-handed.

Balls Bridge was reached at noon without opposition, but as the advance guard of the 2/7th crossed the bridge a heavy fire was opened on them from the front (Pembroke Road) and the flanks. It was a trying ordeal for such young troops, many of whom had only three months' service, especially as it was impossible to see where the enemy, who were concealed in the houses, were firing from.

Most gallantly led by Major Fane, the Battalion continued to advance, their orders being to take the strong position formed by the bridgehead at the end of Northumberland Road. When this was taken the 2/8th were to pass through the captured position and advance up Lower Mount Street towards Merrion Square and College Green.

Meanwhile, Brigade Headquarters were established in the Town Hall at Balls Bridge, where the telephone was utilised to get into touch with the Irish Command at the Royal Hospital, Kilmainham.

As the progress made was very slow, the Brigadier ordered the O.C. 2/8th to detach a company to the right flank in order to endeavour to turn the position at the bridgehead from the direction of Beggars' Bush Barracks. The Irish Command, however, telephoned peremptory orders not to attempt anything on the flank, but to concentrate on the straight route over the bridge.

The company was therefore ordered to come back, but the order did not reach all platoons and a portion of the company reached Beggars' Bush Barracks, where they were retained by the Officer Commanding there, Colonel Sir Frederick Shaw.

The 2/7th, aided by the officers from the bombing school, bombed in the doors of houses known to be occupied by the rebels, but lost heavily all along Northumberland Road. The corner house in Haddington Road was strongly held, and was only bombed and taken after a most gallant attack in which several lives were lost. As the afternoon went on the 2/7th continued to lose heavily; Capt. Dietriechsen and Lieuts. Parry and Hawkins were killed, and several others wounded, including Major Fane, who, however, continued to command his battalion. Capt. Rayner, with a few men, had most gallantly crossed the bridge under a deadly fire, but was unable to hold his position owing to the fire from a barricaded house almost facing the bridge on the opposite side, and the fire from the school on the flank.

A house in Northumberland Road was occupied as a dressing station. Throughout the afternoon and evening the Red Cross ambulance with a lady, Mrs. Chaytor, sitting beside the driver, drove continuously under heavy fire to the dressing station and removed wounded to various hospitals in Dublin. Women also rushed out of houses and dragged the wounded under cover.

Maids also came out of the houses and watched the fight, regardless of the bullets, in Northumberland Road, only to throw their aprons over their heads and run in screaming when a bullet came unpleasantly close.

There was a cattle show going on all the time in the show grounds at Balls Bridge, which continued as if nothing was happening.

Brigade Headquarters, during the afternoon, moved up to the 2/7th Battalion Headquarters, and after several consultations with Major Fane it was clear that the 2/7th, owing to their heavy casualties, could not take the position.

The Brigadier therefore returned to the telephone at Balls Bridge and asked the Irish Command if the situation was sufficiently serious to demand the taking of the position at all costs. He explained that he could take it with another battalion, but that it would entail heavy casualties. The reply was " to come through at all costs."

The Brigadier sent for Lieut.-Col. Oates and ordered him, at dusk, to form up his battalion in sections at intervals across Northumberland Road, and at a given signal to charge right through and take the schools on the right and the Bridgehead. One weak company was to be left in reserve.

The battalion was then spread out along Northumberland Road under a desultory fire, and at a signal from the Brigadier charged, gallantly led by their Commanding Officer. They were joined by officers and men of the 2/7th as they went forward.

The schools were taken by 7.30 p.m., and an attempt made to storm the house (Clanwilliam House) on the further side of the bridge, but Lieut. Daffen, who led across the bridge, was killed, and 2nd Lieut. Browne so severely wounded that he died of his wounds next day. Lieut.-Col. Oates then sent for the reserve company, as " ' B ' Company as a fighting unit had practically ceased to exist, all its officers, its sergeant-major, and all the sergeants being either killed or wounded."*

Eventually a most gallant charge across the bridge was led by Capt. Quibell, of the 2/8th, followed by Lieut. Hewitt, 2/8th, Lieut. Foster, 2/7th, and Captains Cursham and Branston, of the 2/8th. Capt. Quibell and Lieut. Foster succeeded in entering the building by breaking a window, and with the aid of bombs attacked the defenders, Lieut. Foster bayonetting three men on the stairs. The house then caught fire and lit up the whole district.

Firing shortly after died down, and the Brigadier went forward and up Lower Mount Street into Merrion Square, from where an officer was sent to Trinity College to report to the Irish Command that the position had been taken and the route through to Merrion Square occupied.

* *Lieut.-Col. Oates' History of the 2/8th Battalion.*

That the general feeling of the people was against the Sinn Feiners was clear from the fact that they streamed out from alleys and courtyards and cheered "the Ginerel" as the Brigade Commander went up Lower Mount Street, which was brilliantly illuminated by the flames from Clan-William House.

In this action the casualties sustained by the Brigade in this one street were—

	Killed.	Died of Wounds.	Wounded.
Officers	4	1	14
Other Ranks ...	20	5	118

a total casualty list of 19 officers and 143 other ranks.

It was not possible to estimate the casualties of the Sinn Feiners, as they were taken away by their friends, but they were probably few, as they were under cover. About twenty prisoners were taken in houses captured.

As soon as the position was taken dispositions were at once made to collect the units, and detail parties to occupy all corner houses and other important points.

Brigade Headquarters and the Headquarters of the 2/8th occupied a house near the schools in Northumberland Road, where the residents provided food and beds.

At 10 p.m. orders were received from Brig.-General Carleton, who had arrived at Balls Bridge by this time with a portion of the Staffords' Brigade and assumed command, that the Sherwood Foresters' Brigade were to hand over the position they had taken to a battalion of the Staffordshire Brigade in the morning and march from Balls Bridge by the South Circular Road to the Royal Hospital, Kilmainham.

As reports were received that the Sinn Feiners were crawling along the roofs and evidently intended to resume the offensive in the morning, the Brigadier thought it advisable to carry out the transfer before daylight, to avoid having to retire tired troops under fire. This was done, and the half Brigade arrived at Balls Bridge before dawn on Thursday, the 27th April.

After resting the troops and arranging for them to have a meal, the "cookers" having arrived by this time, a start was made.

Reports were received that Leeson Bridge and Square were held in force.

A naval officer had "rigged up" a gun on a cart by this time, and, not wishing to have a repetition of the events of the day before, the Brigadier "borrowed" the gun from Brig.-General Carleton, promising to return it when Leeson Bridge was cleared.

The officer in charge of the gun asked the Brigadier to be very careful, as if the gun was fired the cart would collapse!

A section of R.E. also accompanied the column. The gun was given a very prominent place in the column, and paraded round the open space on the further side of Leeson Square Bridge until the column had passed. The gun was too much for the Sinn Feiners if they really were in occupation of the bridgehead, and nothing occurred. The gun was then returned to Brig.-General Carleton.

On this day the 2/8th led, with the 2/7th in reserve and as escort to the transport. About 2 p.m. fire was opened on the column in the vicinity of Rialto Street, and this caused the horses of the R.E. to stampede, the result being considerable confusion in the column. Firing also started from a rhubarb field on the left, and a long halt had to be made while the 2/8th cleared the route. Sniping also began in the rear of the column, and Lieut. Charlton, 2/7th, was wounded whilst searching a suspected house in a side street.

The people in this neighbourhood were evidently in sympathy with the Sinn Feiners, and the offer of a glass of water by a woman to the Brigadier on his horse was apparently a signal, as on her return to her cottage fire was opened on the Brigade staff from the houses and garden walls opposite. The shooting was very indifferent, and the houses and gardens were cleared by the troops.

As soon as the 2/8th were established on the Rialto Bridge over the canal, where Lieut.-Col. Oates established his Headquarters, the 2/7th and transport were marched through the 2/8th and on to the Royal Hospital at Kilmainham, where they arrived without incurring any casualties from the sniping which continued until they were clear of the bridge.

Meanwhile the 2/8th had been heavily engaged. The South Dublin Union was flying the Sinn Fein flag and was strongly occupied. Lieut.-Col. Oates ordered Capts. Martyn and Oates to attack this building and thus clear the right flank, as the fire from the Union commanded the bridge. Some fierce fighting occurred, but with great gallantry Capts. Martyn and Oates succeeded in making a breach in the wall and then held a portion of the Union, which caused the enemy's fire to slacken and enabled the rest of the Brigade to pass over the bridge, as recorded before.

Capt. Martyn was granted the M.C. for his very gallant action on this occasion. When the column had passed through Lieut.-Col. Oates withdrew, not without difficulty as far as the Union was concerned, and the battalion arrived at the Royal Hospital at 10 p.m. This battalion had two killed and seven wounded this day, and accounted for many of the enemy. The 2/8th casualties during the two days' fighting were:—Officers: 1 killed, 1 died of wounds, 6 wounded; Other Ranks: 7 killed, 4 died of wounds, and 50 wounded. They were splendidly led by their officers, and carried their objective on each day.

The Brigade had behaved most gallantly in very trying circumstances, and deserved the compliment afterwards paid them by a well-known and patriotic London preacher who said in a sermon that "God and the gallant Sherwood Foresters saved Ireland for the Empire."

On arrival at the Royal Hospital on the evening of the 27th, the Brigadier met Brig.-General Lowe, who was commanding, and was informed of the situation. The city was divided into sections, under the command of different officers. Corner houses were occupied in each section, and movement from one section to another was prevented. As troops were available and able the sections were closing in round the Sinn Feiners. The 2/5th of the 178th Brigade was holding Kingsbridge Station, just below the Royal Hospital, under Lieut.-Col. Aitchison, and a portion of the 2/6th, under Major Hodgkin, had been sent into the city and were holding a section about Capel Street. The latter battalion came in for a good deal of fighting, and well maintained the honour and reputation of the Brigade. They lost one other rank killed and five wounded. The 5th Battalion had only to keep down sniping, and had no casualties.

The few troops at the disposal of the Irish Command before the arrival of the Sherwood Foresters had been very hard pressed, and had lost heavily. They had borne the brunt of the first rising on Easter Monday, and had been fighting for two days before the latter arrived. This account can, however, only deal with the part taken by the Sherwood Foresters.

The Brigadier was ordered to dispatch the 2/8th immediately on its arrival that night to Athlone, where a rising was reported. He, however, pointed out that the men had not had a night's rest since Sunday night and it was now Thursday night, whilst meals had been of the sketchiest description. If the troops were to be of any use on arrival at Athlone it was essential that they should have a night's rest. The move was therefore postponed till the next morning.

The accommodation in the Royal Hospital was limited and the sanitary arrangements very inadequate for such a large body of troops, but the best arrangements possible were made. The transport was parked in the grounds of the Royal Hospital, where it was subjected to a good deal of sniping.

Incessant firing and a terrific din continued all that night and the next day and night, whilst the fires in the city lit up the sky for miles round.

The 2/8th Battalion entrained the next morning, Lieut.-Col. Oates being given command of a mobile column under the direct orders of the Irish Command, and thus the battalion passed out of the Brigade for the time being. The battalion did excellent work, the C.O. taking a very strong line throughout, and any attempt at disturbance was very promptly quashed and many prisoners taken.

At the Royal Hospital arrangements were made to hold 500 men always ready, with ammunition and two days' rations, to go wherever required at a moment's notice. So much advantage was taken of this arrangement by the

Irish Command that by the evening of the 28th the Brigade consisted of the Headquarters of the Brigade and the Quartermasters' stores of the battalions only.

On Saturday, the 29th, the rebellion collapsed, and firing almost ceased in the afternoon. Prisoners began to come in in large numbers, and a party from the Brigade was sent to Richmond Barracks to guard them.

By the time the rebellion collapsed there was considerable shortage of food in Dublin, and bread carts were looted in full view of the guards at the Royal Hospital. The Sinn Fein flag flew on the South Dublin Union for several days, and sniping at anyone who showed his head above the ramparts at Kilmainham was indulged in.

Meanwhile, General Sir John Maxwell had arrived at the Royal Hospital with plenary powers as Commander-in-Chief. Major-General Sandbach, with the Headquarters of the Division, also arrived, and was appointed to the command of all troops in Dublin.

All Sunday, the 30th April, prisoners continued to come in in large numbers, and were confined in the jails. A large body of them, escorted by detachments from the Brigade, were marched to the North Wall and despatched to England that night.

On the 1st May all was quiet in the city, and the 6th Battalion rejoined the Brigade in the Royal Hospital, but a cordon system was organised round the city on which duty a portion of the Brigade was employed.

On the 2nd May General Sir John Maxwell inspected the 2/7th Battalion and addressed them. He complimented them very highly on their gallant behaviour on the 26th.

It was much regretted that the 2/8th were unable to be present also, owing to their absence on the Mobile Column.

At 3 a.m. on the 3rd May three of the ringleaders of the rebellion were shot, the execution being carried out by the Brigade. They met their fate bravely.

The Brigadier was appointed President of a Field General Court Martial for trying rebels. He was employed on this duty daily until the 6th, when an officer was sent over from England to conduct the remaining trials.

At the conclusion of the trial of one of the chief ringleaders and instigators of the rebellion, the President of the Court asked the prisoner if he would mind stating "what he was fighting for." His reply, given with dignity, was: "I was fighting to defend the rights of the people of Ireland." He was then asked: "Was anyone attacking those rights?" His reply was: "No; but somebody might have been."

This appeared to be a sorry reason for shooting down perfectly inoffensive citizens in the streets.

This prisoner also did his best to exonerate the so-called Irish Volunteers, saying that they were called out without any idea of what was going to happen, which was probably true.

Four more ringleaders were shot at dawn on the 4th May.

On the 3rd May 450 men of the 2/6th Battalion were ordered to Longford, and on the 5th an escort of 400 men was sent to the North Wall with prisoners.

On the 6th May the 2/5th Battalion moved up from Kingsbridge Station to the Royal Hospital, where they remained until the 16th, when they went into camp in the Phœnix Park.

On the 11th May Major Goodman, Royal Irish Regt., arrived, and succeeded Capt. Lee as Brigade Major. Capt. Lee was appointed to the 6th Division in France. His departure was much regretted by the Brigade Headquarters, where he had served with ability from the first formation of the Brigade.

Major Goodman had been in France since the begining of the War, and had been severely wounded. His experience was of the greatest value in the training of the Brigade.

On the 16th May the Brigadier was appointed President of a Court of Enquiry on alleged cases of the shooting of civilians in the rebellion. The enquiry was very lengthy and lasted until the 27th. The result was to absolve the troops from all blame.

During the enquiry a party of women had to be taken out in taxis to Straffan to endeavour to identify men of the Staffordshire Brigade against whom charges were brought. Two thousand men were paraded. One lady, arrayed in a fur coat evidently looted during the burning of Sackville Street, wished to be supplied with whisky before she started, and shouted for it when passing public-houses. When passing along the ranks she remarked: "Shure, I feel just like Queen Victoria reviewing the troops."

Two men were identified, one of whom had evidently made great friends with the ladies of the party, whom he had helped to bring to a place of safety at great personal risk.

The Brigade was ordered to concentrate at the Curragh on the 27th, with the 2/7th detached at Oranmore, near Galway. This was done and normal training resumed.

For the part the Brigade took in the Irish Rebellion the following are some of the honours afterwards granted:—

Col. Maconchy was promoted Brigadier General on the 6th June, 1916.

In the "London Gazette" of the 25th January, 1917:—

Brigadier General Maconchy, C.M.G.
Lieut.-Col. Fane, 2/7th, C.M.G.
Capt. Rayner, 2/7th, D.S.O.
Capt. Quibell, 2/8th, D.S.O.
Capt. Martyn, 2/8th, M.C.
Capt. Oates, 2/8th, M.C.

On arrival at the Curragh the Brigade had to provide a mobile column, to be always ready to move in case of disturbances in the country; but its services were never required.

A much needed course of musketry was carried through, and the training facilities at the Curragh were utilised to their full extent, whilst the Wicklow Mountains provided an ideal practice ground for the Divisional Artillery, amidst glorious scenery at Glen Imaal, and the battalions went out there in turns to practise the attack from and on trenches in conjunction with Artillery barrage.

The bombing trenches also afforded much useful practice, only marred by the bombing officer, Lieut. Prince, 2/5th, getting a piece of a bomb in his leg the first time bombing was practised with regulation precautions!

The presence of the Divisional Headquarters on the spot was another great source of advantage, and Divisional exercises, staff rides, etc., were practised.

The training of the 2/7th Battalion was carried out at Oranmore, where they were frequently inspected by the Brigadier and Brigade Major.

Galway was reported to be very disaffected, and special instructions were given to the battalion to be tactful in their behaviour. The people were sullen at first, but it says much for Lieut.-Col. Fane and his officers that the battalion soon became very popular, and when they left the town the long causeway over which the railway runs into Galway was packed with cheering crowds bidding them good-bye.

On July 11th Lieut.-Col. Oates was detailed by the Irish Command to proceed with a battalion to Athlone, where cattle driving was rife. He was sent with his own battalion, the 2/8th, and dealt with the situation in an able and effectual manner, returning to the Curragh on the 8th August.

On the 26th July the Brigade was inspected by General Sir J. Maxwell, who expressed himself as being very pleased with its training, and on August 3rd he again inspected the Brigade at Glen Imaal in a spectacular trench attack in combination with the Artillery.

On August 16th it was inspected by Field Marshal Lord French, who ordered the Brigadier to publish an order saying that he was extremely pleased with the Brigade. Probably as a result of the fine appearance of the Brigade, ten days later drafts of 200 men per battalion were ordered to be sent out to France. This was a very severe blow, as it meant training fresh recruits and that they would not be sent to the front for a considerable time.

The drafts were inspected and addressed by Major-General Sandbach on the 31st, and left the Curragh on September 2nd.

Investiture by H.M. The King, at Fovant, 13th February, 1917.

Major Goodman left the Brigade early in October to join a Division in France, and was succeeded as Brigade Major by Major J. Benskin, D.S.O., R.E.

Lieut.-Col. Fane, 2/7th, also left the Brigade for the front, and Major Rayner, of that battalion, was appointed Lieut.-Colonel commanding in his place.

On December 11th the transport horses of the Brigade were inspected in order to be handed over to the Artillery. This was a great disappointment, as the greatest care and trouble had been expended in keeping them in good condition, with the result that they were very much fitter than the horses in the Artillery.

During the month orders were received for the Division to move to Fovant, near Salisbury, but the Brigade did not actually move until the 11th January, arriving at Hurdcott camp on the evening of the 12th.

On the 16th January the Brigade was inspected by General Sir Henry Sclater, C.-in-C. Southern Command. Very severe frost and snow prevailed during most of the time spent at Fovant, which interfered with training. Lieut.-Col. Aitchison was succeeded in the command of the 2/5th Battalion by Lieut.-Col. Leger St. Hill. Lieut.-Col. Aitchison had been with the battalion since it was formed, and had brought it to a high state of efficiency.

On February 1st the advanced parties of the Brigade with Major Staniforth, that most efficient Staff Captain, were ordered to proceed to France.

On Sunday, the 11th February, the Brigade went by train into Salisbury, and marched through the city to the Cathedral to attend a service and address by the Bishop of Southwell. After the service they were formed up in the Close and addressed by the C.-in-C., General Sir Henry Sclater, and afterwards by the Duke of Portland, Lord Lieutenant of the County of Nottingham. They then trained back to Fovant.

On the 13th the Brigade was inspected by His Majesty the King, attended by the Duke of Rutland, Field Marshal Lord French, General Sir Henry Sclater, Major-General Sandbach and others. The battalions filed past at a cross road in Fovant, and the C.O.'s of battalions were presented to H.M.

His Majesty then presented the decorations earned in Ireland. It was perhaps unique that troops should be presented with rewards before going abroad, and was probably the only occasion on which it was done during the War.

Orders had been received that no photographs were to be taken, but His Majesty most graciously remarked on the absence of a photographer and asked for photos to be taken, knowing how gratifying it would be to the recipients of the decorations. A camera was produced and photographs taken.

On the 24th February the Brigade began to entrain for France, the Headquarters and details embarking at Southampton for Havre on the 25th, the battalions proceeding via Folkestone and Boulogne.

By March 3rd the Brigade was concentrated at Warfusée, on the Amiens—St. Quentin Road, the Division being posted to the 3rd Corps of the Fourth Army (Sir H. Rawlinson).

On the 9th, Brigade Headquarters advanced to Foucaucourt with three battalions, the 2/8th being at Proyart.

On the 14th advance platoons went into the trenches, and on the evening of the 15th the 2/6th took their place in the front line.

The rest of the Brigade, with Headquarters, were to have gone into the trenches on the 17th, but it was found that the Germans had evacuated their trenches and retired beyond the Somme, destroying villages and the bridges as they went. Our front line advanced about one and a half miles and reconnaissances were made further to the front.

On the 18th the 2/8th Battalion was moved up to Foucaucourt, and on the 19th the 1st Division, on the left of the Brigade, crossed the Somme at St. Christ, the 2/6th Battalion also crossing at the same time.

On the 21st the whole Brigade crossed the Somme at Villers Carbonnel, where Headquarters were established, the battalions occupying old German trenches on the plateau beyond.

The weather was very bad, snow and rain, and the men had a very uncomfortable time of it, as the transport could not be got across the temporary bridge at this point. The Brigadier motored some miles to the front and came on a village with the first French refugees left by the Germans. They were in a state of great destitution.

On the 27th the Brigade moved to Bouvincourt, with the battalions forming outposts in front.

On the 30th orders were received to advance and take Vendelles and Jeancourt, at the foot of the ridge and spur running up to a strong position of the Germans at Le Verguier on the top of the ridge.

Brigade Headquarters were advanced to Bernes, which had been completely demolished by the Germans, and accommodation was only available in cellars, into which the water poured. The weather was atrocious, with constant rain and sleet.

Orders were issued for the attack to take place on the 31st, the 2/6th to lead the attack with the 2/8th in reserve. As the Germans were known to have a wired trench running out from a farm on the right flank which would enfilade the advance, the 2/8th were ordered to send a company on the night of the 30th to the ground occupied by the Division on the right, the 61st, and to advance so as to outflank this trench and the farm. The 61st Division during the night advanced and occupied the village of Soyecourt, farther on the right flank.

The advance was to be covered by the Divisional Artillery.

Before dawn a patrol of the company of the 2/8th, under Captain Oates, M.C., advanced and was able to get close to Vendelles, which appeared to be unoccupied.

The Artillery bombardment began at 12.30 p.m. on the 31st March, and the advance was made at 1.30 p.m.

The 2/6th advanced very steadily in open order through rifle and shell fire on Jeancourt, and drove the Germans from that village and up the slopes of the ridge beyond. At the same time Capt. Oates rushed his company through a heavy enemy barrage and occupied the right edge of Vendelles.

At 2.30, no report having been received from the 2/6th, and heavy firing continuing, the Brigadier ordered the 2/8th to advance. Lieut.-Col. Oates advanced on the right of the line of the 2/6th, occupied Vendelles, and linked up with Captain Oates' company.

At 4.30, as the situation was very obscure, the Brigadier went down to Vendelles.

It was found that Lieut.-Col. Hodgkin had taken Jeancourt, but considered it untenable as it lay in a cup completely commanded by the ridge above. He was then retiring on to a ridge between Jeancourt and Vendelles, under heavy shell fire.

The 2/6th were ordered to occupy some old German trenches on this ridge, and the 2/8th to consolidate their position in and round Vendelles and to strengthen their right flank where there was a gap between them and the 61st Division.

Jeancourt was occupied again that night by small posts from the 2/6th.

The attack had been most gallantly and successfully carried out, and the Brigade was congratulated by the Corps Commander in Corps Orders.

Forty casualties were incurred during the operation. The line was heavily shelled all that night and all the next day, whilst the conditions for the men were wretched. The trenches were little better than mud pies, and afforded little protection against either the weather or shell fire.

On the night of April 1st orders were received to attack and capture the strong position of Le Verguier, on the top of the ridge with one battalion only.

The Germans could be seen consolidating their position, the wire was uncut, and the position was evidently held in great strength.

The 2/7th Battalion, under Lieut.-Col. Rayner, was detailed for the operation, and moved down to Vendelles on the evening of the 2nd April, Lieut.-Col. Rayner spending the day reconnoitring the position and making his preparations.

He decided to send one company under Capt. La Rose up the ridge from Jeancourt to turn the main position, while the remainder of the battalion advanced up the main spur from Vendelles.

The attack was unfortunately a failure. The company from Jeancourt made a most gallant attack, but were hung up by the uncut wire, Capt. La Rose, Lieuts. Gascoigne and Downer being killed and the company practically annihilated.

The Brigadier went down to Vendelles at 1 a.m. and found that the remainder of the battalion had lost its way in the rain and darkness on the spur and had got nowhere. Lieut.-Col. Rayner was then retiring his men and nothing further could be done that night. The officers and men were very despondent at their failure, but the task was an almost impossible one, especially for untried troops in their first attack.

On the 3rd April orders were received for another attack to be made on Le Verguier with another battalion on the 4th—by day this time.

The 2/5th Battalion, under Lieut.-Col. St. Hill, was detailed for the attack.

More Artillery was supplied by the Corps, and the advance was preceded by a heavy barrage.

The attack started at 7 a.m., and was watched by the Brigadier and also officers from Corps Headquarters from the top of a huge crater close to Vendelles.

All seemed to go well and the troops advanced gallantly under a heavy fire. At 9 a.m. figures could be seen moving about in the position, which were believed to be the 2/5th men. The Brigadier-General Commanding the Artillery also reported that our men were in occupation, and he could not go on shelling the position.

The real position was very different. The advancing line had been suddenly caught in a cross fire from machine guns in carefully prepared positions, and were mown down, many officers and men being killed. Lieut.-Col. St. Hill decided to retire his men under cover of a blinding blizzard of snow, and the attack was again a failure.

Brig.-General Stansfeld succeeded to the command of the Brigade, but pending his arrival Le Verguier was again attacked by the 2/8th Battalion, but could not be taken.

It was evacuated by the Germans on the 9th April in their general retirement.

By COLONEL T. W. STANSFELD, C.M.G., D.S.O.

I have been asked by Colonel Bradbridge to write an account of the Infantry in the 59th Division from a general point of view. It is now ten years since I took over command of the 178th Brigade, and, having no diary or notes, I am afraid that what I say will be more from a personal point of view and chiefly about the 178th Brigade.

In April, 1917, I was Commandant of the 4th Army Infantry School at Flexicourt, and I was offered the command of a brigade in the First Army. I naturally accepted this. The day before I was due to take over command I went over to Fourth Army Headquarters to say goodbye to the late General Sir Henry Rawlinson. On my arrival Major-General Archie Montgomery told me that the Army commander found that he had a vacancy for a brigade commander in his Army, and that he wanted to know whether I would prefer to take that brigade and stay in his Army, or to go to an Army that I did not know so well as his. Of course, I accepted his offer, and the whole thing was fixed up on the telephone with G.H.Q. in about ten minutes. I went to join my brigade the following day.

On my way I called at Corps H.Q., the Corps Commander being General Pulteney, and his B.G.G.S., General Romer, who, as is well known, took over the Division about a week afterwards. I was accompanied by Colonel Luckock, who was G.S.O. 1 Training, Fourth Army, and he introduced me to the personnel of Brigade Headquarters. At that time the Brigade Major was Major Benskin, R.E., and the Staff Captain was Capt. Staniforth. Major Benskin did not stay very long with the brigade, as he received a higher appointment shortly after my arrival. Capt. Staniforth, however, remained with me for nearly a year, when he went to G.H.Q. We always used to call him "Purry," and I am quite sure there was not a better Staff Captain in France. His first thought was always for the comfort of the men.

On my arrival at Brigade Headquarters I was told that the brigade had to carry out a night attack on Le Verguier, but the Divisional Commander told me, as I did not know the country, I need not take command of the brigade until the attack was over. Colonel Coape Oates was temporarily in command of the brigade, and remained so until next morning.

On the afternoon of my arrival I walked up to the front-line, which was then only a series of posts with practically no trenches dug, and had a look at the objective which the brigade was to take. I noticed that the wire was uncut, and I came across some young gunner officers and pointed it out to them. They said it would be all right, as the wire would be cut during the preliminary bombardment. I thought this was rather extraordinary, as I had taken part in other battles previous to this, including Loos, and I knew how difficult it was to cut wire after the Artillery had been doing it systematically for days on end. I always wish now that I had referred the matter to Divisional Headquarters, but being new to the ground and the brigade, and not knowing exactly what the plans of the attack were, I did not do so.

That night I rather selfishly went to bed in a ruined village called Vendelles, and was awakened about dawn by Col. Oates, who told me that the attack had been unsuccessful, there had been a lot of casualties, and his own son was missing. Luckily, his son turned up about a couple of hours afterwards.

During the next few days the brigade was pulled out of the line, and we were given a chance of cleaning up and doing some training in our rest place. During this period I was told that my brigade had to attack Hargicourt Quarries in about a week's time, so, with the aid of trench maps, aeroplane photographs, etc., I had our own trenches and the German trenches taped out on an area near our rest billets, and the 2/8th Sherwood Foresters, whom I had detailed for the attack, practised it over this flagged course for several days. This attack, as stated by General Romer in his narrative, was to a great extent successful, and I shall always remember how the tails of the whole brigade went up on having this success, because up to now the Division, although they had been following the Bosche back in his retirement and gained new ground, as a rule were always unsuccessful when they attacked, with the exception of the attack of the 177th Brigade on Villeret.

It was during the fighting at Hargicourt Quarries that Capt. Oates (who during the war received the D.S.O. and M.C.), the son of Colonel Oates, spotted a covey of partridges in No-man's-land. He proceeded to snipe them with a rifle, and killed one; he shot it through the head. He retrieved it himself after dark, and his father ate it the following night.

Brigade Headquarters at that time were established at Roisel, and I remember so well the house that they occupied. It was one of the few that the Bosche had not blown up and was the enemy side of the village. I lived in it in fear and trembling for about ten days or a fortnight, in spite of the fact that the sappers pronounced that they had examined it and could find no trace of any of the delay-action mines mentioned by General Romer. Nevertheless, I was very glad when we left it.

From there we moved as a Division and took over a section of trenches near Havrincourt Wood. It was here that Colonel St. Hill was killed by one of the enemy snipers when going round his front line one day. He was a most gallant officer, with a great sense of humour and had a fund of stories. While we were here, General James, who commanded the 177th Brigade, put the wind up me properly when I had to take over his sector of the trenches on relieving his brigade. He was one of the most fearless men (I called it foolish) I ever met, and, instead of walking down a perfectly good communication trench to see his front line, he insisted on walking over the top in broad daylight, as he said it was much quicker. It is true that that part of the line was what was known as "quiet," and that the Bosche trenches were perhaps 300 or 400 yards from ours. All the same, I was wondering the whole time whether a Bosche sniper was not looking at us through a telescopic sight. Equally rash was Lieut.-Col. Martyn, who would persist in taking me round, about dusk, to see how the new front-line trenches were getting on. Colonel Martyn was usually known as "Mickie," and was one of the best friends I had in the brigade.

During the time we were at Havrincourt, most of the Infantry were employed in digging this new system of front-line trenches. We then moved to the Barastre area and spent a few weeks there. The training that we were enabled to carry out was invaluable. All the men were delighted with the rest, and we were really quite comfortable. One day when I was in the brigade office, which was a canvas hut, with "By-gum-and-by-crike," my Brigade Major, whom General Romer has already mentioned (and, incidentally, he was reported to be the handsomest man in the British Army, and was an expert at mixing cocktails) was sitting at his table telephoning to either a battalion or the Division. At the time there was a terrible thunderstorm going on, and I suddenly saw him being shot from his chair to the other end of the room, and discovered that a tree within ten yards of the Mess had been struck and that he received a fairly severe shock from it. However, I think a cocktail put him right. I should not like to see in print the language that he used. The period spent here was uneventful except for the races, rifle meetings, etc., that have all been already mentioned.

From here we went into the Ypres salient, where we had very comfortable billets. We detrained at a place which all the men called "Gertie Wears Velvet." I think it was spelt Godewaersvelde. Most of our time was spent in training, and also reconnoitring the part of the line on which we had to make an attack, which I think was on the 26th September. I remember very well all the officers of the brigade being taken by General Sir Hubert Gough to see a model of the battlefield, which was marked out on the ground and which gave one an extraordinarily good idea of the country over which we should have to attack. Every pill-box and every trench was shown. The size of the model was about half that of a tennis court. Most of the senior officers in the brigade also dined with the Corps Commander, General Hunter Weston, who, after an excellent dinner, used to give us a lecture on the impending battle.

We took over from a brigade of the 55th Division during the night of 25th/26th September, and my Advance Brigade Headquarters were in an old German pill-box, which was called Capricorn Keep. I was ordered by the

Divisional Commander to go there that night. It was actually on the jumping-off line of leading troops. My Rear Headquarters was in a very large and very deep dug-out at Weiltje, and about midnight I telephoned to the Divisional General asking if I could remain there until I knew whether our first objective had been taken, because the shelling at the time was intense, and I thought that, if the attack was not successful, Brigade Headquarters would be of no use amongst the foremost troops. This the General agreed to. Also the counter barrage would have come down (which it did) on the line the pill-box was in. The attack went according to plan, and " By-gum-and-by-crike " and I went forward to this pill-box about half-an-hour after dawn. When we arrived there we found an absolute shambles, as, being a German pill-box, naturally all the entrances to it, which were only wooden doors, were facing the Bosche, and this pill-box, which was occupied by the battalion, got a direct hit on the door. The brigade captured all its objectives, as did the 177th Brigade on our right.

After the objectives were taken, things were fairly quiet until 5 o'clock in the evening. I had orders to take over the front of the brigade which was attacking on my left on the night of the 26th/27th. For this purpose I had been loaned a battalion of the 176th Brigade, and I was supposed to carry the relief out at dusk. As a matter of fact it did not take place until about 3 o'clock on the morning of the 27th, the reason being that about 5 o'clock the Bosche heavily counter-attacked, as has already been described by General Romer. The counter-attack, I must say, was a most unpleasant one, but only a small pill-box was recaptured by the enemy. Colonel Martyn, who was in command of the 2/7th Sherwood Foresters, happened to be going round his front-line posts at the time the counter-attack commenced, and it was very largely due to him that the situation, which seemed from the rear to be far more critical than it actually was, was restored.

I had a very unpleasant experience towards the end of the counter-attack on making my way back to the Rear Brigade Headquarters to telephone to the Division the situation in front, for, as I was picking my way across the shell-holes, which were full of water, amidst all the din of the battle I saw little spurts of water coming from the shell-holes. I happened to look up and found a swarm of low-flying aeroplanes, who apparently were firing at anything they could see.

After the counter-attack had died down I was told to give orders for a battalion of the 176th Brigade to take over the brigade front on my left. This took place about 2 or 3 o'clock in the morning. The Division on the left had reported that it had captured all its objectives, but when the officer commanding the battalion referred to had been round his new line he came and reported to me that this was not the case and that they were about 400 yards short of their original objective. I reported this to the Division, and about 10 o'clock the next morning the brigade commander of the brigade that I had relieved came to me and said that he had had it reported to him that all his objectives had been taken, and was my report true. I replied that I had not been round myself to see, but had no reason to doubt the commanding officer's report. He himself then went out to reconnoitre the line, and came back and admitted that what I had reported was true. This was rather a good lesson in map-reading, as the objectives for that particular brigade, as far as I remember, were three farms. Of course, in the salient at that time few signs of these farms existed. According to the map, about 400 yards in rear of these three farms were three other farms, and the company or battalion commanders who had reported their objectives as being taken had read their map inaccurately.

We were eventually relieved by the New Zealand Division, and as Brigade Headquarters, as is well known, could not withdraw until the relief was complete, " By-gum-and-by-crike," who hated anything to do with gas, insisted on the Brigade Gas Sergeant remaining behind to accompany me and himself back to our Rear Headquarters. The reason really was because he found great difficulty in putting his gas-mask on. When he got it over his head he always used to say to me: " I can't find the — — to put in my mouth!"

That night we were put into huts near Poperinghe, and we were very heavily bombed by Bosche aeroplanes. There was a full moon, and it was a most unpleasant experience. One bomb got a direct hit on a hut and killed or wounded thirty men.

We then moved back a long way behind the line for a short period, and were billeted in some comfortable villages, where there was a trout stream. We then moved up to the Lens area. The trenches, which we took over from the 1st Canadian Division, were really excellent ones; the communicating trenches might be compared with Piccadilly to a small country lane. Part of the front line ran actually through the village of Lens, our front-line trench being one side of a street and the Bosche the other. It was a most eerie line to visit at night.

During this period several American officers were attached to various battalions of the Brigade, and we all noticed how keen they were to learn their work and were not the people we expected them to be, viz., come out to the country to teach us what to do.

When we were in Brigade Reserve at Chateau-de-la-Haie we had very comfortable quarters and huts, and could do a good deal of much-needed training with our reinforcements, who had come out after the battle in the salient.

During November I was at home on leave, and I received a wire recalling me. I rejoined the brigade the following night about midnight, and found Mickie Martyn in bed. The Division had moved from the Lens area. Mickie was commanding the brigade in my absence, and he informed me that we were going down to help with the tank attack at Cambrai. He and I then sat down and discussed it over oysters and beer. The former I had brought out from England.

We did not take part in the actual attack at Cambrai; in fact, I think we were the last Division to be used in the Army. We relieved the Guards Division in Bourlon Wood, our Brigade being in Divisional Reserve at Ribecourt.

In this village there were some catacombs which were big enough to hold practically the whole brigade. As regards their origin, I was told that all the stone for the village church had been quarried from here and left a large natural dug-out, which probably the quarriers had never dreamed would be used for such a purpose in later years. With candles stuck about these catacombs, it looked like a fairy grotto.

On 1st December the Hun counter-attack broke through the line of the 29th Division on our right at Gouzeaucourt, and General de Lisle was very nearly captured. As he was withdrawing from his Divisional Headquarters he met Major Robinson, commanding 470th Field Company, marching down the road to join my brigade. He pointed out to Major Robinson where the Huns were and told him to stop them. The Field Company occupied the best position they could, and, with rifle fire and Lewis gun fire (the Lewis guns they found on the ground, and though never trained in using them, they, with the skill of a sapper, soon found out what to do), they kept the Germans back until reinforced by the Guards Division.

As far as I remember, that night we took over part of the line to the right of Flesquieres, having 177th Brigade on our left. An unfortunate affair occurred there, as the dug-out of the Headquarters of the 2/5th Bn. caught fire owing to the Headquarter cook putting a tin of petrol on the fire instead of water. The dug-out was completely burnt out, and two or three men lost their lives, and an officer in the dug-out only just escaped before the flames reached him.

At that period the 2/7th Bn. had been lent to the 176th Brigade, and they had a very difficult operation to perform withdrawing from Bourlon Wood.

After being withdrawn from this part of the line, we went into rest in the Le Cauroy district. This was absolute peace, and we had very good billets. It was terribly cold at the time, and, as far as I remember, we arrived there on Christmas Day. It was while we were here that the organization of the brigade was reduced from four battalions to three, the 2/7th being merged into the 1/7th, who had come from the 46th Division, the command being taken over by Colonel Toller. It was here also that we started the 178th Infantry Brigade Fox Hounds. The origin of this pack was as follows:—Bill Wright, the transport officer, when he was not seeing the rations up to the line used to spend all his nights badger digging or fox digging. When talking about it one night at dinner, I asked him whether, instead of knocking the foxes on the head when he had got them, could we not make better use of them? So the next time he was at home on leave he brought out two and a half couple of Pytchley hounds. These were augmented by various setters, pointers, and other dogs, and we had a pack of about six or seven couple. Then each time that he dug a fox out it was put in a sack and brought back to billets. The following day a drag line was planned, and we ran a drag with this pack for three or four miles. (We could not hunt a bagged fox for any distance on account of the cultivation.) At the end of the drag some open space was usually selected where Bill's servant, with the fox in the bag, let it loose. In addition to our pack we had what we called our " storm troops." This was a pointer nearly as big as a donkey, which would have killed anything. It used to accompany Bill's servant with the fox, and when the fox was released it was given about 100 yards start, and the " storm troops " was let loose, followed by the pack which had been running the drag. It sounds rather cruel, but the diversion was most pleasant. In all we killed eleven foxes in this way, and several young officers were blooded.

We all thoroughly enjoyed our rest at Le Cauroy, and carried out some very valuable training.

From there we went into the line at Bullecourt, and were kept very busy digging new lines in preparation for the big German attack in March. We were constantly being asked to try and get identifications from the German line, and the 176th Brigade carried out a successful daylight raid. It was ingeniously thought out, and was planned somewhat as follows:—

A portion of the front-line trench was within about fifty yards of the Bosche trench. From observation the 176th Brigade had noticed that there was a Bosche post opposite them, and that the men of this post used to come out of their dug-out and have breakfast regularly about 8 o'clock in the morning. They accordingly systematically trench-mortared that part of the trench for about a week from dawn for about half an hour. The Bosche trench was heavily wired, and the difficulty was to know how to cut the wire as it could not be done by Artillery. It was decided, therefore, that a Bangalore-torpedo should be carried out at night, placed under the wire opposite the Bosche post referred to, and an electric lead brought back into our trenches. On the morning of the raid the trench-mortaring continued as usual, but, if I remember rightly, the target was behind the Bosche post. Eventually a dud trench-mortar shell was put in the mortar and fired at the post. Immediately it was seen to fall into the Bosche line the button was pressed on the electric lead; up went the Bangalore-torpedo, the wire was cut, the Bosche, who was eating his breakfast—thinking it was a trench-mortar shell that had burst—disappeared down into the dugout. The raiding party jumped over our front line, rushed across No-man's-land, and brought back three prisoners from the dug-out. A most valuable identification.

At that time the Division had two brigades in the line, one in reserve, and the Brigade Headquarters were quite the healthiest I had been in for some time. We were practically never shelled, and used to sleep in beds in elephant shelters. We had various rumours of the date when the Bosche would attack us, and on the night of 20/21st March every gun on the Divisional front seemed to be firing. Between 4 and 5 on the morning of the 21st March an intense bombardment from the enemy guns was opened. Our healthy Headquarters at once became one of the unhealthiest I have ever been in. They were in a sunken road at Noreuil, and the stream of shells were making an extraordinary good group on this sunken road. I got out of my blankets and dressed hurriedly, and I remember my servant brought me a cup of tea. I then went into the Brigade Major's shelter, and found the next one to him had had a direct hit on it and that Bill Wright was badly wounded, and there had been several other casualties amongst the men of the Brigade Headquarters. I then told my brigade staff that we had better get into a dug-out which had been completed the day before, which was about thirty yards away. So we dashed down the sunken road to the dug-out, and on our way a Bosche shell burst between us and the dug-out. It wounded my acting Brigade Major (Capt. Nadin) in the wrist. However, we eventually got all the wounded down to the dug-out, and remained there until the shelling had died down. Poor Nadin eventually died from the effects of this wound.

The line was held by the 178th Brigade, with the 2/7th on the right and the 2/6th on the left, with the 2/5th in reserve. All these three battalions had a terrible time from the Bosche bombardment. As soon as the shelling began in the morning we got on by telephone to the 2/6th, but as soon as they answered us the line was cut. I had various messages by runner from the three battalions, but the situation was really very obscure, and all one knew was that the Germans were attacking in force. The brigade held on to their position until about 2 or 3 in the afternoon, by which time they were practically wiped out. Just in front of Brigade Headquarters was a section of machine guns, which did most extraordinarily good work and did tremendous execution amongst the Huns in the Noreuil valley.

About 3 o'clock in the afternoon I telephoned to the Divisional Commander (my line back to the Division had only been broken once or twice during the day and our signallers had repaired it each time) and told him that our front system had gone, that the Huns were within 400 or 500 yards of my Brigade Headquarters, that the men of the Brigade Headquarters were manning their posts outside, and that I thought that, with the aid of this M.G. section, we could stay there till dark, but he ordered me to withdraw Headquarters to others which had been prepared a little distance behind in another sunken road.

I forgot to mention that when I found Nadin was wounded, I telephoned to the Division and asked for someone to replace him. About mid-day, down into the dug-out came a most spick-and-span officer with a coat warm British with a fur collar, and gloves on his hands. This was Trollope, of the Suffolk Regiment, who had been sent to me and who had been acting as G.S.O. 3 to a division in the rear. He remained with the brigade until the end of the War, and did sterling work.

When I got back to my new Brigade Headquarters I found that out of about 2,000 men of the brigade who started in the battle, there were only 53 left—all the rest had been killed, wounded, or taken prisoner, and about 70 per cent. of the prisoners were wounded.

Here I must say what extraordinarily good work the runners from battalions did. They always got their messages back, and I think many of them must have been killed or wounded on trying to rejoin their battalions. There was one man in particular (I am afraid I have forgotten his name) who brought me messages about three or four times from the front line. He was one of the three other ranks of the 2/5th Battalion who were with us that night, and was complimented by His Majesty the King when we were visited by him a few days afterwards.

On my way back to my new Brigade Headquarters I passed through several of our batteries, who were firing their guns as only British gunners can. There I saw General Stirling on a horse, encouraging his gunners and taking not the slightest notice of the enemy shells, which were bursting all round.

My original Brigade Headquarters were never taken until the next day, the machine gun section referred to above denying them to the enemy, and we were actually able that night, under cover of darkness, to send a G.S. waggon there and collect our kits, which we had left behind.

It was with feelings of relief that those that remained of us marched back on the night of 22nd/23rd to Achiet-le-Grand, and even then we were followed by shells fired from enemy long-range guns, and when we arrived at our destination we went into an encampment of huts which were also being shelled at intervals by the same guns.

We then moved to the salient again, where the brigade was made up to strength once more. The officers and men who came out as drafts belonged to various regiments of the British Army, but they were of magnificent material, and, after about a week, the brigade had the makings of as good a brigade as could be desired. General Plumer inspected us and gave all the officers a short resumé of what had taken place since 21st March, and what he expected of us.

The 176th and 177th Brigades took over the line in the Ypres salient, and we were held in reserve.

H.M. THE KING, escorted by Lieut.-Col. R. B. RICKMAN, inspecting the remnants of the Robin Hoods at Hermin after the Battle of Bullecourt, March, 1918.

Imperial War Museum Photo, Crown Copyright.

H.M. THE KING, accompanied by Lieut.-Col. R. B. RICKMAN and Capt. W. FOSTER, M.C., interrogating Pte. DENNY and the remainder of the Robin Hoods at Hermin, after the battle of Bullecourt, March, 1918.

Imperial War Museum Photo, Crown Copyright.

While I was out one morning reconnoitring the line in rear of the other two brigades with a view to counter-attacking if necessary, an orderly on a motor-cycle rode up and said that orders had been received for the brigade to move at once, and that by the time I got back it would probably be on the move.

I rejoined them as quickly as I could and found that we had received orders to come under command of the G.O.C. 19th Division, and that we were to march to Kemmel and report to the senior brigadier there.

We arrived there that evening, and I reported to Brig.-Gen. Tom Cubitt. He had already been fighting in that area for, I think, five days, and had under him the remnants of his own brigade, a brigade of South Africans, and a brigade from the Ulster Division, and another brigade. The 178th Brigade, being up to strength, was a most welcome addition to his command.

We were under his orders for seven days and seven nights, and, although the fighting was most unpleasant, I have seldom enjoyed from my own personal point of view—if you can call it enjoying it—a battle more, as General Cubitt was a host in himself, and, although being a most capable soldier, he always saw the humorous side of a situation. He had a nick-name for all the brigadiers and most of the officers in his brigade. Some were complimentary and others were not.

A French Division relieved us at Kemmel, and they were very angry at having been called to fill a part of the British line. One of the officers insinuated that we could not hold our own line. However, we had held Kemmel then for about ten days, and the Bosche took it about two days after the French took over from us.

The night we were relieved I was sitting with General Cubitt in a shelter in rear of the line and he was rung up by the G.S.O.1, who happened to be a Marine, and was ordered to carry out some task which he, General Cubitt, thought was impossible. After a long conversation, he told the Marine he thought he had better go and join his ship!

The brigade was then withdrawn into billets and farms in rear of Mont Rouge, and it was about that time that Colonel Crossman relieved Colonel Gorton. Colonel Crossman was an old friend of mine, as he was, at the beginning of the war, Brigade-Major to the 21st Brigade, of which my regiment, the Green Howards, formed part.

The 59th Division was soon after broken up at St. Omer, and it was a very sad day for me to see the Sherwood Foresters marching away to their new Divisions. I was personally then sent to run a Senior Officers' School on the coast. This school was for prospective commanding officers, and the courses lasted a fortnight or three weeks. We had a house to ourselves, with a good mess, plenty of sea bathing, and practically all our work was making out tactical schemes for the use of company commanders while they were training behind the line. I stayed there about six weeks, and rejoined the Division, to find that it had been re-formed with B.2 units, who, I think, came from England. Later on in this book there is an order issued by the Corps Commander (General Haking) saying that after certain operations which the Division took part in, it was never to be described as a "B" Division in the 11th Corps. They became extraordinarily efficient, but it took a longish time to weed out the men who were really of no use to us; for instance, one got men who were half blind, deaf, and men with practically no teeth, and as Napoleon said that an army marched on its stomach, the men with no teeth were not of much use to us. General Whigham was commanding the Division at that time.

The attack referred to by General Smythe on 30th September, 1918, was carried out by the 11th Bn. Royal Scots Fusiliers of my brigade. It captured all its objectives, and what I remember chiefly about the attack was that it was very difficult to get an efficient artillery barrage owing to the proximity of the Bosche lines to ours. General Smythe, therefore, gave me all the light trench-mortars of the Division to supplement the artillery barrage. They were most effective and their shooting was very accurate. We then side-slipped down the line to the left and took over trenches that had been German trenches. The fighting was now semi-open warfare.

About 20th October, 178th Brigade were in the line, and patrols at dawn discovered that the Bosche had retired towards Lille. About an hour afterwards civilians came out from Lille, and an old French gentleman and his two daughters arrived at my Brigade Headquarters and presented me with a bunch of flowers which they had picked from the garden of their old house which, of course, had been razed to the ground. The French interpreter who was with me told me that I ought to kiss the girl who gave me the flowers, so I kissed her on both cheeks. I would sooner have kissed her sister, as she was much the better-looking of the two.

As soon as we found the Huns had retired, the battalions in the line promptly followed them up, and we marched through the outskirts of Lille at about 10 o'clock in the morning. On the way there I was riding my horse and my groom was on my other old favourite charger, " Huntsman." He suddenly shouted to me that " Huntsman " was lame. I told him to get off and see if he had a stone in his foot. When he looked at the foot he found that it was not a stone, but a " crow's-foot." A " crow's-foot," for the benefit of the uninitiated, is a military weapon used for putting into fords and on roads, for the purpose of laming horses. It is made of iron and has four spikes to it, and whenever you throw it on the ground one spike always points to the sky. It was most effectual in this particular case, as poor old " Huntsman " had about three inches of iron running through his frog up into his hoof. However, I got him into a stable in Lille, and he was all right in about a week's time.

Our entry into Lille was a most extraordinary affair. Thousands of French people welcomed us; practically every man of the brigade was embraced by the ladies (you simply could not keep them off), and my groom resembled a bridesmaid at a wedding as he carried three or four bunches of flowers. I remained on my horse and only received handshakes.

This triumphal march very soon became serious war again, and no sooner had we got in the country outside Lille than we encountered the enemy and carried on a running fight with them. I made my Brigade Headquarters that day for a short time in an old French Chateau, the occupant being a Count (I am afraid I do not remember his name), who had been there the whole of the war. He was a most courteous old gentleman, and told me that he had been at the Ecole de Guerre with Marshal Foch. I think it was about thirty years before, as a student. He said that his Chateau had been a Hun Corps Headquarters, and that on their arrival there at the beginning of the war the Hun general asked him to dine with him in his own house. This, he said, he refused to do, and from that day until the Germans left four years afterwards the only room he was allowed to use was the kitchen, and he had to sleep in an attic. He said he was half-starved towards the end of the war, and he took me round his chateau and showed me where very valuable pictures had been hanging, which the Huns had sent back to Germany.

A few days after this the 36th Bn. of the Northumberland Fusiliers sent out a fighting patrol of about half a company and had a most successful engagement with the Germans. This was really open warfare. Lieut. Johnson acted most gallantly in this small action, and received the V.C. for it. We had a lot of hard fighting on the Scheldt.

About 2nd November I was given a week's leave to go to Paris, and I rejoined the brigade on the evening of the 10th. The next day our Corps was going to be pinched out of the line, as the front was narrowing. However, as is well known, the Armistice was declared at 11 o'clock that day. The first intimation I got of the Armistice was at 1 p.m. on the 11th, when some staff officers from the Division came to my brigade Headquarters, and I asked them if they had any news, and they replied did I not know there was an armistice. We had no telephonic communication with Divisional Headquarters, as we were constantly on the move, and our only means of communication was either by D/R or wireless, and the latter was not very effective. Naturally we were all delighted with the news, and celebrated it by sharing a bottle of port!—the only liquor we had in the Mess—amongst about 12 officers.

I shall always remember the relief that night, knowing that we need not draw the curtains in our headquarters, —because, of course, at that time we were in that part of

France which was constantly being bombed—and therefore were able to have all the rooms fully lighted, with no fear of enemy attack from the air.

The Division then marched back towards Lille, and we were put into excellent billets on the outskirts of the town. There we had good sport with our Brigade fox hounds, hunting hares on the French artillery practice ground.

From there we moved back to a mining area, and the 178th Brigade was sent down to Dunkirk to form the staff of an embarkation camp for the purposes of demobilization. This perhaps was the hardest work I had in the war, because on arrival there I was shown a large expanse of sand dunes, on which stood a big brick building which could be used as a dining hall for about 2,000 men, the only other signs of a camp being a few ablution benches, etc., which had been erected by the Sappers. After the brigade had been there two days the camp opened, and we received our first batch of men for demobilisation. They consisted of a mixed crowd of some 2,000 men. These kept increasing daily, and at one time (it was when the men who were due to return to France from leave refused to embark at Folkestone) I had over 16,000 men in the camp for a week. Part of the camp was mud well over your ankles (I may mention that on the French maps this part of the camp was shown as a marsh), and the men naturally became very restless at there being no boats to take them home. I used to wander round the camp by myself and stand on a packing case and try and explain to them that it was not our fault that they could not get home, but the fault of their comrades who refused to come out again. I think I am right in saying that this embarkation camp was one of the very few that did not have a mutiny of some description at the end of the war. The system of intelligence was extraordinarily good, and if there was talk of anything approaching a mutiny amongst these demobilized men, I knew about it next morning.

We had one very unpleasant incident there, as a battalion of Maoris was sent to Dunkirk by mistake—they should have gone to Havre. Most of the private soldiers carried automatic pistols, and used to go into the town of Dunkirk (which, incidentally, was out of bounds) and hold up the estaminet proprietors and rob their tills. There were only about three white officers with them, and I ordered the C.O., who was a sick man, to have an officers' patrol in the town every night. This he did, with the result that one night the officer in command of the patrol was murdered by one of his men they found in the town. The officer was a Maori.

After about two months the camp became quite habitable. We had three large dining halls capable of accommodating 2,000 to 3,000 men each, and a large "delouser," which was capable of delousing about 800 men in three-quarters of an hour. We had a very fine theatre, made out of an aeroplane hangar, with the latest and most up-to-date stage and lighting. We had a concert party who used to give entertainments practically every night, and also a cinema.

The difficulty in running this camp from the Brigade point of view was that as the Army was being demobilized, so also was the 178th Brigade, and eventually the 176th Brigade had to be sent to reinforce us. The men of the Brigade carried out all duties in the camp, such as dining hall waiters, cooks, sanitary men, etc., and they worked extraordinarily hard.

We had one or two race meetings there and gymkanas, to one of which the Divisional Commander, General Smythe, came by aeroplane, landing on the course. One of the events in one of these gymkanas was a "Mounted Lloyd Lindsay," with teams of four officers. There were, I think, eleven teams entered, and it was won by a team composed of General Smythe, Brig.-Gen. McDouall (who was Base Commander there), Lieut.-Col. Brazier Creagh, and myself. The other teams could not shoot and we could!

I am afraid these reminiscences of mine have been chiefly personal; but, as I said at the beginning, it is very hard to remember events ten years after they have happened, and I will only conclude by saying that I never wish to command a finer body of men than the Sherwood Forester Brigade of the 59th Division.

By BRIG.-GEN. J. W. STIRLING, C.B., D.S.O.

(Since deceased, June, 1926).

On the 21st March, 1918, the 59th Division, commanded by Major-General Romer, C.B., C.M.G., as part of the 6th Corps, occupied a position facing the German Hindenburg line, and extending from Bullecourt on the left to a point in the Hirondelle Valley about 1,500 yards E. by N. of Noreuil, and covering a front of about 3,400 yards.

The Hirondelle Valley was the Corps boundary which ran S. of Noreuil, the 6th Division being on the right. The 59th Division had taken their position on 12th February, 1918, and had done a lot of defence work.

The Infantry was disposed with 176th and 178th Brigades in the front line, with B.H.Q. at L'Homme Mort and Vraucourt respectively. The 177th Brigade formed the Division reserve.

The Artillery covering the Division consisted of the Divisional Artillery, the 295th and 296th Brigades R.F.A., plus the 26th Army Brigade (one Battery of the latter, however, the 117th, commanded by Major Hilditch, M.C., was retained as a mobile reserve), and the Divisional Trench Mortar Batteries.

It was divided into two groups in liaison with the two Infantry Brigades holding the line as follows:—

Right Group, Lt.-Col. Hinton, C.M.G., 26th Army Brigade. H.Q., Vraucourt.

- A, B and C Batteries, 295th Brigade, 18 Pdr.
- 116th Battery, 26th Army Brigade, 18 Pdr.
- D, 295th Brigade, 4.5 How.
- Half of Division Trench Mortars.

Left Group, Lt.-Col. Shaw Stewart, C.M.G.

- A, B, and C Batteries, 296th Brigade, 18 Pdr.
- A, 26th Brigade, 18 Pdr.
- D, 296th Brigade, 4.5 How.
- Half of Division Trench Mortars.

These Batteries were in echelon in the Hirondelle and Ecoust-L'Homme Mort Valleys respectively.

The Trench Mortars were dug in in front of the Railway reserve trench in two groups, one around Bullecourt, the other on the right or south flank.

In conjunction with the Divisional Machine Gun Battalion, the S.O.S. line of guns, howitzers and trench mortars covered the front of the Division.

During the night of 20th-21st March, owing to the reports received of enemy movement and massing of guns, all Batteries were engaged in an extensive programme of harassing fire, to which the enemy made little reply until between 4.45 and 5 a.m., when the storm broke.

The whole of the first line defence from Bullecourt to Noreuil, including the supports and reserves at L'Homme Mort and Vraucourt, was subjected to an intense bombardment. Owing to the fog and dust observation was most difficult, and all overhead telephone wires were practically useless. Fortunately, buried cables had just been completed in the Hirondelle Valley, and from L'Homme Mort to the Infantry Battalion H.Q.'s in the Railway Reserve Trench, and by means of the Artillery Liason Officers with the Infantry Battalions the O.s'C. of groups were able to learn the happenings in the front line. These, however, were most confused, but we gathered that the main enemy attack on our front was developed through the Hirondelle Valley, and they swept along the rear of the Railway Reserve Trench, where fierce hand-to-hand fighting took place, and also advanced on Noreuil. The Liaison Officer with one Battalion H.Q., in Railway Reserve Trench, Lieut. Spite, gave information as to the enemy's progress until at last he started: " The Huns are coming down the dug-out stairs. Goodbye; I am breaking the 'phone." Another Liaison Officer, Lieut. St. Leger, D/295, attached to the left battalion 178th Brigade, was severely wounded, and subsequently died of wounds; he behaved in a most gallant manner. Col. Hodgkin, the Battalion Commander, who was taken prisoner, wrote of him: "Lieut. St. Leger fought with a rifle all the time, and he was continually getting wounded. When he was taken he was alive, but suffering from a badly broken jaw and several wounds in the body."

The enemy also broke through in the neighbourhood of Bullecourt, and from there attacked Ecoust.

By 9.30 a.m. the enemy was in possession of the Railway Reserve Trench, and the whole of the Infantry of the two Brigades in the first line had been cut off. The forces available for defence now consisted of three battalions of the 177th Brigade in reserve near Mory. At 11 a.m. the enemy had occupied Ecoust and Noreuil and was advancing on Vraucourt Copse. The advanced sections, as well as the whole of the trench mortars, had been overrun, but in nearly every case they had expended the whole of their ammunition, and had also put the guns out of action.

Instructions had been given that when it was necessary to destroy guns, the best way would be to jam an H.E. shell in the muzzle and fire another with a long lanyard. After the Armistice, Major Maudsley, M.C., who was with his advanced section of the 295th Brigade in Noreuil, told me that this method was most effective, and that the chase of the guns split up into two or three pieces.

This officer, who with a rifle kept back the Germans in the outskirts of Noreuil, was unfortunately taken prisoner. He sent back two of his subalterns with all unwounded men. Lieut. Godfrey, who was severely wounded shortly after, and Lieut. Scott, a most gallant young officer, who was unfortunately killed at Quesnoy Farm a few days after, and he himself went down to tell the wounded men who had been placed in a dug-out that they were forced to retire, but on coming out he found himself surrounded by Germans, and had no alternative but to surrender. At about 11 o'clock, as the information received at Divisional Headquarters was most meagre, I sent my orderly officer, Lieut. Lascelles, to the Headquarters of the Left group to ascertain the position there. He returned about 2 p.m., stating that Lieut.-Col. Shaw Stewart, C.M.G., 296th Brigade R.F.A., had been severely wounded about 5 a.m.; that the Adjutant, Capt. Watson, had carried on the control of the group until the arrival of Major Curran, M.C., 296th Brigade, and that the general situation was as described in the previous paragraph.

This information was most valuable, and the way in which Lieut. Lascelles carried out the duty under heavy fire was most creditable.

The evacuation of the Hirondelle Valley position is described in the report of Major Bates, D.S.O., M.C. (attached).

This officer, wounded in the shoulder, after handing over the personnel of his Battery to Lieut. Sitwell, came to Division Headquarters (Behagnies) and reported on the situation before going to the dressing station, and in this way added greatly to the services he had rendered in the retirement from the Hirondelle Valley.

The wisdom of the plan by which silent Batteries in concealed positions had been arranged for was now apparent, the only Artillery available for keeping back the enemy advance in the Hirondelle Valley being the six guns of A.295, carefully dug in in the outskirts of Vraucourt, and two guns of B.295, at another point. This section suffered severely. Lieut. Wilson, in charge, was killed, and Lieut. Scott, who had retired from the advanced section in Noreuil, took command about mid-day and kept up a continuous fire until dusk, when the guns were withdrawn.

The 117th Battery, 26th Army Brigade, less two guns attached to left group, commanded by Major Hilditch, M.C., had been held in mobile reserve under the orders of Brigadier-General commanding the 177th Infantry Brigade, which formed the Divisional Reserve. About 3 p.m. one section took up a position near the Sugar Factory at Vraucourt in support of the above-mentioned Artillery of the right group. Lieut.-Col. Hinton, C.M.G., commanding the right group, personally directed their action, and their guns, together with A/295 and the guns of B/295, by their continuous fire, stopped the enemy's advance in the Hirondelle Valley and their debouchment from Vraucourt Copse. The remaining two guns of 117th Battery, under Lieut. Millar, took a position near Mory.

At about 5 p.m., no information having been received as to the situation at Vraucourt, the C.R.A., accompanied by Lieut. Lascelles, proceeded to the Right Group Headquarters and found that the Infantry Brigade Headquarters had been withdrawn to the previously prepared position in the sunken road south of Mory, and no formed body of Infantry was to be seen in the neighbourhood, and on proceeding to the position of the section of 117th Battery, near the Sugar Factory, it was found that Col. Hinton, C.M.G., had just been killed. It was therefore arranged that as soon as it was dark the six guns of A/295, the two guns of B/295, and the two guns of 117th Battery should be withdrawn to the south of Mory, and this was successfully done.

Orders were also sent to Major Akerman, D.S.O., M.C. to take command of all available guns of 295th and 296th Brigades, which had been directed to a position where dumps of ammunition had been prepared.

To return to the Left Group. By mid-day the enemy had occupied Ecoust and Longatte, and pushed out parties with machine guns along the ridges on N.W. and S.E. of the valley in which the Batteries were echeloned. B/296, the most advanced Battery, was the first to feel the effect of this action, and Capt. Godwin, who at about 11 a.m. took over command from Major Curran, proceeded to Group H.Q. to take the place of Col. Shaw Stewart, wounded, was obliged at about 1.45 p.m. to evacuate the position. Two of the guns were already out of action through hostile fire, and the remainder were disabled.

He proceeded with his gunners to the position of A/26, and found that Battery about to retire, so that the personnel of both Batteries fell back on D/296. This Battery had suffered heavily. Capt. Montague and Lieut. Rous had both been wounded, and 2nd Lieut. Moore was in command. A stand was made on the ridge in rear of D/296 Battery, where a Battalion of Infantry was in position, but as the guns were under machine gun fire, Capt. Goodwin decided to abandon them, having first got all the wounded men away and disabled the howitzers. C/296 was evacuated about the same time.

Between 3 and 4 p.m. the enemy, who had evidently been strongly reinforced, made a determined attempt to advance from Ecoust and Longatte, offering a splendid target to A/296, under Capt. MacGuinness, and the section of 117th Battery, with 106 fuses; these were used with tremendous effect, and completely broke up the attack. After dark these guns retired on Mory.

Lieut. Williams, C/296, who was on duty at the O.P. west of Ecoust on the morning of the 21st March, rendered very valuable assistance during the whole day, first by sending information as to the enemy's movements, and also by collecting stragglers from Batteries and Infantry, with whom he held successive positions on the ridge N.W. of the valley which runs between Ecoust and L'Homme Mort. For his gallant conduct he was recommended by the Infantry Brigadier of the 179th Infantry Brigade for a M.C., which was subsequently awarded to him.

By 9.30 p.m. on the 21st all the guns (20) of the 295th and 296th Brigades which had been saved were concentrated at Mory under the command of Major Akerman, D.S.O., M.C.

No less than forty-six guns and howitzers, in addition to trench mortars, had fallen into the enemy's hands; but in making this sacrifice the 59th Division Artillery may claim to have shared with the Infantry of the Division (which had suffered so terribly) the honour of holding the German attacks on that fateful day (21st March, 1918), and so allowing the reinforcing Divisions, the 40th and 42nd, to form a new line of defence.

The action of the combined Brigade of the twenty guns available under the command of Major W. P. Akerman, D.S.O., M.C., during the 22nd, 23rd, 24th and 25th March are contained in that officer's report attached.

On the 23rd the 59th D.A. passed under the orders of the 40th Division Headquarters, near Bucquoy, and was transferred to the 4th Corps.

On the 25th the H.Q. of 59th D.A. moved to Ablainzevelle, the administrative portion, with Staff Captain, forming a rear headquarters at Bienvillers.

On the 26th March so many guns and howitzers had been obtained for the Division, through the efforts of

Major Parker-Jervis, M.C., the Staff Captain, that it was possible to reform the Divisional Artillery into two Brigades, which formed a group under the 42nd Division, commanded by the O.C. 59th D.A., with H.Q. at Essarts.

The Batteries were placed in position on the northern slopes of the ridges running from Quesnoy Farm to Douchy, with S.O.S. lines passing through Ablainzevelle, which was occupied by the enemy, and covering the northern portion of the position passing through Bucquoy, which was held by the 42nd Division.

On 3rd of April this position was subjected to a very heavy bombardment, and again on the 5th April, when the Germans attacked Bucquoy in force; fortunately, their attack failed, the Infantry of the 42nd Division maintaining all their positions.

Subsequent to this date the situation became stabilized and settled down into trench warfare with periodical bombardments.

In connection with the incidents of the 21st March and subsequent days, honours were awarded to the under-mentioned officers:—

Major Bates, Bar to M.C.
Capt. Godwin, M.C.
Capt. Watson, Bar to M.C.
Capt. Archibald, R.A.M.C,. M.C.
Lieut. Cross, M.C.
Capt. Cumming, M.C.
Capt. MacGuinness, M.C.
Lieut. Williams, M.C.

And in addition to these and the officers already referred to, special mention should be made of Capt. H. O. H. Eden, M.C., Brigade-Major 59th D.A., recommended for D.S.O., though it was decided that as a Captain he was not eligible for that honour.

Major V. C. Hilditch, commanding 117th Battery, 26th Army Brigade, attached 59th D.A., who received a D.S.O. in recognition of his services. A born soldier, he enlisted as a gunner in 1914 and rose to the rank of Lieut.-Colonel in four years, having been awarded a D.S.O. and

M.C. with two bars. After his return to England, on appointment to the School of Gunnery, he succumbed to an attack of pneumonia following influenza, to the great regret of all who knew him.

Major W. P. J. Akerman, D.S.O., M.C., of whom the C.R.A., 59th Division, reported to the 4th Corps as follows:—

"I think the able manner in which this officer gathered up the debris of the different Batteries, and commanded them as a fighting organisation from the evening of the 21st until the 26th March, is most praiseworthy, and marks him out as an exceptional leader of men. His courage, judgment and quiet manner are unsurpassed, and I hope that his conduct may receive some special mark of approval."

I believe that he subsequently received a Bar to the D.S.O. on account of his gallant conduct.

REPORT OF MAJOR A. G. BATES, D.S.O., M.C., COMMANDING D/295.

From about 2 a.m. onwards the Battery was engaged with counter preparation at stated intervals. At 4.45 a.m. the weather was very thick; so thick that "C" Battery flashes 150 yards away were only just visible, and some difficulty was experienced in seeing aiming post lights. At 5 a.m. a heavy and remarkably accurate barrage of 5.9 H.E. and 77mm. gas was put down on the battery position, and from the general noise, on our front line as well. To verify this I got through to my forward section, who told me that they also were being heavily barraged, but with H.E. only, and that the front line was also being very heavily shelled. They further told me that the weather was far too thick to see any Very lights or S.O.S. signals. Communication with group had gone, so I opened a slow rate on S.O.S. lines.

This state of affairs continued until 7 a.m., when, still having got no news, I sent out an officer's patrol to get in touch with the nearest support Battalion.

This patrol, on reaching its destination, sent back word that the Infantry there had had no news of any kind from the front line, but that there was still a very heavy barrage on front and support lines and Noreuil village.

By 8 a.m. the mist and smoke were so thick that I had still failed to get into touch with group H.Q. or my forward section by lamp. I then received an orderly from Group H.Q. ordering me to fire on Counter Preparation "A." This I did, at the same time informing Group that we could see no S.O.S. signals owing to mist.

Gas shelling then ceased, while H.E. continued, but not so heavily. An orderly from forward section brought the following news from 2nd Lieut. White, who had taken command when Lieut. Cocks was wounded. He had been in communication with Major Trench, of the Support Battalion, near Iggaree Corner. They had had no news of any kind from the front line. Support line was getting very heavily shelled. I then saw a company of Infantry of the

6th Division going back along the half-dug communication trench just south and parallel to the Noreuil-Vaulx Road.

I spoke to the officer in charge, who told me:—

(1) That the enemy had attacked on his Divisional front, and that he was under orders to occupy the Corps line.

(2) That he formed part of a Support Battalion, some of which were ordered to remain in the Sunk Road south of Noreuil, and others to garrison the Corps line.

On this I went back on to S.O.S. lines.

Next, on information received from the 178th Brigade I.O., I barraged in front of Railway Reserve.

Next, the personnel of my forward section arrived and informed me:—

(1) That the enemy were in Noreuil.
(2) That they had fired all their ammunition.
(3) That they had blown up their guns.
(4) That approximately half their detachments were out of action.
(5) That 116th Battery forward section had done same half-an-hour previously.

Next, I could see that a fight was taking place near Iggaree Corner. It was some minutes before I could see clearly what was happening; meanwhile Lieut. Beddington, B/295, arrived with the personnel of his section.

I could see that a fight was taking place in Noreuil Switch, about 100 yards east of where it joined the Sunk Road, in which my section was situated. Further, that Iggaree Corner and the Sunken Road near it were packed with Huns. These were immediately engaged, and, I think, successfully.

Next, Huns began to come out from village and reached a point at the top of the valley east of Noreuil. About two companies of our Infantry were making their way along the ridge going east. The Huns at the top of the valley were engaged with gas shell and one 5 Ch. bag, since first Ch. would not clear at the range of 700 to 800 yards. These Huns were also engaged with a Lewis Gun and a Vickers, also rifles, and were forced to retire towards Noreuil in haste. The two guns which had been on these were now put back on to Iggaree Corner, where much movement was apparent.

The situation looked a little better, since apparently another company was moving up.

C/295 Battery personnel arrived next, reporting Huns in force. They could not be seen from my position, but preparation was made to meet them.

The decisive factor was the appearance of a large force of enemy over the crest N.W. of Vraucourt Copse. The Battery was subjected to a heavy enfilade M.G. fire from this direction, and parties of enemy very quickly made their way down to 116th Battery position. At this moment I had with me, besides the remainder of my own personnel, those of Lieut. Beddington's section of B/295 and C Battery—altogether some seven officers and about thirty to forty men. I had very little time at my disposal, and ordered the temporary disablement of my own guns. Having burnt the secret file of papers, I gave orders to rendezvous in the Corps line five hundred yards down the road.

The enemy's M.G. fire was getting very accurate, and several men were hit.

Having reached the Corps line, I handed over D/295 to Sitwell, and went down to Mory via Vaulx and Group H.Q. Here I found Tyson, 116th Battery (Group H.Q. and 178th H.Q. had gone), and I proceeded to Division H.Q. at Behagnies.

REPORT OF MAJOR W. P. J. AKERMAN, D.S.O., M.C., A/295.

March 21st. I received orders from C.R.A., 29th Division, at 6.30 p.m. on March 21st to take over the remainder of the three Brigades. I was then acting as Senior Liaison Officer at L'Homme Mort. I found my way to the mixed H.Q. of the 295th and 296th Brigades at Mory about 9 p.m.

The Batteries were then all in action, or coming into action.

The Batteries and their Commanders were:—

117th Battery (Major Hilditch, M.C.), six guns.
A/295 Brigade (Capt. Pratt), six guns.
B/295 Brigade (Lieut. Beddington), two guns.
A/296 Brigade (Capt. McGuinness), six guns.

March 22nd. The night was quiet, and in the morning the light was poor, and there was no movement to be observed except of our own troops. Wire communication with the Infantry and the Liaison Officer of the 117th Battery was cut, and observation had to be relied upon. In the afternoon the light improved, and the enemy were seen moving in small bodies, but considerable numbers, along the Vraucourt-Noreuil-Lagnicourt ridge. These were actively engaged by all Batteries, and casualties seen to be inflicted. The 117th Battery profited from their position near the crest for easy command, while the other Batteries in their previously prepared positions were better off for ammunition.

Confused movement from the Sugar Factory on and to the north-east of the St. Leger Road proved to be our Infantry throwing back their right flank.

The situation on the right was obviously obscure, and having received orders to retire to Behagnies, I considered it best to reconnoitre first. Major Hilditch accompanied me, and we visited the Infantry line east of the Bengnâtre-Sugar Factory Road. The enemy were seen making their way singly and in small parties through Vraucourt down the valley. The Infantry were not firing at them, although within 800 yards. I then proceeded to Behagnies, after giving Major Hilditch instructions for the Batteries to fire all the ammunition, if possible, before retiring, in accordance with orders, engaging movement and harassing the Noreuil Valley approaches to Vraucourt.

There was very little enemy Artillery fire, in spite of many low-flying aeroplanes.

By 9.0 p.m. all Batteries were in action in front of Division H.Q. at Behagnies.

During the night we received orders stating that, in consequence of the enemy occupation of Mory, we should have to withdraw to Gomiecourt.

March 23rd. All Infantry Headquarters withdrew from Behagnies in the early morning.

Before daylight I ordered all the Batteries to move into positions N.W. of Gomiecourt to engage the Mory-Ervillers-Behagnies area.

Aware of the difficulty and responsibility attached to distinguishing friend from foe, I gave the task of engaging enemy movement from Mory to Major Hilditch with two guns of 117th Battery.

The Batteries left behind one officer each to receive any orders following on my reconnaissance by daylight.

Daylight showed our Infantry retiring N.W. and S.W. from Mory, engaged by machine gun fire from line Mory-Mort Copse. I enquired from the Infantry Battalion Commanders, 177th Brigade, and found that the intention was to line and dig in on the Ervillers-Behagnies Road, pushing forward their left flank to rejoin the flank of the Division on their left.

There was still touch to the right front to the Army line, and a switch trench was being dug back from there. I then retired to rejoin the Batteries, and fire was opened on Mory and the Mory-L'Homme Mort Road, observation being obtained later from Ervillers.

Observation was possible but not easy, and movement was very confused; so much so that I did not consider it possible to fire on any other targets than the ones mentioned.

The 26th Army Brigade was now under the command of O.C. 177th Infantry Brigade, and 295th and 296th as a sub-Group under O.C. 178th Infantry Brigade, and I did not obtain touch again with them satisfactorily.

A night O.P. was manned at Behagnies, and communication established there by wire.

There was very little Artillery fire from the enemy.

March 24th. The morning opened quietly, and positions were reconnoitred for a move forward by all three Brigades. I visited the Infantry line with Capt. Watson, M.C., and could see the enemy machine gun posts. Our machine guns then engaged them from the sunken road, and could easily have silenced them for a counter attack.

Ammunition supply was becoming difficult, the dump at Gomiecourt becoming exhausted.

In the afternoon the enemy's Artillery and low-flying planes became active.

In the afternoon Capt. O'Brien (C/295) reported that he had six guns in action.

(Note.—During the morning D/296 received three new howitzers, and took up a position in front of the Railway on the Courcelles-Ervillers Road. This position they left in the early hours of the morning of the 25th and retired to Essarts.)

At about 10 p.m. a message was received from B.M., R.A., 42nd Division, that the enemy was reported across the Behagnies-Bapaume Road near Sapignies, and we were to retire at once to Courcelles. I issued these orders to Batteries, and recalled Lieut. Hilton, M.C., from night O.P. at Behagnies, in spite of the fact that all patrols reported quiet on the right flank.

I then returned to discover what the other Brigades were doing. 178th Brigade informed me that Major Hilditch had reconnoitred the whole line on horseback and reported all quiet.

March 25th, 12.15 a.m. I therefore rode after the Batteries and issued orders for the re-occupation of our old positions by all guns, less three of B/295 (one received that morning), which came into action behind the railway.

All Batteries sent men out for a continued patrol until daylight, and the day opened quietly.

Enemy artillery became much more active during the morning against the environs of Gomiecourt.

At 2 p.m., in accordance with orders received and the retirement of our Infantry on the right, which was visible from south of Gomiecourt, I ordered the Batteries to retire.

The Batteries took up positions here in line facing the Gomiecourt-Achiet-le-Grand line, an O.P. being at once established.

The situation was confused, and enemy advance appeared to be confined to the Biefvillers-Bihucourt-Achiet-le-Grand line of approach, which is well wooded.

The Batteries did not fire, but remained in observation.

A/295 Brigade R.F.A. was bombed by one of our aeroplanes when moving into this position.

In the evening the C.R.A., 59th Division, took command, and under orders received, I reconnoitred positions for 295th Brigade, R.F.A., and the Batteries moved there at dawn.

March 26th. Later in the morning we moved under orders to positions near Douchy, and established O.P.'s on the Douchy-Quesnoy Farm ridge.

By LIEUT.-COL. K. C. BRAZIER-CREAGH, T.D.

Towards the end of January, 1915, the 46th Divisional Artillery (1st N. Midland Division Artillery) were instructed to send their respective T.F. Brigade Depots, the surplus officers and men of their War Establishments, also all the permanent Staff Instructors, to form the Second Line Division (59th).

Col. Phillpotts (retired R.H.A.) was appointed C.R.A. without any staff. He spotted a sound business man in Capt. E. M. Parker-Jervis, who had been a land agent, for his Staff Captain. The Headquarters were started in the empty upper rooms of The Prudential Buildings, Luton. Empty packing cases and locally purchased stationery, two Midland Railway clerks and a master tailor—this was the original office which had to cope with the organisation and equipment, etc., of 900 recruits, which arrived from the aforesaid T.F. Brigade Depots, the first week in February. Major K. C. Brazier-Creagh, who had been Staff Captain to the 46th Divisional Artillery, reported for duty as Brigade Major. When these recruits were paraded on arrival, some were so flat-footed they could not march; two or three had glass eyes; and a number had minor injuries to hands and feet, which would not pass them for Infantry, but evidently they were considered fit to be gunners by the Medical and Recruiting Officers of those days. Having no guns or rifles, logs of wood on civilian wagon wheels and broom handles were used to start training until March, 1915. The 46th Divisional Artillery, having gone to France, instructions were received to send officers to Bishops Stortford area, and bring to Luton the discarded impedimenta and civilian transport, etc., they had left behind. As this was never properly handed over (as laid down in King's Regulations), it was the source of months of correspondence between the 46th and 59th Divisional Staffs, War Office, and the Territorial Force Associations of Staffordshire, Lincolnshire and Derbyshire, and tens of thousands of pounds were eventually struck off, as the Equipment and Clothing Ledgers of the 46th Divisional Artillery were incomplete or *non est*.

One, Major E. U. Bradbridge, the genial D.A.Q.M.G. of 59th Division H.Q., acted the Solomon-like arbitrator between the above contending Units and Associations by interviews along the line of least resistance. Recruits poured in, overflowing Biscot Camp, and as all the Permanent Staff Instructors, except one, had been wangled to France with the 46th Division, the N.C.O.'s had to be improvised. School boys and professional men who had influence enough to get them commissions reported daily, but no horses or guns or limbers came to train these. Colonel Phillpotts induced Major Honner (an old gunner) to come from Ireland, and Capt. Anson (Chief Constable of Staffordshire) to take command of the Lincs. and Staffs. Brigades respectively. Capt. Arkwright commanded the Derby (Howitzer) Brigade, and Sir Montague Bradley was sent by the War Office to command the Stoke-on-Trent Batteries. Major Mottram commanded the Staffs. R.G.A., which was attached. A number of debilitated horses were received from Veterinary Hospitals (labelled for light duty only), and 90 m/m muzzle loading guns from some French Museum were sent to train the recruits in driving and gun drill. Just as the training had been organised properly, orders were received to provide drafts for each Brigade of the 46th Divisional Artillery (our first line) of officers and men. This dashed all hopes of the second line ever going on service overseas as a Division. However, after inspection by General Rundle and the urgent representations of Colonel Phillpotts for proper guns to train the officers and men in gunnery, the 1st Home Counties (Howitzer), 59th Brigade, under Col. S. Thomas, and the 1st Wessex R.G.A., under Col. Williams (who were fully equipped), arrived at Luton for combined training of all units. Differences arose daily over the lending and using of these guns by the 59th Batteries, but Col. Williams (being an old gunner) arranged matters eventually with Col. Phillpotts and Majors Honner and Anson (who had all been at " the shop " together). The French curio guns were returned to Woolwich, and 15 pounders, discarded by a Territorial Artillery Division proceeding to India, were received minus dial sights, etc., but were welcomed with joy, as were a few hundred Japanese rifles. However, these rifles were annexed for our

Divisional Infantry a few weeks after by Col. Carleton. The Artillery was ordered to march to Hemel Hempstead, as Luton was overcrowded. We marched and got the impedimenta, guns, etc., to Hemel Hempstead without more animals. By the assistance of Capt. Coe (the cheery Veterinary Surgeon in charge of Stockwood Veterinary Hospital, who later on was A.D.V.S. to 59th Division), we obtained horses to transport the Brigades by stages to Hemel Hempstead. There the Artillery spent the wet winter of 1915-16 in misery. There was no proper drainage to the camp, and the surplus water flooded the huts, messes and cookhouses. The horse-lines were seas of mud. Very little training, except route marching, could be done. We had a couple of field days for the War Office Brass Hats, who came down chiefly to inspect the Infantry. The Artillery were allotted some confined space where no artillery formation could be arranged. Infantry Commanders rarely understand that Artillery must have space to manœuvre. The chief feature learned at these inspections was "how not to do things," and counter-orders arriving every minute by a cheery eccentric sportsman of an A.D.C.—Captain Bagot Chester—to the Divisional G.O.C., who darted about from unit to unit with orders, like a swallow catching flies. Any explanations of, or about the orders, were quite beyond him, and he gave them like an excited rustic viewing a fox breaking covert. Weary months passed of entraining and detraining tactics, and also route marches, enlivened only by a trip to Lark Hill for gun practice, under the keen eye of one, General Brunker, who quickly squashed all the assumed knowledge of gunnery the officers and N.C.O.'s thought they had acquired. As one of the men who had been invalided from France said: "Old Frosty-face didn't half put the wind up them officers and Non-Coms." On returning to camp the Division was suddenly ordered to prepare to entrain for East Coast defence on receipt of telephone orders in one code word. Weeks passed; "nothing doing" on that coast. A new C.R.A. and Brigade Major arrived in February, 1916, to take over. Col. Phillpotts proceeded to command the School of Gunnery at Lark Hill, and Major Brazier-Creagh to form and command the D.A.C. at Luton. The new C.R.A. (Col. L.

Graham) did not remain long; Col. Peel replaced him. The new Brigade Major, Major McLean, who was invalided from France, gave the officers some knowledge of what was expected of them in trench warfare. New Brigade Commanders came to take over the 295th and 296th Brigades, as they were now called, from Cols. Anson and Honner (viz., Major Bridges and Col. Tayor), also a couple of Battery Commanders. General Brunker, after his inspection, recommended that officers who had been Overseas should be sent to the Batteries. Also, the Batteries were made up to establishment in horses, and 15-pounder guns and 5.9 howitzers were replaced by 18-pounders and 4.5 howitzers. On the 26th April, 1916, orders were suddenly sent for the 59th Divisional Artillery to proceed to Ireland to quell the rebellion which had broken out in Dublin. The Batteries entrained at Boxmoor, Watford, and Berkhampstead for Liverpool, and on arriving at Kingstown proceeded by road to Ballsbridge to support the Divisional Infantry. The Batteries came into action, but no firing was done, as the rebellion had fizzled out. The 295th Brigade proceeded to Dublin minus its doctor, so Capt. Grummitt, who was on leave, was telegraphed for to proceed to Dublin and take over his duties. A few days later the 297th Brigade proceeded to Coolmaney, Co. Wicklow, 295th to Kildare, and 296th Brigade camped in Phœnix Park. After a practice camp at Coolmaney, the Brigades were dispersed—297th to Dundalk, 295th to Kildare, and 296th Brigade had a battery at Cahir, Fermoy and Limerick. The 59th D.A.C. having been formed at Luton, were ordered to Ireland to take over the D.A. Columns of the 295th, 296th and 297th, which consisted of all the "dud" N.C.O.'s, men, animals and equipment of the Batteries. As there were twice the number of N.C.O.'s that the establishment allowed, weeding out of the inefficient was a trying ordeal (as the Territorial Regulations do not allow of N.C.O.'s being degraded unless proved inefficient). A few had been sergeants because they had helped to recruit men in their district, but were hopeless at drill, training, or inculcating discipline into their subordinates. The taking over of units was, during the War, a very trying business, as both officers and Quarter-master-Sergeants had very sketchy ideas of Army book-keeping; so much so that units proceeding Overseas are known to have thrown their books overboard on leaving Southampton, but as they omitted to add weights to sink them, they were picked up by patrol boats, who forwarded them to the War Office.

The 59th Divisional Artillery spent a dismal wet winter in Ireland, very discontented at no prospects of ever going on active service. Col. Granet replaced Col. Peel as C.R.A., and both Col. Peel and Brigade-Major McLean proceeded to France to join other Divisional Artilleries. Col. Ouseley and Major Heather replaced them. Very little training was possible, the units being so scattered doing garrison work, and so the winter of our discontent passed. In January, 1917, orders arrived for the Division to proceed to Salisbury Downs, and we were relieved by 63rd Division. There the Division was equipped, etc., to war establishment, and a complete change came over everyone. Keenness and energy became the order of the day, as at last we were to go Overseas, and the finding of drafts for the 46th Division had ceased. After the final practice camp (at which General Brunker so far relented his frosty attitude to Terriers as to compliment some officers on their good shooting, "taking up gun positions," and the men on their driving, etc.), the Divisional Artillery received orders to entrain at Amesbury for Southampton and France early in March. The last units (the D.A.C. and a Battery of the 298th Brigade, which had been made up at Lark Hill during February, under Col. De Satge), arrived at Le Havre on 17th March (St. Patrick's Day) and proceeded to Amiens area for the Somme. The Divisional Artillery was jammed straight into the firing line of that devastated area without any chance of learning trench warfare conditions, and as the Huns were then evacuating their positions on the Somme, the Division was ordered to pursue them. The roads from Foucaucourt through Estrees and Villiers-Carbonnel to Brie, on the Somme river, were blown to pieces, having been No Man's Land for two and a half years. It snowed or rained every day, and froze hard every night; men and animals suffered horribly, as there was no shelter. The Huns, in retreating, had blown in their dug-outs and all the houses in every village. As mechanical transport could not be used owing to the state of the roads and frost conditions, the D.A.C. had to work night and day drawing road metal and, later, timber, to build the bridges over the Somme at Brie; also to assist the A.S.C. to feed the units who were over the Somme in pursuit of the Boche rear-guards at Cartigny, Bouvincourt and Vraignes, over 25 kilometres ahead of their supply railhead depot. All through April the Artillery advanced over the worst country they encountered in France (except at Passchendaele in Ypres salient in September, 1917), through Roisel, Hervilly, and Jeancourt to Ronssoy, Hargicourt and Hesbecourt, facing the Hindenburg line, supporting their Infantry when attacking Le Verguier, the trenches and outposts in front of Villeret. Supplying ammunition to the batteries from the dumps at Proyart and Sars, to the Infantry from near Foucaucourt, over 30 kilometres behind, was fearfully arduous work—motor lorries not being able to work over the roads between Brie and Estrees, and no railway or Deccaville to the Somme until the end of April, when the railway reached Peronne, and during May and June was pushed on to Roisel. Early in April our G.O.C. R.A. (Ouseley) had a bad fall from his horse, bruising his face, and had to go to hospital, and Col. Stirling took over command. In May things had again settled down to trench warfare, raids, etc., as there were no reserve troops behind the Division for attacks. All the horses of the batteries were now becoming emaciated and debilitated, and were sent to the D.A.C. and replaced by horses and mules from that unit, thus rendering it immobile, but gained the advantage of the batteries not losing their good and favourite horses, which they would have had to do had they been sent to rear Veterinary Stationary Hospitals. During June numerous clovers and lucerne patches, sown by the Boches on land that had been cultivated for years for sugar-beet, were cut by the units and used to fatten up these debilitated animals, under Major Coe's (A.D.V.S.) supervision. The 59th Infantry moved northward in the end of May to Rocquigny and Flers area. The 59th Divisional Artillery and D.A.C. were in the area of Cavalry Corps, who relieved the 59th Division, and things were quiet, so all horse transport was used to collect up Hun and British debris and ammunition from devastated areas round the Somme and Roisel dumps. A Divisional Horse Show and Sports were held, and all units had competitions to select their best horses, drivers, and equipment, etc.—a welcome recreation after three and a half months' trekking and fighting. The Army and Corps Staff congratulated General Stirling on the turn-out of the Batteries, men and horses, etc., with the result that the Division was "earmarked" for fresh fields and pastures new. The first honour won by the Artillery was given to a Corporal Kidd, of the D.A.C., for rallying his party when heavily shelled at night, taking up ammunition to Ronssoy Wood, when the mules stampeded, several of them having been killed and their drivers wounded.

At the end of August orders were received to entrain at Peronne for Proven and Poperinghe, in the Ypres salient, and we relieved the 5th Australian Division in front of the Menin Gate and Cambridge Road positions the first week in September. During the weeks that followed there was heavy fighting and the loss of numerous officers and men, including Majors Davenport, McConnel, Capts. Darbyshire, Westby and Marshall (all were blown to bits by shellfire), besides a large number of wounded. Major Davenport had just received his D.S.O., after gaining his M.C. only a month before. His death was mourned by all, as he had been in the 2nd North Midland Division Artillery Brigade since 1908, and the 59th Divisional Artillery since its formation; so also was Capt. Darbyshire in the 4th North Midland (Howitzer) Brigade. The shelling of the gun positions was continuous, and at times so intense as to be made untenable; gunners had to move to other guns in alternative positions and re-open fire when the enemy's "barrages" modified or switched. The Hun Artillery fire, heavy, medium, and field, was accurate—explosive and gas shells mixed—our guns and limbers being overturned or hit, daily showed how excellent was their aeriel observation and sound-range firing. The Hun aeroplanes were even more active than ours, especially at night, bombing all camps and horselines between Ypres and "Pop.," causing numerous casualties of men and animals in the artillery wagon-lines and the D.A.C. Getting huge quantities of shell to the gun positions was a most difficult and arduous job, all having to be packed on mules and led along winding tracks between shell holes. No vehicles could travel over such shelled area as lay between Zonnebeke and the Passechendaele Ridge. Over 200 mules and some horses worked nightly by relays. Work by day was rendered almost impossible by shell fire. Fifty to sixty mules were also constantly employed packing S.A.A. to the Infantry. About 20,000 shells and half-a-million rounds of S.A.A. were transported daily from Stanley, Oxford, Pickering, Overton and Toronto Ammunition Dumps to the firing line during the last weeks of September. During the second week of October we were relieved by the Canadian Division, and moved through "Pop." and Hazebrouck to Lens and Servins area by road. The Artillery lost 20 per cent. of officers and over 25 per cent. of men and animals during their stay in the Ypres salient. After a month's rest and refitting, the Artillery moved through Arras and Bapaume to Flesquieres and Ribecourt (south-west of Cambrai) into the Boche trenches of the Hindenburg line in front of Marcoing, covering the Infantry pushed back from Cambrai by the Boche after the failure of that "stunt" of the "Bing Boys" Army. For this, and our good work in the Ypres salient, several Battery Commanders and Lieutenants with the batteries received M.C.'s or D.S.O.'s in the New Year Honours, 1918. In December the 59th Divisional Artillery went into reserve troops, and after Christmas at Ruyaulcourt, to billets near Doullens. A Divisional Football Competition for the G.O.C.'s Cup kept the men cheery and fit; every unit entered a team, and in the final the 2nd/7th Sherwood Foresters beat the Divisional Ammunition Column by one goal to none (extra time had to be played) amidst great excitement. The weather was bitter, snow and hard frosts every night; animals suffered and lost condition owing to no shelter, except for the gun team horses.

In February, 1918, the Artillery were back in the Hindenburg trenches at Bullecourt, Ecoust and Noreuil (in front of Queant), fortifying same and barbed wiring in the gun positions to prevent, if possible (which it did not), the Huns (who were massing in thousands from Russia and other fronts) from rushing the guns, and over 1,000 rounds per gun were placed in the gun positions and a forward ammunition dump (Sucie) formed near Vraucourt of 6,000 rounds. Army and Corps Staffs issued orders for every unit to plough vegetable plots and plant same during March; and also the wire defences and old trenches were cleared round Gomiecourt, Achiet-le-Grand, Moyenneville, Bucquoy and Miraumont, where petrol tractors were ploughing for sowing of spring corn, etc. This wire would have been invaluable to Infantry for defence to stop the Hun advance six weeks later. During the first week in March, aerial and other information told everyone that the Huns intended to smash through. During the night 20/21 March the Artillery laid down an intensive barrage and counter battery fire, to which the Hun replied with intense fire on our front line from 4.45 a.m. till 9 a.m. on the 21st, overwhelming same, and rushed our obliterated positions, driving the Division back to Ecoust, and later to Ervillers. On the 21st some forward guns which were wired in were lost, and the other guns were brought out that night by the pluck of Majors Akerman and Crossman, and other Battery Commanders. The heaviest guns retreated to Gomiecourt and took up marked positions on the Willow line, which had no defences. Infantry and other units came retreating towards Courcelles. The Artillery took up positions near Ervillers, and shelled the advancing lines from Ecoust and Mory, and held them in check. Sucie ammunition dump fell into the hands of the enemy almost intact, but Behagnies ammunition dump was emptied of 20,000 rounds by the D.A.C. and Battery wagons and supplied to the Batteries; also Achiet-le-Grand and Moyenneville dumps. The 34th Division supported our overwhelmed Infantry, and suffered heavy losses. Five officers and nearly half of the 59th Trench Mortar Unit were taken prisoners, as were a number of the battery officers and men. The horses and ammunition wagons, by luck and great pluck of their drivers and officers, were all got away to Courcelles, which enabled large quantities of ammunition from the aforesaid dumps to be placed in the reserve gun positions on the railway embankment near Courcelles and Achiet, to which the batteries retreated on the nights of the 22nd and 23rd. The 40th and 42nd Divisions, coming to relieve our tired-out and broken

Infantry Brigades, drove the Boches from Ervillers, and gave all units of the 34th and 59th and other Divisions time to retreat in fair order all night on the 23rd to Ayette. Corps and our Division having annexed all the motor lorries when they retreated hurriedly on the 22nd March, hampered the ammunition supply, and left the G.O.C.R.A. and his staff and the 59th Artillery in the air. Our Division having disappeared, the Artillery were left to be attached to each successive Division which came into the line, viz., 40th, 42nd, 62nd, and later on the 39th Division, General Stirling taking on the position of a Group Commander and living with Batteries in the line like the good plucked gunner officer he always was. The Huns, having met a stiff opposition of Artillery and Infantry fire from Ablainzevelle, Bucquoy and Courcelles (where the Air Force burnt their large aerodrome on the 22nd and departed tout suite), were stopped at Achiet-le-Grand and Achiet-le-Petit. The retreat of the broken-up units of the 34th, 59th, 40th Divisions, etc., from Douchy-les-Ayette through Monchy and Bucquoy was done in excellent order, but the chaos at Ayette caused by the marching of relieving troops advancing, and retreating, broken, wearied troops after four days' continuous hard fighting, was awful and distressing. Things were left to Brigade Commanders and Field Officers to sort out their units. Had a few Hun aeroplanes come over Ayette, using machine gun fire or bombs, it would have been a shambles on the 24th March, 1918. By the 25th March things had somewhat straightened themselves out. Our Artillery had got good positions on a line from Monchy-au-Bois to Bucquoy, which they held in spite of intense Boche gas and explosive shell of all descriptions for two months (when they were relieved by 57th Division), and assisted in annihilating thousands of Huns on the numerous attempts to advance from Logeast Wood to Ablainzevelle, which never succeeded. At Souastre some officers and men galloped in with the false information that the Hun cavalry and armoured cars had broken through our Infantry at Hebuterne from Miraumont and were coming on. An enterprising 59th Artillery officer, bidding his unit to stand fast and await his return, started out on the road to Sailly-au-Bois to see if such was true. On reaching Chateau-de-la-Haie, half-way between Foncquevillers and Sailly-au-Bois, he did see what might be an armoured car or lorry, and dismounting, saw through his glasses smoke coming from it. Visibility was poor owing to a smoke haze, but eventually he discovered it to be a steam roller which its plucky driver had been driving for three days and two nights from Achiet-le-Grand with ammunition boxes, old logs, etc. He remarked: "I brought the old girl out from Norwich, and I'm going to take her back. No b—— Boche is going to have her." So rejoiced was this officer at discovering from this engine driver that he had seen no Huns since he left Puisieux-au-Mont the day before, when our Infantry (25th Division, he thought) were being pushed back; but saw only a few mounted British soldiers galloping past him on a parallel road early that morning in the same direction he was going, that he galloped back to Souastre without ascertaining this plucky engine-driver's name and unit—a thing he still regrets and ever will—for this man certainly deserved recommending for honours. On returning to Souastre this Artillery officer found his unit gone. They had been ordered to Pas-en-Artois by some Staff Officer. There were wagons overturned and abandoned all along the roads to Pas and St. Amand, two Artillery guns with breech blocks removed near Gaudiempre (which a party arrived to recover at midnight from the 59th D.A.C., who had taken possession of them meanwhile). Heavy Artillery and three D.A.C.'s were trotting towards Pas and went on to Doullens; all this nearly ten kilometres behind the firing line. Had Corps sent the control officers to Souastre, Bienvillers, and other villages in this area, such a panic would not have occurred. Two days before this the curious sight of a well-known Scotch laird was seen on the road to Monchy from Courcelles (he was Town Major of one of the villages), who was trundling a peasant's wheelbarrow with all his belongings, together with a case of Peter Dawson's whisky on top. He received much chaff from the Tommies and the officers who knew him (he was a weird but cheery senior officer with great ideas of his importance to the Army). During these last days of March, 1918, the great difficulty was the supply of ammunition to the Infantry and Batteries; Division and Corps kept changing and D.A.C.'s were travelling 20 to 30 kilometres a day in search of ammunition dumps, only to find they were emptied or belonged to a Corps who allowed no unit not under their command to load ammunition thereat, no matter how urgently it was required. This neglect of Army Instructions and Regulations, and selfishness, was the cause of many lives being lost, and used up horses and transport, and wasted time shamefully. VI. Corps would not allow animals of IV. Corps to water in their area at Gaudiempre, where there was water sufficient for an Army Corps, pumped by an engine capable of raising 2,000 gallons an hour. Consequently there was a great loss of animals, who had to go ten miles to water from the Souastre-Bienvillers area. When General Foch was made Generalissimo, on 25th March, at the meeting of Army Commanders at Doullens, things were straightened out, and all these panicky units were sent back to their respective map reference in the front line. During the whole of April and May hard fighting and heavy shelling continued from Arras to Albert, but that line was never shifted, and the enemy admit having suffered immense losses, especially south of Arras. The 59th Division Artillery lost over twenty officers and 300 men; but it speaks well for the pluck and determination of the men that sick parades were scantily attended—some units had none for days at a time. During this trying period Col. Stirling and his Brigade Major were badly gassed, and Major Crossman took the latter's place when he went to hospital later. Col. Stirling refused to leave, and recovered wonderfully. The Staff Captain (Parker-Jervis) worked night and day to keep things going, and deserved the M.C. he received later, as did Majors Akerman and Crossman, who received D.S.O.'s; likewise Capts. Watson, Cumming, Halcombe, McGuinness, and others who got M.C.'s for their excellent gunnery. Much " kudos " was received by the 59th Artillery from the Army when they came out of this front and proceeded in June to the 1st Army (Houdain area). It did not remain there long, having been ordered to join the 5th Army (now reformed under General Birdwood) to occupy positions in the Nieppe Forest facing Merville and Neuf Berguin, from which the Portugese had been driven out. Here General Stirling left, and General Joe Laycock took command. This forest reeked of gas and was heavily shelled, causing casualties daily in the Batteries, including Lieut. G. P. Eyre, who was badly gassed and burnt whilst rendering first-aid to his Battery Commander (Major Langford), who had two legs smashed by a gas shell and died a few hours after. Early in August, 1918, the Huns retired from Estaires, Sailly-sur-la-Lys and Laventie, and our Artillery took up positions in front and south of Armentieres from the 74th Division Artillery. During this month and September the D.A.C. and the Battery wagons salved 100,000 rounds of shell, millions of S.A.A., grenades, trench mortar ammunition, etc., between St. Venant and Estaires, which had been abandoned by our troops and the Portugese in their retreat, in addition to hundreds of thousands of brass shell-cases (British and Hun); in fact, cleaned up that area. The first week in October our Infantry forced the Hun back from Armentieres and advanced towards Lille, and the Division entered this town through Lomme and St. Andre on the 17th October. A French interpreter, an Artillery officer and an Infantry officer entered Lille on the evening of the 16th, having met with some inhabitants of Lille at Lomme and St. Andre, who informed them that the Boches were evacuating Lille. These adventurous individuals were fairly mobbed with " beaucoup embraces " by the poor Lillios, who could hardly realize their troubles, misery and slavery were over. When the Infantry marched through Lille the women and children rushed the columns and transport, likewise the Artillery guns and wagons like ants in their joy, regardless of being kicked or run over. Every person seemed to be waving an Allies' flag or " Tricolor," which had been sold to them by the Germans before they left. (Such is the mentality of the Boche.) The Division advanced through Roubaix and Tourcoing, the Artillery via Flers, Hem and Sailly to Templeuve, pursuing the Hun rearguards to and across the Scheldt, where they were held up by the enemy's machine gun fire from Obigies, and Artillery fire from gun positions on both sides of Mont St. Aubert. Here Major Halcombe was killed whilst reconnoitring gun-positions on the Scheldt. Poor Halcombe was our last casualty, and was going on leave the next day; he was one of the best. These gun-positions were found later to be in the Convent Garden and grounds on Mont St. Aubert, which were occupied by nineteen nuns, three of whom were hit by our shells, two killed and the other had her arm and part of her scalp blown off, yet she survived. On the 8th November the Artillery crossed the Scheldt, supporting the Infantry, who were pursuing the flying Huns towards " Ath.," on the road to Brussels, where hundreds of French refugees were met who had been released by the enemy rushing for the Rhine. Instructions were received the day after the Armistice (which the troops regretted, all wishing to go on to Brussels) that the Division was not chosen to be one of the Army for the Rhine, and were to return to the Lille area, where they remained until the end of November, assisting to rehabitate the peasants and gathering in their roots, potatoes, etc., which the Hun had made them grow (for Hans' and Fritz's support during the coming winter by forced labour), and now became their property. The Artillery marched back across the devastated area of Lens and La Bassee to Bethune area, where they spent the rest of the winter salvaging the above-mentioned devastated area, and replacing the inhabitants thereon in tents, huts and shelters.

Towards the end of December, 1918, miners, pivotal and slipmen (Z32's) were released from the Artillery for demobilization to the key industries. During January and February, 1919, began demobilization of animals by grading; officers' chargers and sound mares for breeding marched to Boulogne to be sent to England, geldings (passed sound) for Rhine Army, the remainder for sale, locally; likewise all mules. During March and April the Artillery were gradually reduced to "cadre " strength (i.e., sufficient to take gun, wagons, equipment, and stores to England). General Laycock proceeded to England, Brigade-Major Crossman to the Rhine Army, and Staff Captain Parker-Jervis to England to be demobbed—a very sad parting, as they were very popular. During May each unit's stores and equipment was checked over and brought up to War establishment by indents on Ordnance, etc.—a farce, the use of which to the Army was never fathomed, as on reaching the Demobbing Station in England no real handing over or checking was done. The issuing of this new equipment and stores in France bit by bit to units and taken back by Ordnance in the same manner in England, did not improve them, and made extra work for the Ordnance and everyone. All animals sold to the peasants and public locally made excellent prices.

At the end of May the Artillery entrained at Noeux-les-Mines Station (Bethune area) to Dunkirk Camp, where they were deloused! and remained for nearly three weeks awaiting embarkation—shipping being very scarce, only two transports a week. The last unit to leave Dunkirk was the D.A.C. under Lieut.-Col. Brazier-Creagh (on the 14th June), who had remained from mobilization on August 4th, 1914, until demobilization of the whole 59th Divisional Artillery, which ceased to exist on the 18th June, 1919.

THE LAST FIGHTS OF THE 59th DIVISION, THE LIBERATORS OF LILLE.

By MAJOR-GENERAL SIR N. M. SMYTH, V.C., K.C.B.

On the 30th September, 1918, the 11th Royal Scots Fusiliers attacked the enemy in front of Fromelles, on the celebrated Aubers Ridge, launching their charge across No Man's Land, which had intervened between the Germans and the Allies from 1914 till the spring of 1918, when the Portugese were driven back by the German offensive, and on the 2nd October the 176th and 177th Brigades advanced into Fromelles and to Fournes en Weppes.

On 10th October, 1918, the 59th Division, which side-slipped to the left on 3rd October, was in possession of Wez Macquart, and slowly and by hard fighting and unremitting aggressive tactics pushed back the German forces West of Lille, with the 47th (2nd London) Division (General Corringe) on its right, and the 40th Division (General Peyton), consisting of Class " B " men echeloned in rear of the front line, on the left.

On this day the Major-General inspected reinforcements for the 178th Brigade. The men were young conscripted Class A.1 soldiers from every part of Great Britain, and had no claim to hail from the recruiting areas of the Northumberland or Scots Fusiliers, or the West Riding Regiment, which were the battalions constituting the Brigade, for at this period of the war it was of more importance to maintain the constant flow of reinforcements to the advancing armies than to permit even an hour's delay for the purpose of sorting the rank and file territorially. The 59th Division was engaged hourly—day and night—with the enemy, and our offensive tactics led to a constant drain in casualties.

The Cameron Highlanders of the 40th Division were situated just behind the British front line trenches and No Man's Land east of Armentieres, which trenches had been held from 1914 till April, 1918. These Highlanders' advanced posts were visited by the Major-General of the

59th Division, in order to arrange for combined action and a refusion of the flank on the left of the 59th Division, and this was eventually accomplished entirely by a detachment of the Divisional Machine Gun Battalion, which faced due north. On this night, the wind being favourable, a thousand gas projectors, which had been previously placed in position, were discharged at the enemy's advanced lines and machine gun positions in front of Capinghem. The sound of the discharge was drowned by our simultaneous bombardment of the enemy's artillery positions, and by our indirect machine gun fire directed on selected targets. The discharge illumined the landscape as by a flash of lightning, and the deadly gas containers hurtled through the air and crashed among the enemy.

Some prisoners captured the next day, on being cross-questioned, reported for the first time that it was rumoured that the Kaiser and Crown Prince had been told to abdicate by their ministers.

On the 14th October the Division made a further advance, killing many of the enemy, capturing 23 prisoners and two machine guns. The prisoners confirmed the belief that the 120th German Brigade had been relieved by the 121st Brigade the night before. The Major-General was at the Headquarters of the 178th Brigade, near La Vesée, when it was heavily shelled with gas shells. This was a common experience, for the enemy aimed a gas shell concentration at some point of our area four or more times daily at this period.

On the 16th October the 57th Division (General R. Barnes) took over the right Division sector from the 47th (London) Division, which withdrew to get ready to rail to Italy. Eventually, owing to the situation on the Western front, the 47th Division was brought back to the Fifth Army and entered Lille on 28th October, to be acclaimed as its deliverers on tricoloured posters.

On Thursday, the 17th October, the 59th Division, whose strong patrols were constantly pressing the enemy back, closely supported by the advance of the whole attacking system of the front line, machine guns, supports, reserves and artillery, succeeded in advancing as far as Lille, astride the Bailleul-Armentieres-Lille Road, and by the evening the Haute Deule Canal and river had been crossed to the north of Lille according to plan, and the enemy retiring from La Madéleine was effectively followed by our contact patrols.

Orders had been issued prohibiting anyone in the 59th Division from entering Lille. The city was to be encircled, and it was the task of the 59th Division to pass it on the north and pursue the enemy beyond.

Every bridge leading into Lille or towards the east had been blown up by the enemy, but by working all night the Divisional Engineers had bridged the Haute Deule Canal and river by 5.50 a.m., and on the 18th October Lille was encircled completely by the victorious British.

The enemy took with them in their retreat every able-bodied man, all horses, cattle and food. There were no men of the age or physique fit to bear arms left in French or Belgian territory west of the Scheldt. Every boy over twelve years of age had been marched off by the Germans, carrying on his back what food or sustenance he could collect for a ten days' march, and carrying with him a blanket or rug.

The entire industries of the country had been destroyed by the removal or destruction of all machinery. In their retreat the Germans blew up the railways, bridges, cross-roads and defiles; but our advance was yet too rapid to allow of the completion of their nefarious schemes.

Thousands of women greeted the stalwart and bronzed soldiers of the 59th Division, and hundreds of anæmic children accompanied the marching columns and stood around the British guns whenever they came into action and cheered in ecstasy when the guns fired. Every house from Lambersart, on the west of Lille, as far as the Scheldt, displayed a French or Belgian flag or a combination of the flags of the Allies, and our aeroplanes and patrols were able to report the exact progress of the German retreat by the clearly visible flag-bedecked houses. These flags had doubtless been kept in concealment, and had been secretly sewn together by the weary fingers of half-starved but still hopeful women and girls during long years of degradation under the tyranny of Kaiserdom.

The relentless pursuit continued, the heroic advanced patrols of the 59th continued to take prisoners, to slay the dishonoured foe, and to thrust between and in the teeth of the Germans' machine guns and artillery fire. The relation by the unhappy inhabitants of their ill-treatment inspired our men to redoubled efforts, and they pressed upon the Germans, many of whom were routed and, disencumbering themselves of shrapnel helmets and accoutrements, sought safety in disgraceful flight.

The 59th Division, which was now constituted the advanced guard of the 11th Corps (General Haking), was reinforced by the 2nd King Edward's Horse (Colonel Dick), the Divisional Cyclists, Heavy Artillery, while the Portuguese Artillery and three Portuguese battalions were held in reserve.

On the 18th October the Headquarters of the Division were established in the Mansion at La Madéleine, on the Lille-Tourcoing Road, which had been inhabited during the war by the notorious, the brutal and despicable Prince Rupert of Bavaria, who had covertly ordered the murder of prisoners of war and the persecution of women and children.

As the 59th Division pressed back the enemy, who continued to put up a stubborn but ineffective resistance beyond Lille, the 57th Division guarded the exits of the city in order to prevent movement of civilians on the roads.

On the 18th and 19th the enemy retired sullenly, putting up a well-correlated machine gun defence, but our men were not to be denied and drove the enemy back to the Scheldt. The Scots Fusiliers pursued the enemy at a rapid pace, and outstripping the mounted troops, entered Froyennes, on the outskirts of Tournai, and captured some of the enemy who were drinking there. Fighting across the open, our Brigades converted the enemy's rear-guard action into a flight.

On the 20th October, the 25th King's Liverpool Regt. (Lieut.-Col. C. E. Lembcke), of the 176th Brigade, which had marched from Wez Macquart, where it had been rallied in reserve, passed Lille to the Scheldt, a distance of 21 miles, in 20 hours, crossed the river in the face of strong

THE LAST FIGHTS OF THE 59th DIVISION.

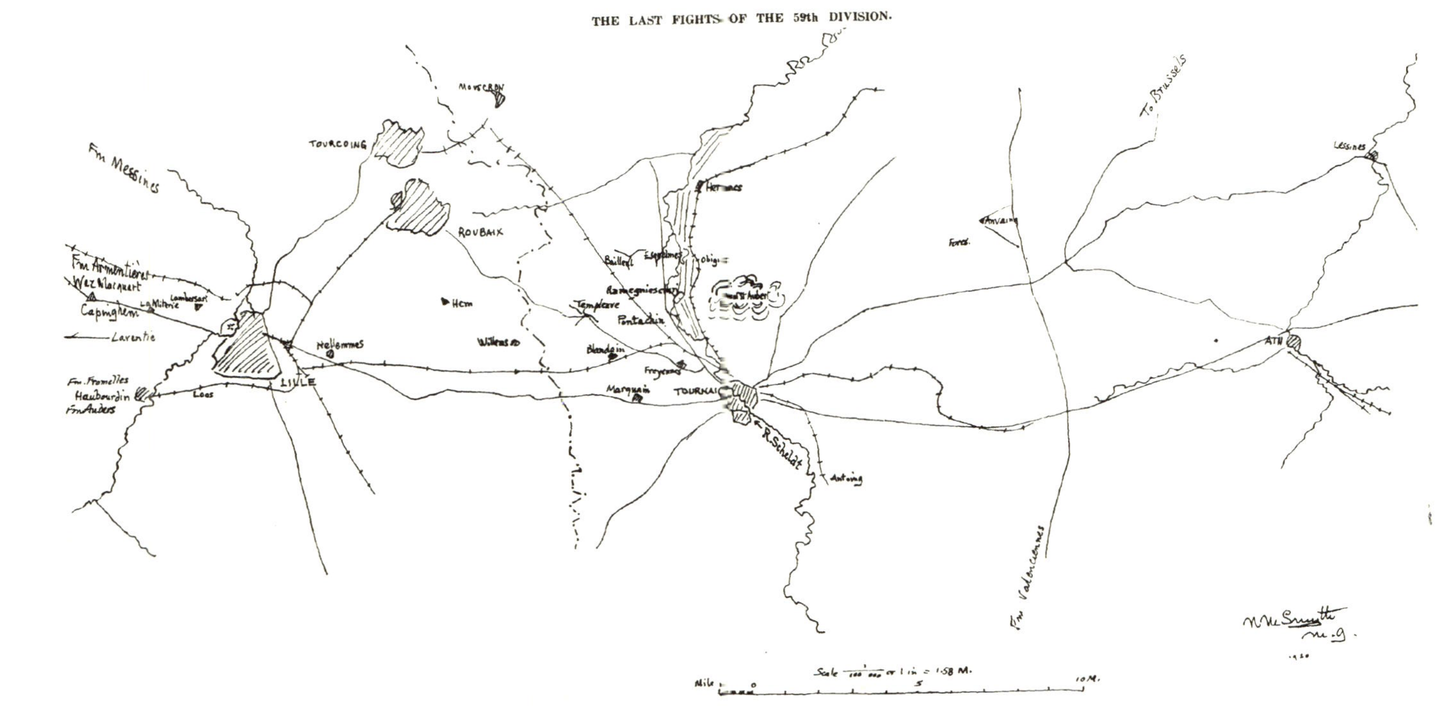

opposition from all arms, and formed three bridge-heads to cover two foot bridges and a ferry which they had thrown in the face of the enemy to the right bank near Ramegnies Chin and Esquelmes. At the same time the 178th Brigade crossed at Pont-a-Chin and formed a bridge-head about 100 yards beyond the bridge, which was handed over next day to the 57th Division to hold when the 59th Division once again side-slipped to the left, handing over results of its fighting to another Division to hold which was weaker in numbers.

Thus the 59th Division were the first of the Allies to cross the Scheldt.

During the next few days, by a series of vigorous raids, resulting in many captures of enemy prisoners and machine guns, our bridge-heads were extended under the shadow of the strongly-defended Mont St. Aubert, from which the enemy looked down upon us.

At last, on the 7th November, the situation was so far prepared that the Major-General crossed to the Tournai-Herinnes Railway, carried a reconnaissance, and brought the troops to the heights on the right bank covered by the Divisional and Portuguese Artillery. On the 9th November the 178th and 176th Brigades advanced to Auvaing, ten miles east of the river, driving the enemy before them.

At the eleventh hour of the eleventh day of the eleventh month all firing ceased. The Armistice found the advanced posts of the Division in front of Lessines, with a detachment of the Northumberland Fusiliers and Royal Engineers at Ath and Leuze for the purpose of mending the railway and viaducts.

Thousands of released prisoners of the Allies, including Italians, and the French and Belgian lads who had been herded eastwards during the last days of the tyrant's domination, poured westwards in a continuous stream; ragged, starved, emaciated, yet jubilant, singing and marching under the Allies' flags; a strange contrast to the calmly working, dour and disciplined soldiers who bore the sacred emblem of King Offa's Cross, of which they had indeed proved worthy, for in the hour of victory there was no excess, no unseemly exultation, no vain glory; each man's character, built upon the foundation of duty, remained honourable, gentle, merciful, and, as always, cheerful.

A BRIEF DESCRIPTION OF THE D.A.D.O.S. BRANCH OF THE 59th DIVISION.

By LIEUT.-COL. J. DODDS, O.B.E., AND CONDUCTOR RICHARDSON.

The Division was formed at Luton, Bedfordshire.

Starting with very small beginnings, it was the first 2nd line Division ready to proceed Overseas. The D.A.D.O.S. at that time was Captain G. Webster. Sudden secret orders were received on April 23rd, 1916 (Easter Monday), for the Division to move to Liverpool at once; 178th Brigade moved first. Arriving at Liverpool, the Brigade embarked on board two boats and were taken to Kingstown, Ireland. During the following days the rest of the Division followed. The D.A.D.O.S. opened a dump at Kingstown, and supplied all stores and ammunition required. One B.W.O. was in Ireland with the 178th Brigade, and he functioned direct to the C.O.O., Dublin, drawing stores and ammunition under strong guards, as continual street fighting was going on.

When the rebellion was subdued, the D.A.D.O.S. moved to Phœnix Park, Dublin, with D.H.Q. 176th Brigade was also in Dublin. 177th Brigade was moved to Limerick and district, whilst 178th Brigade moved to the Curragh, the B.W.O. in each case being with the B.H.Q. and administering there for Ordnance stores and questions relating thereto, the D.A.D.O.S. being in telephonic communication with them and visiting them constantly in his car. On 6th August, 1916, Capt. Jackson Dodds was sent in relief to Capt. Webster.

The Division remained in Ireland until January, 1917, when it was moved to Salisbury Plain.

No transport was taken to Salisbury, a transfer of vehicles being made with units of the 73rd Division.

The final equipping was made at Tidworth—all stores being drawn from C.O.O., Tidworth, whose help during a strenuous time made smooth working, and was much appreciated.

The D.A.D.O.S. went to France February 13th, 1917, to make preparations for the move of the Division, etc. The remainder of his staff followed on the 23rd February. The first dump was opened at Saleux. Arrangements were made for the second blanket per man and all winter clothing, trench stores, etc., required and allowed to a Division in France.

The dump was moved to Bayonvillers on February 28th, about four miles behind the trenches held by the Division at Foucaucourt. With no addition to the D.A.D.O.S. staff, all winter clothing, including gumboots, waterproof capes, field boots, waterproof cap covers, were issued here. It involved very hard work and long hours for the whole staff. The dump was moved to Proyart, where we took over from the 50th Division. The billets and storage accommodation were good.

The Divisional workshops were opened, armourers, blacksmiths, boot-makers, tailors and gumboot repairers being attached from Battalions.

The armourers very quickly received plenty of work in the repair and overhaul of rifles and machine guns.

The latter were repaired when possible, and if beyond repair, were stripped—the spare parts used for the repair of others. Thus when two guns were badly hit one gun could be made out of the two; this relieved the Base workshops.

During this period the enemy retreated towards St. Quentin. The roads at this time were in a very bad state, and it was impossible to establish a complete dump forward.

On 30th March a small dump was opened at Prusle, and under great difficulties through bad roads and congested traffic, necessary stores were taken from the main dump at

Proyart, and issues were made to units from there in their own transport. The weather was very bad—snow, rain and bitter cold—and the dump at Prusle, which was simply a tarpaulin on tentpoles, was a sea of mud, and work was carried out under great difficulties.

On April 9th we crossed the Somme and opened a dump at Estree-en-Chaussee. The village was practically demolished by the enemy, but a small farmhouse, which had more or less escaped ruin, was used as a dump. Mines having been left in ruined buildings, the office and men's billets were moved from the farmhouse under canvas.

During the push forward the workshops were discontinued and the N.C.O.'s and men returned to their Battalions, with the exception of cycle fitters.

Divisional workshops proved to be more or less useless then, and afterwards, when troops were moving forward. Only during a prolonged stay at any one place are they a success.

Conferences were held weekly by the A.D.O.S. of the III. Corps of the D.A.D.O.S. of each Division for the purpose of exchanging views and making suggestions for the better running of work for Divisions situated under the same conditions.

During May the second blankets were withdrawn from units and returned to the Base for cleaning and packing for the ensuing winter.

A move was made on 24th May to Equancourt, but the conditions were not suitable, and the dump was moved to Ytres on the 26th. The dump and billets were all under canvas. A road was quickly built into the camp, and the site was a good one. D.A.D.O.S. here gave a demonstration in the use of the Yukon pack.

The Division was moved to the Ypres sector on September 17th. D.A.D.O.S. staff remained at Winnezeele, and got the Division thoroughly equipped. On 22nd the dump was moved to Poperinghe.

The third battle of Ypres was then in progress. We lost heavily in machine guns, and three times a lorry had to be sent up to St. Jean at night to deliver both Vickers and Lewis guns.

We were congratulated by the Staff Captains for the quick response to their demands. On the receipt of the demands by wire, often with little enough information, lorries were sent off to the gun park, and within a few hours of receiving the wire the new guns were handed over.

The journey these lorries had to make was most perilous, being under gunfire the whole time. On one occasion the men ran into gas, but no serious casualties resulted.

The bombing at Poperinghe was the worst experienced up to this time. On the 29th (a brilliant moonlight night) 250 bombs were dropped on the town, and although pieces were knocked out of the buildings we occupied, no casualties occurred; 26 bombs fell within 100 yards of the office in four to five hours.

On October 1st we very thankfully left Poperinghe and went to the sleepy little village of Steenbecque, and we occupied a farm and had a very comfortable time for a few days. However, we were not long left in peace. On October 6th we moved to Greuppe, and after a few days again moved, this time to Estree-Cauchie, in the Lens sector. We were very comfortable here, but the A.D.O.S. thought we were too far from the line, and again we moved to Carency, some distance in advance of Divisional Headquarters. The move happened at a critical time; all winter clothing was arriving, and the only site possible had no buildings. Store tents were erected in a sea of mud. The weather was very stormy, and one night the tents were blown down and the chaos was indescribable. Jerkins, field boots, blankets, horse rugs, as well as the normal stores, were in heaps in the rain and mud. Our staff was small, and everybody had to work all night with the aid of torches in a high wind and blinding rain. We stuck to it next day and endeavoured to issue to units as well as to get the camp in order. It was then, when we were looking forward to a good night's sleep, that a train-load of tent bottoms arrived. Again we worked the greater part of the night, and I cannot speak too highly of the way the worn-out men worked. This was one of the occasions when the issue of rum to the men really did good. I feel sure half the men would have been sick afterwards in their wet and soaking condition had it not been for the "tot."

Later the R.E.'s got to work and built stores, offices, roads and accommodation, and before we left the camp was nearly ideal. On November 17th we picked up our traps and moved on—this time to Barlin; we travelled light, shedding all stores except actual necessities, and a few days later we found ourselves at Beaumetz-les-Loges, from there to Achiet-le-Petit, and again on to Nurlu, and a day later to Etricourt—all within a week. During this period all work was done direct from the lorries, and although great difficulties were experienced, we kept the troops supplied the whole time.

We knew by this time that something special was afoot, but such secrecy was kept that until a few hours before it actually happened we were not aware that we were taking part in the great thrust for Cambrai.

On December 1st we had to move very quickly. Our attack had failed, and the Hun had broken through at Gouzeacourt, which was not far from the dump. We had a forward dump, with two storemen issuing. These men had a rough time, but stuck to their job well.

The D.A.D.O.S. visited them, and incidentally gave up his own steel helmet to one of the men, as the shelling was heavy. Eventually it got too hot, and we all had to get out. We loaded all stores at the double, and only one thing was lost—a pair of gloves. This afterwards proved to be a record, as practically all Divisions in the vicinity lost large quantities of stores.

We moved to Fremicourt at night, and the dump consisted of one tent and some tarpaulins. Gumboots and blankets were arriving, and the weather was bitterly cold. To add to our troubles, the Hun was bombing and firing his machine guns down the road, and we had a poor time.

A few days later things had become quiet. Our Division were defending Bourlon Wood, and we took up our quarters at Ytres. After a few days we were moved to Bus, where we remained until two days before Christmas. The Division was then so badly cut up that they were brought out to rest, and we picked our dump in a schoolroom at Houvin Houvigneul. This was the first time troops had seen civilians for a long time, and they made merry.

We only remained a few days, and transferred to Etrée-Wamin, the next village. This was found necessary, as the weather had turned frosty and heavy snow fell, and it was found impossible to run lorries. A railway line from Frévent ran into Wamin, and we were able to collect direct from the train. On December 21st another dump was opened at Doullens for the Artillery, who had now come out to rest for the first time. They required re-equipping very badly, and this was taken in hand at once; it was found to be a big job, but in a short time we were able to have everything up-to-date.

On February 11th the Division was moved south of Arras, near Bullecourt, and the dump was opened at Ervillers. We took over a large barn in a very bad state of repair, but ("our friends") the R.E.'s got to work and made the place watertight. The dump was taken over from the 40th Division, but it was a month before we got the place up to our standard. Huts were built, old ones demolished, roads made up and dug-outs cleared, etc. Before the fateful 21st March the depot was as near as perfect as we could get it, so near the line. The Hun used to worry us a good deal from the air, and one night he managed to hit two lorries and make 26 holes in the office in which two men were sleeping and sixteen in the D.A.D.O.S. mess, and very nearly caught the D.A.D.O.S. and an officer that had been sent from the Base to learn the working of the Divisional system. I might add that the latter officer did not stop very long, and he returned to the Base with a lasting memento of his trip to the front, as his clothes were simply riddled. On the whole, the detachment was particularly lucky, considering the number of times we were bombed and shelled. We had no actual casualties.

We passed a most uneventful time until the morning of the 21st March. We were certainly expecting a very big push, and the atmosphere had been full of electricity for some days. About 4 o'clock on the morning of the 21st we were awakened by a fearful bombardment; there was a ground mist, but it was not too thick for us to see our own gunners firing their guns as fast as they could go. There were guns in front and guns behind us, and it was a sight to be remembered.

There was hard fighting during the day, and twice new guns were obtained and sent up the line.

At night orders were received to move to Bucquoy at the double. This was carried out in perfect style, and all stores were brought away. Very few other Divisions on this part of the line were successful in getting away without loss of stores.

We quickly moved from Bucquoy to Bouzincourt, where we stayed two days, but the Huns were still advancing, and we moved on to Contay, and from there to Franvillers the following day. We remained at the latter place a few hours only and proceeded to Mingoval, and a few days later on to Proven.

The Division, or what remained of it, had been taken out of the line. Reinforcements arrived, and the Division was once again up to full strength.

Practically the whole of the equipment of the Infantry units had been lost, and instructions were received to re-equip them at once.

The D.A.D.O.S. left for the Ordnance Base at Calais at 9 p.m., and arranged for priority of issue, and within 24 hours eight lorry-loads of stores arrived.

This necessitated the staff working all night on the 3rd and 4th April. The stores were all issued and in the hands of units, and the dump was transferred to Broidhoeck by the 5th.

The Divisional Commander, General Romer, ordered a parade of all the Ordnance staff on 10th April. He personally thanked the D.A.D.O.S. and the whole of the staff on the excellent way that units had been re-equipped in record time, and the general good work of the Ordnance staff during the whole of the operations. We moved the dump to Watou on the 13th, and on to 5 Camp on the 19th. We remained here only a few days and went on to Bambecque, from there on to Kruystraete, and on the 7th May we moved to St. Omer. Whilst at St. Omer the Division was ordered to break up.

A large jute factory was taken over as a dump, and all Infantry battalions and the M.G.C. battalion and Pioneer battalion both returned the whole of their equipment.

Work commenced on the 8th inst., units bringing in and laying out their stores, where it was checked by a warrant officer and receipts given.

All stores were then packed in cases and sacks by the Ordnance staff, sent to railhead and loaded in trucks, detailed lists being made out. Serviceable and unserviceable were sent separately. Nine ten-ton trucks were required. All winter clothing and blankets had previously been disposed of.

Machine guns were sent to the gun park by lorry, and ten three-ton lorries were required to complete the move.

The work took 45 men thirty actual working hours, and the amount of stores (which had to be handled many times) was estimated at 150 tons.

The Division was then reformed as a B1 Division, and a new dump was opened at Diéval on May 11th.

We moved again to Crepy on June 17th, and the Division was in training and the work was merely routine.

The Division was not sent to the line until the end of July, and on the 25th a dump was opened at Gouy-en-Artois. The part of the line held was very quiet, and on the 25th August the dump was moved to La Goulee, and from there to Busnes. On September 6th the dump opened at Beaupré, near Laventie.

Here the dump was both shelled and bombed, but although some fell close enough to be unpleasant, no casualties occurred.

The D.D.O.S., 5th Army, and Col. K. S. Dunsterville, C.B., from the War Office, called and inspected the dump. At various times officers were sent for instruction, and were taken through the whole system of supply.

We moved to Laventie on October 10th, Laventie to Hem on the 22nd, and then to Templeuve on the 11th November. The armistice was announced on this day, and from then onwards the work was wholly routine. Units were withdrawn from the line and were re-equipped and made up-to-date, the same method of accounting as when in the field being adhered to. This is being stopped shortly, and ledgers will be kept. On Armistice Day the D.A.D.O.S., Major Jackson Dodds, was made A.D.O.S., VI. Army Corps, with the acting rank of Lieut.-Colonel, and proceeded to that unit to arrange for the march into Germany. Major Bacon was appointed D.A.D.O.S., 59th Division, and continued to hold that appointment until the Division was disbanded.

Decorations, etc., gained:—M.S.M. A/Condr. S. E. Richardson, R.A.O.C., also mentioned in despatches; Private Leslie Higman, R.A.O.C., mentioned in despatches; A/Major (T/Capt.) Jackson Dodds, O.B.E. (Military Division), mentioned in despatches four times in succession.

NOTES ON THE 2/1st NORTH MIDLAND (59th) DIVISION

By S.Q.M.S. L. H. GOADBY (Div. H.Q.).

Recruiting was commenced in September and October, 1914, for the units which afterwards formed the 2/1st (North Midland) Division. The Infantry Battalions were raised by Companies being recruited in the towns and villages in Staffordshire, Lincolnshire, Leicestershire, Nottinghamshire and Derbyshire.

As recruiting proceeded the men were instructed in foot drill, physical training, company drill, etc. The greatest difficulty was experienced in getting uniform, and most of the recruits paraded in civilian clothes, or partly in civilian and partly in uniform, for many weeks.

At the end of 1914 the Companies were mobilised at Battalion Headquarters, and training proceeded with as far as the limited number of arms, etc., available would permit.

At the end of January and in February, 1915, units were concentrated in the Luton area and formed into the 2/1st (North Midland) Division, which was composed as follows:—

Staffordshire Infantry Brigade (afterwards numbered the 176th Infantry Brigade).—Brig.-Gen. Chandos-Pole-Gell.

2/5th Bn. South Staffs. Regt.
2/6th do.
2/5th Bn. North Staffs. Regt.
2/6th do.

Lincs. & Leicester Infantry Brigade (afterwards 177th Infantry Brigade).—Brig.-Gen. G. M. Jackson.

2/4th Bn. Lincolnshire Regt.
2/5th do.
2/4th Bn. Leicester Regt.
2/5th do.

Notts. & Derby Infantry Brigade (afterwards 178th Infantry Brigade).—Brig.-Gen. W. Bemrose.

2/5th Bn. Notts. & Derby Regt.
2/6th do.
2/7th do. "The Robin Hoods."
2/8th Bn. Notts. & Derby Regt.

2/1st (N.M.) Divisional Artillery.

2/1st N.M. Brigade R.F.A.
2/2nd do.
2/3rd do.
2/4th N.M. (How.) Bde. R.F.A.

2/1st N.M. Field Coy. R.E. (afterwards 467th Field Coy R.E.).
2/2nd N.M. Field Coy. R.E. (afterwards 469th Field Coy R.E.).
2/3rd N.M. Field Coy. R.E. (afterwards 470th Field Coy R.E.).
2/1st N.M. Divisional Signal Coy. R.E.
2/1st N.M. Field Ambulance.
2/2nd do.
2/3rd do.
No. 1 Coy. A.S.C. 2/1st N.M. Divisional Train.
No. 2 Coy. do.
No. 3 Coy. do.
No. 4 Coy. do.

A Divisional Headquarters was formed at the end of January, 1915, with offices in the Library, Luton.

Brig.-Gen. H. B. McCall, C.B., was appointed Divisional Commander.

Major C. Heyworth-Savage was appointed G.S.O. 2nd Grade.

Major E. U. Bradbridge was appointed D.A.A. & Q.M.G.

With three men from Infantry Battalions to act as Clerks—

Sergt. (?)
Private Wilmot, Lincs. Regt.
" Goadby, L. H., 2/5th Leics. Regt.

The troops at this time were billeted in private houses, rations being drawn from unit stores and cooked in the billets.

Early in February the details (unfit and Home Service Men) of the 1/1st N.M. Division arrived at Luton and joined their respective units. Colonel Fearon, who was in charge, assumed duty as A.A. & Q.M.G. of the Division, bringing with him Sergt. Tuckwood and Privates Blancher and Bradley as clerks.

Battalions of the Division were despatched to the Braintree, Ongar, etc. district for short periods of trench digging.

D.H.Q moves into more suitable premises in Prudential Buildings, Luton.

On June 3rd, 1915, there was a mobilization parade of D.H.Q. (1st and 2nd Echelons) at Luton. Brig.-Gen. McCall inspected the parade.

July 1st.—D.H.Q. took part in a Divisional route march, all ranks parading except one officer and one clerk.

July 31st.—D.H.Q. left Luton for St. Albans and opened offices in Donnington House. The whole Division is now quartered in the Watford and St. Albans area, and is ear-marked for Coast Defence at short notice under an elaborate "Railway Entrainment Scheme," under which, as soon as entrainment is ordered, the whole Division will entrain in twenty-four hours.

Major-General R. Reade assumed command of the Division in November, 1915, and Major-General A. E. Sandbach in February, 1916.

In April, 1916, orders were received for the Division to be concentrated at Codford for equipment and preparation for active service. An advance party was sent from Divisional H.Q., but this was recalled, as on the 24th April orders were suddenly received for one Infantry Brigade to proceed at once to Ireland to assist in the suppression of the rebellion which had broken out in Dublin.

At 10.30 p.m. on April 26th, D.H.Q. left St. Albans for Liverpool, arriving there at 7 a.m., 27th; they embarked on the "Patriotic" and started for Kingstown at 8 p.m., arriving there after a very quiet journey at 4 a.m. on April 28th.

On the morning of 29th April D.H.Q. marched to Balls Bridge and opened an office in a Girls' School there. At this time there was still a good deal of irregular fighting going on in the streets.

On May 1st another move was made to a house in North Circular Road, Dublin, the other ranks of H.Q. being billeted and rationed at Marlboro' Barracks.

Towards the end of 1916 orders were received that the Division was to be prepared for early embarkation for France, and at 6 p.m. on January 6th, 1917, D.H.Q. left Curragh Camp for Fovant with this end in view. At the end of January the whole Division was given embarkation leave, special trains being earmarked for this purpose.

On Tuesday, February 13th, His Majesty the King inspected the Division, and presented numerous decorations which had been won in the Irish Rebellion.

At. 10.20 a.m. on February 23rd, D.H.Q. entrained at Fovant Siding for Southampton, embarking at 6 p.m. the same day. The voyage to France was uneventful, but the boat very overcrowded and accommodation bad, and everyone was glad to disembark at Le Havre at midday next day.

After taking over further equipment and stores, D.H.Q. marched to a camp several miles away, where the night was spent in tents, marching back to Le Havre next morning and entraining again at midday. Accommodation on this train was most limited, and the men were in trucks, many of which contained more than forty soldiers fully armed and equipped.

Detraining at Longueau in the early morning of February 26th, D.H.Q. proceeded by motor lorry to Méricourt-Sur-Somme, and H.Q. were established in the Chateau grounds.

The Division is now in the 3rd Corps, and the A. & Q. Branch was very busy in the preparation of returns, which appeared to be demanded by everyone for no apparent purpose.

The 59th Division relieved the 50th Division in the line early in March, and D.H.Q. moved to P.C. Gabrielle (near Foucaucourt) on the 9th March. On 17th March the Germans commenced their retirement on the Somme, and the Division followed them up, crossing the Somme after little opposition on the 19th March. H.Q. moved forward on 28th March to St. Cren and occupied the only house remaining in what was once the village.

On 31st March the first prisoners were captured and brought to D.H.Q. for examination.

Major-General C. F. Romer, C.B., C.M.G., assumed command of the Division on 8th April, 1917.

Another move was made on April 10th to Bouvincourt, where D.H.Q. opened in Cantin Farm. This farm was evacuated later owing to the danger of delay-action mines, and H.Q. were quartered under canvas.

The Division, having been relieved in the line by a Cavalry Division, D.H.Q. moved on May 28th to Equancourt, where a hutted camp had been specially erected. This place was shelled several times by H.V. guns, but little damage done. Two alarms of cloud gas were given whilst D.H.Q. were at Equancourt, but were afterwards reported false.

On July 10th the Division was withdrawn from the line and proceeded to the Barastre area for training, with D.H.Q. at Barastre.

Orders having been received that the Division was to move North to take part in the attacks near Ypres, D.H.Q. moved to Acheux by road on 23rd August. On 31st August D.H.Q. entrained at Albert for Proven, and on arrival there proceeded by march route to Winnezeele, where offices were opened in the Schools.

Lieut.-Col. E. U. Bradbridge having been appointed A.Q.M.G. (IV. Corps), left the Division on 5th September, and Lieut.-Col. R. B. Airey, D.S.O., assumed duty as A.A. & Q.M.G.

On 24th September D.H.Q. moved by lorry to Mersey Camp, near Brandhoek, with advanced H.Q. near the Ramparts at Ypres. The seven days spent at Mersey Camp were marked by heavy night bombing by enemy aircraft, the moon being at its full, but beyond casualties to horses very little damage was done to the Camp.

The Division, having been withdrawn into rest, H.Q. moved to Watou on October 1st, to Steenbecque next day, and subsequently to Bomy on October 6th.

Orders having been received to relieve the 4th Canadian Division in front of Lens, D.H.Q. moved to Chateau-de-la-Haie in the early morning of 14th October. The Division remained in this sector for about a month, when it was withdrawn to take part in the Cambrai battle. On the night of 21st—22nd November, D.H.Q. moved to Achiet le Petit, moving on again to Etricourt on November 23rd. On 29th November an advanced H.Q. was opened at Trescault; this party narrowly escaped being captured on 30th November—the day of the great German counter-attack. On the same day the H.Q. Signal Office caught fire and was burnt to the ground, several men being very severely burned—in some cases fatally. The fire was eventually extinguished by water carried by hand from the Canal du Nord. At this time the situation was very critical, and it was with difficulty that communication was kept up with advanced H.Q.

On 1st December H.Q. moved to a camp in Vallulart Wood, moving again to Little Wood on 5th December.

The Division having been withdrawn from the line, D.H.Q. moved back on December 23rd, the greater part going direct to Le Cauroy, leaving a portion of the "Q" Branch at Achiet le Petit to superintend the move of the Division. On the night of December 23rd a small fire broke out in one of the huts in the camp at Achiet le Petit, which at one time looked like being serious, as only a very few men were available and all water was frozen. However, the flames were subdued by means of snow, and no very great damage was done. On Christmas Day the party at Achiet-le-Petit moved by lorry to Le Cauroy, the whole of the Division now being in rest in this area. Whilst resting here rooms in estaminets and private houses were hired as reading and recreation rooms, and the troops were made as comfortable as possible.

The "A & Q" Branch is now very busy re-organizing the Division on a three-battalion basis, the following battalions being disbanded:—

2/6th North Staffs. Regt.
2/5th Leicestershire Regt.
2/8th Bn. Sherwood Foresters.

Having been thoroughly rested, re-organized and re-equipped, the Division was moved into the line again under IV. Corps in the Bullecourt Area, and D.H.Q. moved to Gomiecourt by lorry on February 10th, moving again to Behagnies on 13th February. On February 18th the enemy made a very heavy air-raid on D.H.Q., killing one man and wounding another by a bomb which fell on the cookhouse. Many horses in H.Q. stables were killed or had to be shot.

The 6/7th Battalion Royal Scots Fusiliers now joins the Division as Pioneer Battalion, and the Machine Gun Companies are re-organized and amalgamated to form the 59th Battalion Machine Gun Corps, Lieut.-Col. E. D. Basden, M.C. (Divisional M.G. Officer), being appointed to command. Elaborate defence schemes are prepared at D.H.Q. in anticipation of a great German attack in the early Spring.

About 4 a.m., on March 21st, the expected attack commenced, and communication with the infantry was lost before midday. D.H.Q. packed up in the afternoon and stood by with lorries under load till 7 a.m. next morning, when a move was made to Bucquoy. On the night of 22nd inst. orders were issued for all transport to retire, and what remained of the Division was withdrawn to be re-fitted, D.H.Q. moving to Bouzincourt. At 2 a.m., on the 25th, D.H.Q. proceeded to Contay, leaving there on the 26th for Fienvillers. On the 28th a further move was made to Villers Chatel (via St. Pol, Frévent, Pernes, Houdain, etc.). His Majesty the King visited Infantry Brigades on March 30th and complimented them on the gallant fight made in the Bullecourt sector. On March 31st orders were received for the Division to move North, and on April 1st H.Q. moved by lorry to Couthove Chateau, near Proven, taking over a sector of the line near Ypres on April 5th, with D.H.Q. in the Ramparts. On April 11th and 12th H.Q. moved back to Brandhoek, moving again to Abeele on 13th.

The Division having been hurriedly thrown into the line near Bailleul, D.H.Q. were constantly on the move for the next few days, offices being opened for short periods in Westoutre, Mont Noir, and farms in the vicinity, only short stays being made at each place owing to enemy shelling.

On 19th April, D.H.Q. fell back once more to Couthove Chateau, leaving there on 21st for the Convent at Vogelje. As the district round the Convent was being heavily shelled, the "G" Branch made a flying move to Bambecque on April 20th, but returned in the evening, as it was no better there.

Early in May, 1918, orders were received for the Division to be reduced to a "Training Cadre" basis, and it was moved to St. Omer about May 6th for this purpose, all the Infantry, except those on the cadres of units (10 officers and 43 other ranks), being sent to their respective Base Depots in the course of the next few days.

On Friday, 10th May, D.H.Q. moved to Hestrus, and whilst in this area various Category "B" battalions and Chinese Labour Companies were attached to the Division, and were employed in making the "B.B." Sector of G.H.Q. Defence Line. Considerable difficulty was experienced owing to the low category of the troops, many being sent to the Base daily by A.D.M.S. as being unfit for the work.

It was subsequently decided to reconstitute the Division as a "B" Division, and the Infantry was grouped as follows:—

176th Infantry Brigade:—
- 25th Bn. Liverpool Regiment.
- 26th Bn. R. Welch Fusiliers.
- 17th Bn. R. Sussex Regiment.

177th Infantry Brigade:—
- 11th Bn. Somerset Light Infantry.
- 15th Bn. Essex Regiment.
- 2/6th Bn. Durham Light Infantry.

178th Infantry Brigade:—
- 36th Bn. Northumberland Fusiliers.
- 11th Bn. R. Scots Fusiliers.
- 13th Bn. W. Riding Regiment.

25th Bn. King's R. Rifle Corps (Pioneers).
200th Bn. M.G. Corps.

The 23rd Bn. Cheshire Regiment, 17th Bn. Worcestershire Regiment, 23rd Bn. Lancashire Fusiliers and the 2nd Bn. R. Irish Regiment, which had been attached to the Division for trench digging, were transferred to the 40th Division, which was being organised on the same lines as the 59th Division.

The 59th Division, having been ordered to the Bomy Area for training, D.H.Q. moved to Bomy on 17th June, subsequently proceeding to Monchy Cayeux on July 11th.

At the end of July the Division was considered fit to take over a quiet sector of the line, and was ordered to relieve the 2nd Canadian Division in the Mercatel sector, D.H.Q. moving on July 26th to Basseux.

The Division having been relieved, D.H.Q. moved to Bavincourt Chateau on 23rd August, 1918, going on to Norrent-Fontes next day and to Busnes on 27th August, 1918, relieving the 74th Division in the Merville Area.

The enemy having commenced his retirement towards Lille, the 59th Division advanced rapidly, D.H.Q. moving to Carvin on 7th September, L'Epinette next day, Rill Works on 4th October, Fleurbaix on 17th, St. Andre on 19th, Hem on 20th, and to Sailly les Lannoy on 31st.

At this time most of the staff were suffering from an epidemic of influenza, and nearly all the A. & Q. staff were down, including the A.A. & Q.M.G., D.A.A.G. (D.A.Q.M.G. was on leave), and most of the clerks. Colonel Browne, A.Q.M.G. XI. Corps, assumed temporary duty as A.A. & Q.M.G., 59th Division, until November 11th.

D.H.Q. reached Esquelmes, near the River Scheldt, on 10th November. Detachments of infantry, cavalry and cyclists had crossed the river and were pushing on very rapidly when the suspension of hostilities was ordered on November 11th.

The 59th Division was withdrawn from the line on November 12th and moved to the Wattignies Area (near Lille), D.H.Q. arriving at Wattignies on 16th November, 1919.

Whilst near Lille it was decided to start a 59th Division Union Jack Club in some empty buildings in the city.

Considerable trouble was taken to make this very comfortable, but it had only just opened when a further move was ordered to the Bethune area, D.H.Q. proceeding to Vaudricourt Chateau on 6th December, 1918.

In the Bethune Area the troops were employed in clearing up the district, salvage, etc.

On December 10th the 178th Infantry Brigade was detached from the Division and proceeded to Dunkirk to take over the Port and Demobilization Centres, and the 177th and 176th Brigades were detached later on for similar duties.

Towards the end of February, 1919, information was received that the Division would not be finally disbanded, but would be retained for duty in the Calais and Dunkirk area, and all units would be made up to strength with personnel not eligible for demobilization. On 8th March, 1919, D.H.Q. moved to Le Beau Marais (near Calais).

Moves of H.Q., 59th Division, in France.

LOCATION.	DATE OF ARRIVAL.			CORPS.	ARMY.
Méricourt-Sur-Somme	26	2	17	III.	Fourth
P.C. Gabriel	9	3	17	III.	„
St. Cren	28	3	17	III.	„
Bouvincourt	10	4	17	III.	„
Equancourt	28	5	17	III.	„
Barastre	10	7	17	III.	„
Acheux	23	8	17		
Winnezeele	1	9	17		
Mersey Camp, Vlamertinghe	24	9	17		
Watou	1	10	17		
Steenbecque	2	10	17		
Bomy	6	10	17		
Chateau-de-la-Haie	14	10	17	I.	First
Hermaville	17	11	17	XVII.	„
Basseux	19	11	17	VI.	„
Achiet le Petit	21	11	17	V.	„
Etricourt	23	11	17	III.	Third
Vallulart Wood, Near Ytres ...	1	12	17	V.	„
Little Wood, Near Ytres ...	5	12	17	V.	„
Chateau, Ytres	16	12	17	V.	„
Achiet le Petit	23	12	17	?	„
Le Cauroy	25	12	17	III.	„

LOCATION.	DATE OF ARRIVAL.			CORPS.	ARMY.
Le Cauroy	1	1	18	VI.	Third
Gomiecourt	10	2	18	VI.	„
Behagnies	13	2	18	VI.	„
Bucquoy	22	3	18	VI.	„
Bouzincourt	23	3	18	VI.	„
Contay	25	3	18	?	?
Fienvillers	26	3	18	?	?
Villers Chatel	28	3	18	I.	First
„ „	29	3	18	XIII.	„
Couthove Chateau, Proven ...	1	4	18	VIII.	Second
Ramparts, Ypres	5	4	18	VIII.	„
Brandhoek	12	4	18	VIII.	„
Abeele	13	4	18	IX.	„
Westoutre, Adv. H.Q. at Mont Noir	14	4	18	IX.	„
Westoutre	16	4	18	IX.	„
Couthove Chateau, Proven ...	19	4	18	VIII.	„
Vogelje Convent	21	4	18	VIII.	„
St. Omer	6	5	18	VIII.	„
Hestrus	19	5	18	X.	First
Bomy	17	6	18	X.	„
„	3	7	18	Canadian	„
Monchy Cayeux Chau	11	7	18	„	„
„ „ „	15	7	18	XVII.	„
Basseux	26	7	18	VI.	Third
Bavincourt Chau.	23	8	18	VI.	„
Norrent Fontes	24	8	18	XI.	Fifth
Busnes	27	8	18	XI.	„
Carvin	7	9	18	XI.	„
L'Epinette	8	9	18	XI.	„
Rill Works	4	10	18	XI.	„
Fleurbaix	17	10	18	XI.	„
St. Andre ... ... Flers	19	10	18	XI.	„
Hem	20	10	18	XI.	„
Sailly-les-Lannoy	31	10	18	XI.	„
Esquelmes	10	11	18	XI.	„
Wattignies	16	11	18	XI.	„
Vaudricourt Chau.	6	12	18	XI.	First
Le Beau Marais	8	3	19	Lines-of-Communication.	

UNVEILING OF MEMORIALS.

"Lincoln Leader," November 27th, 1926.

THE SERVICES CHAPEL, LINCOLN CATHEDRAL.

Cross and Candlesticks for Altar.

Presented at Cathedral Service.

A cross and candlesticks of oak and gilt, to be placed on the centre altar of the Services Chapel in Lincoln Cathedral, was presented to the Dean at a special parade service in the Cathedral on Sunday week by Colonel Bradbridge, representing the 59th Division.

They are of very fine workmanship. The candlesticks are ornamented with the Cross of Offa, which was the Divisional sign of the 59th Division during the War; and the cross bears the inscription:

> "To the glory of God and to the memory of the Officers, N.C.O.'s and Men of the 59th Division who fell in the Great War 1914, from the survivors, 1918."

Memorial in Lincoln Cathedral.

"Leicester Mail" of February 14th, 1927.

MEN WHO HELD THE HUN.

Tablet to the Glorious 59th.

Unveiled in LEICESTER Cathedral.

"We have no memorials to the 59th Division overseas, save the graves of its men in France and Flanders; and I personally am glad we have not, for I think they should be in the churches overlooking the houses from which the men went forth to fight, many of them to die."

This sentiment was expressed by Major-General Sir C. F. Romer, K.B.E., C.B., C.M.G., in unveiling the memorial tablet to the 59th Division (Territorial) in Leicester Cathedral on Saturday afternoon, as briefly reported in our final edition of Saturday evening.

This tablet, said the General, commemorated not only the Leicestershire men of the unit, but all their comrades in it, officers, non-commissioned officers, and men.

From all Professions.

He paid a glowing tribute to the part played by the 59th Terriers in the war, remarking that "there were very few of what one might term professional soldiers amongst them. They were miners, operatives, agricultural workers, every class of civilian life, such men as one sees in your streets and fields at the present moment. They were flung into the biggest war history has ever known, with very little experience or training."

"We know," General Romer went on, "how nobly they displayed the typical English qualities of courage and endurance. Both General Sandbach and myself feel it an honour to come here to-day and express our pride in those officers and men."

Held Back the Hun.

He concluded by describing how in the last big push of March, 1918, when the Stafford and Warwickshire contingents were almost wiped out at Bullecourt, pressed by 45 German divisions with overwhelming artillery, the

Lincoln and Leicester contingents came to the rescue, "and," he declared proudly, "the Germans never did break the line there; the 59th held their ground."

Buglers of a contingent from the 4th Batt. Leicestershire Regiment (under Major Pair), sounded the Last Post and Reveille, and the tablet was dedicated by the Ven. Archdeacon Macnutt, Hon C.F., who led the assembly in prayer.

There were also present, in addition to Major-General A. E. Sandbach, C.B., D.S.O., Col. Sir Ian Colquhoun, Col. E. U. Bradbridge, Colonels Baines, Sarson, Nowell, Atkins, and Astley V. Clarke, Major C. M. Serjeantson, O.B.E., D.L. (secretary of the Leicestershire Territorial Association), Ald. Sir Jonathan North, the Mayor of Leicester (Ald. T. W. Walker), and Ald. J. Russell Frears, who was Mayor at the time the 2/4th and 2/5th Leicesters were being raised.

"Derbyshire Advertiser" of February 18th, 1927.

FIFTY-NINTH DIVISION.

Memorial Tablet Unveiled in All Saints' Church, DERBY.

Officers' Re-Union Dinner.

Tablets in memory of the men who served with the 59th Division during the war and made the supreme sacrifice have been erected in Derby, Leicester, Chesterfield, Lincoln and Stafford, the unveiling ceremony of Derbyshire's taking place on Sunday morning.

Previous to the unveiling of the memorial in All Saints' Church a parade was held in the Market Place, under the command of Lieut.-Col. F. Beaumont-Checkland, M.C., T.D., and was attended by former members of the 59th Division; band and drums of the 5th Batt. the Sherwood Foresters; 46th North Midland Division Royal Artillery, under Capt. Kay; No. 1 Company R.C. of S., under Capt. Briggs; Derby Companies 5th Batt. the Sherwood Foresters, with colours, under Capt. J. W. Potter, D.S.O.; Legion of Frontiersmen; Veterans' Association, under Sergt. Kelly; and the Nursing Division of the St. John Ambulance Brigade.

Noticed among the congregation were the Sheriff of Derbyshire (Captain G. M. Buckston), the Mayor of Derby (Coun. A. H. Domleo), members of the Town Council, the Town Clerk (Mr. G. Trevelyan Lee), and the Chief Constable (Capt. Rawlings), Major-General Van Straubenzee, C.B., C.M.G., Lieut.-Col. J. Hunter, Lieut.-Col. G. A. Lewis, C.M.G., Capt. FitzHerbert Wright, and Capt. Thornton, M.C.

The Vicar (Canon H. Ham) said the service that morning, with its atmosphere of 1917-18, came as a shock. The associations of war had not been deliberately forgotten or consciously pushed to one side, but the growing generation was looking to the future. The lesson of the war was an activity to see that such a thing did not happen again. The idea of progress had captured and controlled the modern mind, and it was hard to realise that things were not always so.

The tablet bore the inscription:—"59th (North Midland) Division, T.F. To the glory of God, in memory of the dead, and to record the services of the Division in the Great War, 1914-1918. Ypres, 1917. Menin Road, Polygon Wood, Cambrai, 1917. St. Quentin, First Battle of Kemmel, Albert, 1918."

Major-General Sir C. F. Romer, K.B.E., C.B., C.M.G., who commanded the Division in France, unveiled the tablet. It had been erected, he said, in memory of the 59th Division as a whole and in everlasting memory of their comrades who died. Probably all would agree that far the best place for memorials to men was in churches which overlooked and stood in the midst of their homeland. Hardly any of the men who fought in the 59th Division could have imagined before August, 1914, that they would be taken from their ordinary toil and flung into the horrors of the biggest war in the world's history. As the officer who had the honour to command that Division in France, he, with many brother officers in that church, always took the opportunity of expressing pride and gratitude to the men of the Division; and fellow-citizens would share that pride. The tablet fulfilled two purposes. It enshrined the memory of all ranks of the 59th Division, and would serve as a reminder and an example to all in this and succeeding generations of how, when the call of duty came, it should be met.

Canon Ham dedicated the memorial.

Re-Union Dinner.

On Saturday evening, in the Midland Hotel, Station Street, Derby, the officers of the 59th Division held their annual re-union dinner. Major-General A. E. Sandbach, C.B., D.S.O., presided. Others present included Major-General Sir C. F. Romer, K.B.E., C.B., C.M.G., Major W. McGowan, M.C. (secretary), representing the Staffordshire Territorial Army Association; Lieut.-Col. C. Herbert-Stepney,, D.S.O., D.L. (secretary), representing the Derbyshire Territorial Army Association; Major-Gen. C. C. Van. Straubenzee, C.B., C.M.G. (46th Division T.A.), Major L. V. Wykes, Capt. G. W. Border, Capt. F. Sutherland, Lieut.-Col. J. C. Baines, D.S.O., T.D., Major T. E. A. Carr, Col. R. B. Rickman, Capt. J. S. Turner, Capt. A. Orton, Lieut.-Col. H. G. W. Dawson, Capt. W. Foster, Major A. Holt, Lieut.-Col. H. Johnson, Lieut.-Col. M. C. Martyn, D.S.O., Col. T. W. Stansfeld, C.M.G., D.S.O., Lieut.-Col. H. Porter, Lieut.-Col. A. N. Lee, D.S.O., Lieut.-Col. H. M. Whitehead, Capt. B. H. Brewill, Major R. P. Shea, Brig.-Gen. R. St. G, Gorton, C.M.G., Major E. M. Parker-Jervis, Capt. G. J. Edmunds, Capt. H. P. G. Branston, Major T. E. Tildesley, Major R. A. Henderson, Capt. R. D. Best, Major W. E. V. Tompkins, M.C., Capt. H. A. Hewitt, and Lieut.-Col. E. U. Bradbridge.

Letters of regret at inability to attend were received from, among others, Capt. Dimock, Lieut.-Col. A. B. Wildsmith, Capt. Hart-Davis, Capt. F. W. Watson, Lieut.-Col. W. C. Oates, Col. Anson-German, Col. Weston-Colquhoun, Col. Rayner, Capt. Pocock, Col. Oliver, Capt. K. Neville Moss, Major-General Raymond Reade, Lieut.-Col. Lincoln, Capt. L. L .Cooper, Brig.-General Maconchy, Col. Atkins, Col. A. C. Clarke, Brig.-General Carleton, Capt. Yeomans, and Lieut.-Col. H. Taylor.

One of the rules of the dinner is that there shall be no speeches, and this was strictly observed on Saturday night, for the only speech-making took the form of thanks to all who had helped with the provision of the memorial tablets. Major-General Sandbach said Col. Bradbridge had gone to an enormous amount of trouble with the scheme for the memorials. The chairman also thanked the Territorials of Derby for the part they had played in the scheme.

Major-General Romer remarked there was a movement on foot for the compilation of the Division's history. It was mainly a question of expense. One suggestion had been put forward that the history first be published in serial form in a local newspaper and afterwards printed in book form. After all the memorials had been paid for there would be a balance of £40. Could that money be diverted towards the cost of the publication of the history? Derbyshire, he was glad to inform them, had paid for its own tablets, whilst Staffordshire and Leicestershire had collected nearly the requisite amount.

Remarking that he was no volunteer for the after-dinner speech, Major-General Van Straubenzee stated he had been listening to the speeches and understood they wanted contributions to the history of the Division. He would willingly volunteer for the job. The pedigree he could tell them, for the sire was an Army Council instruction and the mother of it was difficult to answer, but he thought was the 46th Division. He had been closely associated with that " lady " during the past four years, and he could inform them she was in very good shape. (Laughter.) Occasionally, said General Straubenzee, she was a little difficult to handle, but he was sure if they treated her kindly and with sympathy they could get what they wanted out of her if she was called upon by an A.C.I. He was confident she would be able to produce just as good a bouncing boy as she did when she produced the 59th Division. (Applause.)

Replying to the thanks accorded local Territorials, Brig.-General Jackson claimed he was the oldest member of the association. He said he would like to thank all the speakers for what they had said about the 59th Division, which was a baby from the old association. It had been his privilege to command the second line in its infancy, when it was the Lincoln and Leicester Brigade. He had never had such an enjoyable time. By coming to Derbyshire the assembly had done the Territorials a great honour. He hoped they would carry out Major-General Sandbach's suggestion and when holding the dinner in the country always come to Derbyshire.

"The Derbyshire Times," February 19th, 1927.

59th DIVISION MEMORIAL.

Unveiling at CHESTERFIELD by General Sandbach.

Impressive Ceremony.

A memorial to those who served and fell in the 59th (North Midland) Division (T.F.), which comprised the second line units of the Battalions of the 46th Division, was unveiled in Chesterfield Parish Church on Sunday afternoon by Major-General A. E. Sandbach, C.B., D.S.O.

A short appropriate service had been arranged by the Vicar, the Rev. G. H. Clayton, and the beauty of this, the hymns and prayers which struck the right note, the impressive unveiling ceremony, all conduced to make the service one that will be remembered long by all privileged to take part in it.

The memorial tablet, which is of bronze, is erected on the wall on the south of the chancel screen, and bears the inscription:—

59th (NORTH MIDLAND) DIVISION (T.F.)

To the Glory of God, in Memory of the Dead, and to record the service of the Division in the Great War,

1914—1918.

Ypres, 1917. Menin Road. Polygon Wood. Cambrai, 1917. St. Quentin. First Battle of Bapaume, 1918. Bailleul. First Battle of Kemmel. Albert, 1918.

ROYAL ARTILLERY.

295 (2/1 N. Mid.) Bde. (Lincoln).
296 (2/2 N. Mid.) Bde. (Staffs.).
297 (2/3 N. Mid.) Bde. (Staffs.).
298 (2/4 N. Mid.) Bde (Derby).
V. Heavy Trench Mortar Bat.

ROYAL ENGINEERS.

467 Field Coy. (Staffs.).
469 Field Coy. (Staffs.).
470 Field Coy. (Staffs.).
Signal Coy. (Staffs., Notts., Derby, Lincoln and Leicester).
Div. Amm. Col. (Staffs. and Derby).

176th (STAFFS.) INFANTRY BRIGADE.

2/5 Bn. S. Staffs. Regt.
2/6th Bn. S. Staffs. Regt.
2/5th Bn. N. Staffs. Regt.
2/6th Bn. N. Staffs. Regt.
174th Machine Gun Company.
176th Trench Mortar Battery.

177th (LINCS. AND LEICESTER) INFANTRY BRIGADE.

2/4th Bn. Lincoln Regt.
2/5th Bn. Lincoln Regt.
2/4th Bn. Leicester Regt.
2/5th Bn. Leicester Regt.
177th Machine Gun Company.
177th Trench Mortar Battery.

178th (NOTTS. & DERBY) INFANTRY BRIGADE.

2/5th Bn. Notts and Derby Regt.
2/6th Bn. Notts and Derby Regt.
2/7th Notts and Derby Regt.
2/8th Bn. Notts and Derby Regt.
175th Machine Gun Company.
178th Trench Mortar Battery.
200th Machine Gun Company.

A.S.C.

No. 1 Company (Staffs.).
No. 2 Company (Lincoln and Leicester).
No. 3 Company (Staffs.).
No. 4 Company (Notts. and Derby).

R.A.M.C.

2/1st N. Mid. Field Ambulance (Derby).
2/2nd N. Mid. Field Ambulance (Leicester).
2/3rd N. Mid. Field Ambulance (Staffs.).
Sanitary Section (Leicester).

R.A.V.C.

N. Mid. Vet. Section (Lincoln).

250th Divisional Employment Company.

The weather was glorious, and the imposing military procession, which marched from the Drill Hall to the Church, was witnessed by a large number of townspeople. There were between forty and fifty ex-officers, W.O.'s, N.C.O.'s and men of the 59th Division on parade, and although everyone was not in uniform, practically all wore their medals and decorations. Lieut.-Col. F. M. Dick, M.C., T.D., O.C. 6th Sherwood Foresters, was in command of the parade. The Adjutant, Capt. J. D'A. Whicher, was also present, with the following officers of "A" Company:—Capt. H. H. Jackson, M.C., Lieut. A. J. Cook and Lieut. N. E. Carline.

Other officers present included Col. G. D. Goodman, C.M.G., D.S.O., Brig.-Gen. G. M. Jackson, T.D., Col. E. Hall, D.S.O., Major A. W. Shea, D.S.O,, Major E. M. Brooke Taylor, M.C., T.D. (Second-in-command of the 6th), Capt. Basil Darbyshire, Major V. O. Robinson, M.C., Capt. W. Seaton, M.C., D.C.M.

The procession was headed by the drums and band of the 6th Sherwood Foresters, followed by No. 2 Company Royal Corps of Signals, under Captain G. J. Underwood, accompanied by Lieut. Turner. Then came representatives of the 59th Division, the King's Colour of the 2/6th

Battalion being carried by Lieut. R. S. Bury, of Ashbourne, with the colour party, together with "A" and H.Q. Companies of the 6th Sherwood Foresters.

Officers present who served in the 59th Division included Major Welch (Chinley), Major W. E. V. Tompkins, M.C. (Newbury), Capts. H. Douglas (Matlock), F. Brindley, M.C. (Buxton), H. D. Orr, G. J. Edmunds, W. J. Keery, M.B.E., Harold Taylor, M.C. (Chesterfield), J. Farnsworth, E. A. Carlisle (Sheffield), Lieuts. A. P. Lockwood, M.C. (Sheffield), T. O. Colles (Whaley Bridge), H. Brown (Chesterfield), N. A. Pitt. Capt. W. D. Jamieson was unable to be present owing to being in hospital at Manchester.

Lieut. Harold Barnes represented the 24th Derbyshire Yeomanry Armoured Car Company.

Fifty members of the British Legion attended under Lieut.-Col. H. Tylden Wright (the president), who was accompanied by Capt. W. N. Broomhead (chairman).

There were three Grenadier Guardsmen, Sergt. Carter being in charge, and the representatives of the Old Comrades' Association under Sergt. Hall.

Tribute by Chairman of Derbyshire T.A.

Addressing the units at the Drill Hall before the procession formed up, Mr. E. Edmund Barnes said that he wished to make a few remarks to the men on parade as Chairman of the Derbyshire Territorial Association. He was very pleased they had such a good muster on parade, and it showed how great a desire there was amongst them to pay a last tribute to all their comrades and friends of the 59th Division who had sacrificed their lives in the Great War, and to whom the tablet in Chesterfield Parish Church was to be unveiled. It was most appropriate that they should be unveiling the tablet in Derby and at Chesterfield to their memory that day, because in the first place nearly all—he might say all—who joined the Derbyshire units which formed part of the 59th Division were Derbyshiremen. All the units were raised and equipped by the Derbyshire Territorial Association, of which he was then a member, which made it more personal, and it seemed to him that it was most fitting that they should have memorial tablets to their memory in the county.

The Service in Church.

The service in church, which did not last more than half-an-hour, was of a deeply impressive and inspiring nature. There was a large congregation, and the seats reserved for the wives and families of those of the 59th Division who fell or served in the war were practically all occupied.

Major-Gen. Sandbach, Brigadier-Gen. Jackson, Colonel Goodman, Colonel Hall, Ald. E. C. Barnes (Deputy-Lieut. of Derbyshire), Mr. E. Edmund Barnes (Chairman of the County Territorial Association), Lieut.-Col. F. M. Dick, and other officers sat in the seats immediately in front of the memorial tablet.

There were also present the Mayor (Ald. H. Cropper), Aldermen W. H. Edmunds, G. Clark, W. Crossley, T. D. Sims, Councillors H. J. Watson, C. B. Franklin, J. H. Randall, A. W. Swale, H. Harrison, W. Wicks, J. T. Bradley, Mr. W. Jacques, Mr. R. Faulkner, J.P., Mr. A. A. Townrow, J.P., Mr. W. Swindell, J.P. (magistrates), Mr. H. Davies (gas engineer and manager), Supt. Stone (Derbyshire County Constabulary), and others.

In addition to those taking part in the procession, there were in church representatives of the Chesterfield Troop of Girl Guides, members of the 2nd Chesterfield Troop of Scouts and Rovers, under the charge of Scoutmaster C. W. Handford and Assistant Scoutmaster E. Eyre, and members of the 20th Chesterfield (St. Augustine's) Troop of Scouts, with Assistant-Scoutmaster Davison in charge, and also the Chesterfield Parish Church Detachment of the Church Lads' Brigade (King's Royal Rifle Cadets) under the command of Capt. J. Hydes.

In addition to the Vicar (the Rev. G. H. Clayton, C.F.), who conducted the service, there were present the Archdeacon of Chesterfield (Ven. Archdeacon E. F. Crosse, C.F.), and the Rev. G. W. Dymond, M.C. The clergy wore their medals and miltary decorations.

The service opened with the fervent singing of the hymn, " O God, our help in ages past," after which the Lord's Prayer was recited. Then followed special prayers for those who gave their lives for their country; for those who fought in the Great War, particularly those who are disabled; and for the country and Empire. The hymn "God of Our Fathers" was afterwards sung, and the lesson, Revelations xxi., verses 1—7, was read by Colonel Dick.

The Unveiling Ceremony.

At the conclusion of the singing of the hymn, "O Valiant Hearts," Major-Gen. Sandbach, accompanied by the Archdeacon and the Vicar, proceeded to the tablet.

Before releasing the Cross of St. George, which covered the tablet, Major-Gen. Sandbach gave a short address. He remarked:—

"We are met here this afternoon in this church for the unveiling of the memorial to the 59th Division, and before the actual ceremony I am permitted to say a few words. From ancient time it has been the custom in our country to erect memorials in our cathedrals and in our churches to commemorate great events in history and to commemorate the lives of great and good men. We have endeavoured, with the very loyal assistance of the County Territorial Association and of the local Battalion, to erect some record and some memorial in every locality from which the troops of the 59th Division were drawn. In that way the tablet about to be unveiled has been erected in this church, firstly, as a thank-offering to God for mercies vouchsafed to us, in that during the Great War we were spared the horrors of invasion by the enemy; secondly, as a record of the units of the 59th Division which served overseas in France, and of the battles in which they took part; and thirdly, as a memorial to those officers and men of the 59th Division who gave their lives for their King and country in the Great War. Is it not true that throughout the length and breadth of the land during that anxious time there was scarcely one home circle, however humble, which did not mourn the loss of some kinsman, either a father, or a son, or a husband, or a brother? Those men died at the call of duty, and what higher tribute, or what better tribute to their memory can we offer than that we ourselves should make some sacrifice, however small, in our daily lives for the good of others and for the good of our country."

Major-Gen. Sandbach then unveiled the tablet, saying: "In the faith of Jesus Christ we unveil this tablet, to the glory of God and in memory of the officers and men of the 59th Division. In the name of the Father, and of the Son, and of the Holy Ghost.—Amen."

The Archdeacon dedicated the tablet with the following words:—"O Almighty God, Lord of Heaven and Earth, we beseech Thee to bless and hallow this memorial, which here we dedicate to Thee, beseeching Thee to grant unto those whose service is here recorded the forgiveness of their sins and everlasting joy in Thy presence. And give us grace that we may be ever mindful of their sacrifice, and, loving not our lives unto death, may joyfully spend them in the service of our country and Thy Kingdom; through Jesus Christ, our Lord, Who liveth and reigneth with Thee and the Holy Ghost, now and ever.—Amen."

Buglers of the 6th Sherwood Foresters sounded the "Last Post" and the "Reveille," and the service was brought to a close by the hearty singing of the National Anthem to the organ accompaniment played by Dr. J. Frederic Staton.

After the service Major-Gen. A. E. Sandbach inspected the parade. The various units were drawn up in Alpine Gardens and Stephenson Place, and the General shook hands and chatted with numerous individuals, including a diminutive Scout. Afterwards General Sandbach, who was accompanied during the inspection by Col. Goodman, Col. Dick, Capt. D'A. Whicher and Mr. E. E. Barnes, took the salute of the military portion of the parade, and the march past was carried out with commendable smartness.

The procession then marched back to the Drill Hall, where the troops were dismissed.

"The Staffordshire Advertiser," February 19th, 1927.

WAR MEMORIAL DEDICATION AT STAFFORD.

Lord Dartmouth Unveils Tablet to Fallen Territorials.

An impressive ceremony took place at Stafford on Monday afternoon when, in the presence of a large assembly of military and civic representatives, the Earl of Dartmouth, K.C.B. (Lord-Lieutenant of the County and President of the Staffordshire Territorial Army Association) unveiled a handsome bronze tablet which has been placed in the south transept of St. Mary's Church in memory of the officers, non-commissioned officers and men of the 59th North Midland Division of the Territorial Force who laid down their lives in the Great War, 1914-1918, and also to record the services of the Division during that period. The tablet is one of four which have been erected in the principal church in each county in the North Midland area, the others being dedicated at the week-end at Leicester, Derby and Chesterfield. At Lincoln Cathedral the memorial takes the form of a silver cross and candlesticks. The 59th Division was recruited in Staffordshire, Derbyshire, Nottinghamshire, Leicestershire and Lincolnshire as the second line to the 46th North Midland Division. The men of both Divisions acquitted themselves with credit in France during the late war. The 59th Division took a prominent part in checking the great German offensive early in 1918, and suffered heavily.

The inscription on the bronze tablet in St. Mary's Church shows the battles in which the Division took part, and the various regiments engaged.

Civic Procession.

In honour of the occasion the Mayor of Stafford (Ald. W. T. Richardson), who wore his robes and chain of office, attended the service in St. Mary's in civic state, and was accompanied by members of the Corporation, borough magistrates, and officials. Representatives of the 59th and 46th Divisions were present, and the gathering included a good muster of old members of each Division, some of whom had travelled a considerable distance to attend the ceremony.

While the congregation were assembling, Mr. G. P. Matthews, F.R.C.O. (organist), played Mendelsshon's "Funeral March," "Prelude Solennelle" (Mansfield), "Solemn Melody" (Walford Davies), and "Coronach Lament" (Barratt). The Rector (the Rev. L. Lambert), with the choir, awaited the arrival of the military representatives, and the other surpliced clergy present were:—The Revs. J. O. Johnson (curate of St. Mary's), W. H. Shawcross and H. K. Stapleton (Christ Church), A. R. Alsop (Bednall), S. G. V. Allen (Marston), J. C. Bocking (Knosall), G. Hitchings (Walton), R. A. Jones (Brocton), R. St. C. Page (Seighford), and M. F. Page (Eccleshall), and Rose (Coseley).

Guard of Honour Inspected.

Outside the church, immediately in front of the main entrance, a guard of honour formed up, and was furnished by a detachment of the 244th Stafford Battery R.A., under the command of Major H. P. Hunter, O.B.E., with whom was Major W. O. Mackintosh, of the 13th Highland Park Artillery, and Lieut. R. Simpson, 6th North Staffordshire Regiment. A bugle salute heralded the arrival of the Lord-Lieutenant, who was accompanied by Major-General C. C. Van Straubenzee, C.B., C.M.G. (Commanding the 46th North-Midland Division), and Major-General A. E. Sandbach (who commanded the 59th Division in France). Among other officers present were:—Col. J. C. Grant, D.S.O. (Commanding the 137th Staffordshire Infantry Brigade), Lieut.-Col. the Hon. G. A. Anson, C.B.E., M.V.O. (chairman), Mr. J. T. Homer, C.B.E. (vice-chairman), Brig.-General V. W. de Falbe, C.M.G., D.S.O., Lieut.-Col. W. J. Beddows, M.C. (Commanding 62nd North Midland Brigade R.A.), Lieut.-Col. A. F. Nicholson (61st North Midland Brigade R.A.), Lieut.-Col. H. M. Whitehead (late 59th Division), Lieut.-Col. B. E. Coke, O.B.E. (late R.E.), Lieut.-Col. J. Baldwin Webb (46th North Midland Divisional Train, R.A.S.C.), Lieut.-Col. G. C. Lowbridge, M.C. (46th North-Midland Division, R.E.), Lieut.-Col. T. E. Lowe, O.B.E., Major J. C. G. McFerran (late of the 46th North Midland Division, R.E.), Territorial Army Association, with Major W. Cowan, M.C. (secretary), Capt. Sedgwick (assist. secretary), Major L. C. Owen, D.S.O. (46th North Midland Division Staff), Col. H. Johnson, Major

F. E. Wenger, Major T. E. Tildesley, and Major O. C. Bladen (5th North Staffs. Regiment), Capt. J. I. Cheshire and Q.M.S. W. H. Thursfield (5th South Staffs. Regiment), and Capt. Corson (Stafford). Among others present were:—General Sir John Headlam, K.B.E., of Shrewsbury, and Major E. M. Parker-Jervis, of Farndon Hall, Chester (late of the 59th Divisional Artillery).

After inspecting the guard of honour, Lord Dartmouth said he understood that the men had taken a great deal of trouble to parade that day, and that they were filling voluntarily an unusual role. He expressed his personal gratification to the men and complimented them on the successful results of their training. He also congratulated Major Hunter on the smart appearance of the guard of honour, adding that he fully realised that those who had set an example as they had done to others in shooting would always be able to set an example in other ways.

The Unveiling Ceremony.

The seating arrangements in church were in charge of Messrs. F. H. Brown and S. Johnson (churchwardens). Lord Dartmouth and other officers were escorted by the Rector to the south transept. The service began with the singing of the hymn "Nearer my God to Thee," after which Lord Dartmouth pulled a cord and released the Union Jack covering the memorial tablet. His Lordship said: "In the Name of the Father, and of the Son, and of the Holy Ghost, and in grateful memory of the Staffordshire men, who formed part of the 59th Division, and who in the Great War gave their lives for us, I unveil this memorial."

Major-General Sandbach, on behalf of the donors, then asked the Rector's acceptance of the tablet which had been placed in the church "to the Glory of God, and in pious memory of the 59th Division," with the request "that this gift may be solemnly dedicated to the service of Almighty God, and set apart from all unworthy and profane purposes, and for ever be preserved in this church."

The Rector gratefully accepted the gift, and undertook to see that it was jealously preserved for the purpose for which it had been given. Appropriate prayers were then offered, and the memorial was dedicated by the Rector.

Lord Dartmouth on Value of Territorial Army.

Lord Dartmouth, addressing the congregation from the pulpit, reminded them that similar memorials to the one unveiled that afternoon were being dedicated in other county towns which helped to form the 59th North Midland Division —a Territorial Division of the second line. When the movement started they were told that a force like the Territorial Force was and trained like that force was supposed to be trained in time of emergency would, so far from being an asset, be an actual failure, and that the crazy structure that was being formed would collapse under its own weight or give way to something better. He was subjected to a certain amount of ridicule through what was supposed the exaggerated view he took of the value of the Territorial soldier. He had reasons for his belief, and he was proud indeed to-day to feel that however high his opinion of their merits might have been, their existence had been more than justified as the result of the war. Formed when it was decided to duplicate the fourteen divisions of the Territorial Force, the 59th Division completed its quota within a few months, and after a course of intensive training at Luton and St. Albans the men were inspected and returned as fit for service. The first recruits for the Division were a splendid lot, and they in Staffordshire were glad to remember that it was the first county to complete its establishment before the war. The county of Stafford formed part of the North Midland Division, which was the first Division to go overseas during the war, and the 59th Division was the first of the "second line" to prove itself fit for war service. It was unfortunate, his Lordship continued, that the 59th Division in its earlier days was called upon to perform duty in Ireland that ought never to have been required, and what they suffered during those anxious months one hardly liked to think. It was not until 1917 that they actually went to France, and their record was written there. Those who belonged to the 59th Division might feel very proud of the record they made, and the memorial that had been unveiled was a little tribute of respectful affection to those who gave their lives in the war.

"These memorials," Lord Dartmouth proceeded, "are scattered over the whole country; they differ materially in appearance and design. There are many we like and many we do not like, and we are perhaps a little too much inclined to criticize those we do not like, but the inward meaning as well as the outward appearance of these memorials should be borne in mind. Whether they do or do not appeal to the eye; whether they are situated in some little country parish or in a largely populated centre, the message they give is always the same—a message of grateful recognition of the great sacrifice made for us. In the early days of the war it was a common place to talk of sacrifice being made. There was no equality of sacrifice. The service was equal and the willingness to make the sacrifice was equal, but the act of sacrifice was out of our hands. These memorials showed that the sacrifice was not an equal one, and when we welcomed our troops home after the Armistice there were two sides to the picture—one the return of a victorious army with all pomp and ceremony, and the other those who were always looking for a face that they knew would not be there. There was, he repeated, no equality of sacrifice, but to those who had learned the bitter lesson of direct and personal loss he would like to offer one word of consolation. Although there was a gap in their homes that would never be filled, what should console them and what they could rejoice over was the knowledge of the courage and devotion with which that sacrifice was made, and this should surely go a long way to smooth over the rough edges of that gap. They could also take some consolation to themselves from the lines of Old Ben Jonson, written more than 200 years ago, in which he said that 'in small proportion life may perfect be.' It seemed also appropriate on that occasion more than any other to quote the message of an officer whose life was devoted to the men who served under him—"When the Great Scorer comes to write against our name, He will not ask "Did we win?" or "Did we lose?" but "Did we play the game?"'" "That is a question," said his Lordship in conclusion, "we shall have to answer by-and-bye; the day for some of us may not be far distant, but we shall have to find an answer, and I hope, for our sakes, we shall be able to find as complete and as satisfying an answer as was given by those men whose sacrifice we commemorate to-day. We do not need these memorials to remind us. We are not likely to forget. The value of these memorials is that they will be an indication to generations still unborn that when the country had its back against the wall it was saved by the gallantry of its sons. If one could imagine an answer from those whose sacrifice they commemorated that day he thought would be this—'Don't forget that the finest memorial you can put up to those who have fallen is to do what you can for those who are left behind.'"

Following the address the hymn "Fight the good fight" was sung, during which a collection was taken in aid of St. Dunstan's Home. After the Benediction, the National Anthem was sung, and "The Last Post" was sounded by Privates A. Davies and F. Davies, of the 6th North Staffordshire Regt. The service fittingly concluded with Elgar's "Imperial March," played by Mr. Matthews.

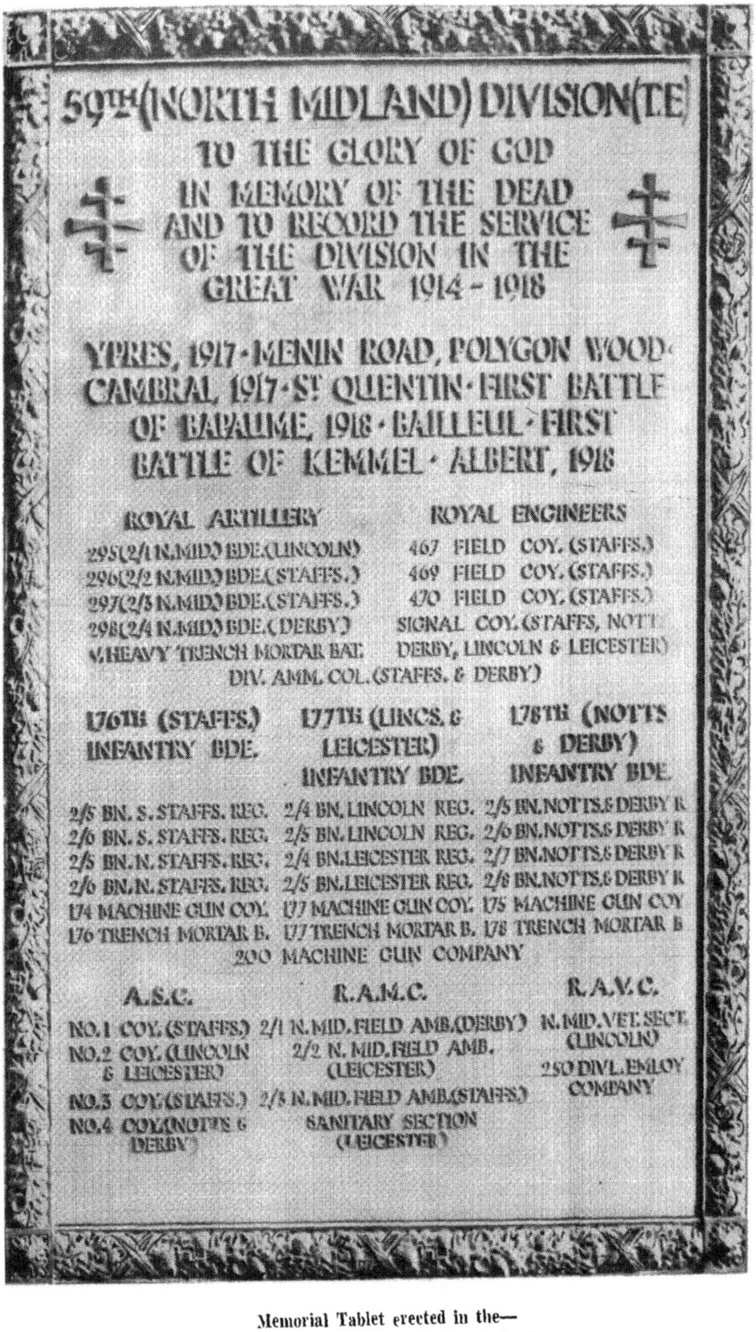

59TH (NORTH MIDLAND) DIVISION (T.F.)

TO THE GLORY OF GOD
IN MEMORY OF THE DEAD
AND TO RECORD THE SERVICE
OF THE DIVISION IN THE
GREAT WAR 1914 – 1918

YPRES, 1917 · MENIN ROAD, POLYGON WOOD · CAMBRAI, 1917 · ST. QUENTIN · FIRST BATTLE OF BAPAUME, 1918 · BAILLEUL · FIRST BATTLE OF KEMMEL · ALBERT, 1918

ROYAL ARTILLERY

295 (2/1 N.MID.) BDE. (LINCOLN)
296 (2/2 N.MID.) BDE. (STAFFS.)
297 (2/3 N.MID.) BDE. (STAFFS.)
298 (2/4 N.MID.) BDE. (DERBY)
V. HEAVY TRENCH MORTAR BAT.

ROYAL ENGINEERS

467 FIELD COY. (STAFFS.)
469 FIELD COY. (STAFFS.)
470 FIELD COY. (STAFFS.)
SIGNAL COY. (STAFFS, NOTTS, DERBY, LINCOLN & LEICESTER)

DIV. AMM. COL. (STAFFS. & DERBY)

176TH (STAFFS.) INFANTRY BDE.

2/5 BN. S. STAFFS. REG.
2/6 BN. S. STAFFS. REG.
2/5 BN. N. STAFFS. REG.
2/6 BN. N. STAFFS. REG.
174 MACHINE GUN COY.
176 TRENCH MORTAR B.

177TH (LINCS. & LEICESTER) INFANTRY BDE.

2/4 BN. LINCOLN REG.
2/5 BN. LINCOLN REG.
2/4 BN. LEICESTER REG.
2/5 BN. LEICESTER REG.
177 MACHINE GUN COY.
177 TRENCH MORTAR B.

178TH (NOTTS & DERBY) INFANTRY BDE.

2/5 BN. NOTTS. & DERBY R.
2/6 BN. NOTTS. & DERBY R.
2/7 BN. NOTTS. & DERBY R.
2/8 BN. NOTTS. & DERBY R.
175 MACHINE GUN COY.
178 TRENCH MORTAR B.

200 MACHINE GUN COMPANY

A.S.C.

NO. 1 COY. (STAFFS.)
NO. 2 COY. (LINCOLN & LEICESTER)
NO. 3 COY. (STAFFS.)
NO. 4 COY. (NOTTS & DERBY)

R.A.M.C.

2/1 N. MID. FIELD AMB. (DERBY)
2/2 N. MID. FIELD AMB. (LEICESTER)
2/3 N. MID. FIELD AMB. (STAFFS.)
SANITARY SECTION (LEICESTER)

R.A.V.C.

N. MID. VET. SECT. (LINCOLN)
250 DIVL. EMPLOY. COMPANY

Memorial Tablet erected in the—
Collegiate Church of St. Martin, Leicester;
St. Mary's Church, Stafford;
All Saints' Church, Derby;
The Parish Church, Chesterfield.

APPENDICES.

Some Papers from Ireland, Collected by Lieut.-Col. E. U. BRADBRIDGE.

G. R.

A PROCLAMATION.

Regulations to be observed under Martial Law.

I, Major-General, the Right Hon. L. B. Friend, C.B., Commanding the Troops in Ireland, hereby command that

(1) All persons in Dublin City and County shall keep within their houses between the hours of 7.30 p.m. in the evening and 5.30 a.m. on the next morning, on all days till further notice; unless provided with the written permission of the Military Authorities; or, unless in the case of fully qualified medical practitioners or medical nurses in uniform in the discharge of urgent duties.

(2) All persons other than members of His Majesty's Forces or Police, or acting in aid of said forces, who are seen carrying arms, are liable to be fired upon by the military without warning.

(3) All persons shall give all information in their possession as to stores of arms, ammunition, or explosives, or of the movement of hostile bodies, to the nearest military authority, or to the nearest police barracks.

(4) All well-disposed persons are hereby warned and advised to keep away from the vicinity of all places where military operations are in progress, or where hostile bodies are moving, and persons who enter such areas do so at their own risk.

Dated at Headquarters, Irish Command,
Park Gate, Dublin, 26th April, 1916.

L. B. FRIEND,
Major-General, Commanding Troops,
Ireland.

PUBLIC NOTICE.

Passengers Leaving Ireland.

I, General Sir John Grenfell Maxwell, K.C.B., K.C.M.G., C.V.O., D.S.O., Commanding in Chief His Majesty's Forces in Ireland, hereby Order that no person shall embark as a passenger on board any vessel except at one of the following ports, viz: Dublin (North Wall), Kingstown, Belfast, and Greenore. Each passenger must produce satisfactory credentials or proofs of identity to the Military Embarkation Officer or Police Authorities at the place of intended embarkation and give valid reasons for the intended journey.

J. G. MAXWELL, General,
Commanding-in-Chief,
The Forces in Ireland.

Headquarters, Irish Command,
2nd May, 1916.

PUBLIC NOTICE.

Arms and Ammunition.

I, General Sir John Grenfell Maxwell, K.C.B., K.C.M.G., C.V.O., D.S.O., Commanding in Chief His Majesty's Forces in Ireland, hereby Order that all members of the Irish Volunteer Sinn Fein Organization, or of the Citizen Army, shall forthwith surrender all arms, ammunition and explosives in their possession to the nearest Military Authority or the nearest Police Barracks.

Any member of either of these organizations found in possession of any arms, ammunition, or explosives, after 6th May, 1916, will be severly dealt with.

J. G. MAXWELL, General,
Commanding-in-Chief,
The Forces in Ireland.

Headquarters, Irish Command,
2nd May, 1916.

SPECIAL IRISH COMMAND ORDER

by

General Sir J. G. Maxwell, K.C.B., K.C.M.G., C.V.O., D.S.O., Colonel Royal Highlanders, Commanding in Chief the Forces in Ireland.

Headquarters,
Parkgate, Dublin,
5th May, 1916.

Message from H.M. the King.

The following message has been received from His Majesty the King:—

General Sir John Maxwell,
G.O.C.-in-C., Irish Command, Dublin.

Now that the recent lamentable outbreak has finally been quelled I wish to express to my gallant troops in Ireland, to the Royal Irish Constabulary and to the Dublin Metropolitan Police my deep sense of the whole-hearted devotion to duty and spirit of self-sacrifice with which throughout they have acted.

GEORGE R. I.

L. B. FRIEND, Major-General,
i/c of Administration,
Irish Command.

SIR JOHN MAXWELL'S THANKS.

Sir John Maxwell issued the following General Order to the troops:—

"I desire to thank the troops which have been engaged in the City of Dublin for their splendid behaviour under the trying conditions of street fighting which I have found it necessary to order them to undertake. Owing to the excellent direction of the Officers and the tireless effort of the troops, all the surviving rebels in Dublin have now surrendered unconditionally.

"I especially wish to express my gratitude to those Irish regiments which have so largely helped to crush this rising.

"Many incidents of very gallant behaviour have been brought to my notice, which I am unable to refer to in this Order, but I must express my admiration of the conduct of a small detachment from the 6th Reserve Cavalry Regiment, which, when conveying ammunition, was attacked in Charles Street, and after a splendid defence for three and a half days, during which their leaders were struck down, safely delivered the ammunition."

J. G. MAXWELL,

General Commanding-in-Chief the Forces in Ireland,
Headquarters, "Irish Command."

May 1st, 1916.

59th DIVISION OPERATION ORDER, No. 4.

28-4-16.

1. The Division will move to Balls Bridge to-morrow.
2. The G.O.C. 177th Infantry Brigade will take over with 5th Lincolnshire Regiment and a Battalion to be detailed by him the line Trinity College (exclusive) to Balls Bridge from the G.O.C. 176th Infantry Brigade.
3. The Battalion detailed by the G.O.C. 177th Infantry Brigade will leave Kingstown at 6 a.m. to-morrow with such of its transport as is available.
4. A Battalion of the 177th Infantry Brigade (less one Company), and the 1/3rd Field Company, R.E., will march at 10 a.m. to Balls Bridge under the command of the O.C. Battalion, who will issue the necessary orders.
5. A Battalion 177th Infantry Brigade will remain at Kingstown and will be responsible for its defence.
6. The Field Artillery Brigade Headquarters and such of their Batteries as may have disembarked at Kingstown will march to Balls Bridge, starting not later than 3 p.m. The Infantry escort will be the Company mentioned in 4 above.

7. "C" Squadron Northumberland Hussars will march to Balls Bridge at 5 p.m., and will act as escort to any transport that may have landed.
8. One day's reserve rations will be issued to-night to be carried on the man if train transport is not available.
9. Billeting parties laid down in standing orders will meet the D.A.A. & Q.M.G. at Divisional Headquarters at 8.30 a.m.
10. The Divisional Headquarters will close at Kingstown at 12 noon to-morrow and will open at Balls Bridge at the same hour.

C. HEYWORTH SAVAGE, Lieut.-Col.,
G.S. 59th Division.

Kingstown.

By the King.

A PROCLAMATION

For Suspending in Ireland the Operation of Section One of the Defence of the Realm (Amendment) Act, 1915 (Right of British Subject Charged with Offence to be Tried by Civil Court).

GEORGE R.I.

Whereas by subsection (7) of section one of the Defence of the Realm (Amendment) Act, 1915, it is enacted that in the event of invasion or other special military emergency arising out of the present War, We may, by Proclamation, forthwith suspend the operation of the said section, either generally or as respects any area specified therein:

And whereas the present state of affairs in Ireland is such as to constitute such a special military emergency as aforesaid:

Now, therefore, We, in pursuance of the powers so conferred on Us, do hereby order that the operation of the said section be suspended in Ireland until We see fit to revoke this Our Proclamation.

Given at Our Court at Windsor Castle, this Twenty-sixth day of April, in the year of our Lord One thousand nine hundred and sixteen, and in the Sixth year of our reign.

GOD SAVE THE KING.

SPECIAL DIVISIONAL ORDER
BY
MAJOR-GENERAL A. E. SANDBACH, C.B., D.S.O.,
Commanding 59th Division.

18th August, 1916.

The Field Marshal, Commander-in-Chief of the Home Forces, has desired the Divisional Commander to notify to all ranks of the 59th Division his great pleasure, during his recent inspections at DUBLIN, THE CURRAGH and FERMOY, in seeing the high state of efficiency which the Division has reached.

Lord French considers that the general turn-out and soldierly bearing on parade, and the marching and discipline reflect the greatest credit on all those responsible for the training of the various Units.

The Divisional Commander congratulates every Officer and soldier in the Division on the excellent result of the inspection, which he recognises has only been attained by constant and continuous hard work and strict attention to duty, which will sooner or later bring its sure reward.

R. St. G. GORTON, Lieut.-Colonel,
G.S. 59th Division.

ISSUED TO ALL RANKS ON EMBARKATION FOR FRANCE.

To..

.........Batt...................................Regt.

To every soldier now going overseas from the 59th Division, I send a copy of Lord Kitchener's message to the original British Expeditionary Force when they left England's shores in 1914.

Read it and act up to it, and you will bring credit and honour not only to your own home and county, but also to the 59th Division, where you have been trained. May God speed you and protect you.

A. E. SANDBACH,
Major-General Commanding 59th Division.

Curragh Camp,
29-8-16.

Field Marshal the Rt. Hon. Lord Kitchener's

Message to the British Expeditionary Force.

You are ordered abroad as a soldier of the King to help our French comrades against the invasion of the common Enemy. You have to perform a task which will need your courage, your energy, your patience. Remember that the honour of the British Army depends on your individual conduct. It will be your duty not only to set an example of discipline and perfect steadiness under fire, but also to maintain the most friendly relations with those whom you are helping in this struggle. The operations in which you are engaged will, for the most part, take place in a friendly country, and you can do your own country no better service than in showing yourself in France and Belgium in the true character of a British soldier.

Be invariably courteous, considerate and kind. Never do anything likely to injure or destroy property, and always look upon looting as a disgraceful act. You are sure to meet with a welcome and to be trusted; your conduct must justify that welcome and that trust. Your duty cannot be done unless your health is sound. So keep constantly on your guard against excesses. In this new experience you may find temptations both in wine and women. You must entirely resist both temptations, and, while treating all women with perfect courtesy, you should avoid any intimacy. Do your duty bravely.

Fear God. Honour the King.

KITCHENER,

Field-Marshal.

August, 1914.

SOME PAPERS FROM FRANCE COLLECTED BY LIEUT.-COL. E. U. BRADBRIDGE.

Issued by the G.O.C. the Division to individuals who performed notably brave actions.

59th (NORTH MIDLAND) DIVISION.

To No.......... Rank......... Name................................

Unit..

Your Commanding Officer and Brigade Commander have informed me that you have distinguished yourself by conspicuous bravery in the field.

I have read their reports with much pleasure.

British Army in France.

Date.................... ....

Major-General,
Commanding 59th Division.

....

....

....

....

PROGRAMME.

178th Infantry Brigade.

RACE MEETING,
Saturday, July 28th, 1917,
at
Four Winds Farm.

Patrons:

Major-General C. F. Romer, C.B., C.M.G., A.D.C.
Brigadier-General T. W. Stansfeld, D.S.O.

Stewards:

Major-General C. F. Romer, C.B., C.M.G., A.D.C.
Brig.-Genl. T. W. Stansfeld, D.S.O., Lieut.-Col. W. Coape-Oates,
Lieut.-Col. H. S. Hodgkin, D.S.O., Lieut.-Col. M. C. Martyn, M.C.

Committee:

Lieut.-Col. H. S. Hodgkin, D.S.O., Major H. Welch,
Capt. W. N. Wright, Lieut. J. Williamson, Lieut. J. M. Jordan,
Lieut. E. J. Friend.

Judges:

Lieut.-Col. W. Coape-Oates, Major G. C. S. Hodgson.

Starter:

Lieut. A. T. Prince.

Clerk of the Course:

Lieut. H. L. Kerrick.

Clerk of the Scales:

Lieut. H. L. Kerrick.

Hon. Secretary and Stakeholder:

Capt. W. N. Wright.

3 p.m. I.—RUFFORD PLATE. Distance about 5 furlongs. Catch weights over 12 stones. Winner of any race 7-lbs. extra. Open to G.O.C. and Staff, C.O.'s, 2nds in Command, Adjutants, Q.M.'s, T.O.'s and M.O.'s in 178th Brigade. Owners up. Entrance, 5 francs and 5 francs extra for starters.

First, 150 francs; Second, 50 francs; Third, 25 francs.

Capt. H. K. Goddard's chestnut mare, aged......... A Bit of Fluff.
Major Fisher's bay gelding, aged .... Dicky.
Capt. Robinson's brown mare, aged .... Jenny.
Capt. F. Carr's bay gelding, aged .... Prince.
Capt. F. Pragnell's brown gelding, aged .... Indian.
Capt. T. H. L. Stebbings' chestnut mare, 8 yrs. ... Mabel.
Capt. C. T. Trench's black gelding, aged .... Jack Johnson.
Capt. T. Mearns' bay mare, 8 yrs. .... Tiny.
Lieut. H. Spendlove's black mare, 7 yrs. .... Queenie.
Capt. T. S. Elliott's brown mare, aged .... Averham.
Capt. W. N. Wright's brown gelding, 5 yrs. ...... Templecombe.
Lieut. W. H. Brierley's bay gelding, aged .... Mickie.
Major H. Welch's bay mare, 7 yrs. .... Ivy.
Lieut. G. E. Titchener's brown gelding, aged ...... Teddy.
Brig.-Gen. T. Stansfeld's, D.S.O., brown gelding, aged .... Huntsman.
Major G. C. S. Hodgson's, M.C., chestnut gelding, 8 yrs. .... It.

Capt. H. L. Paddock's brown mare, 7 yrs. .... Jane.
Lt.-Col. H. S. Hodgkin's, D.S.O., brown gelding, aged .... Okeover.
Lt.-Col. H. S. Hodgkin's, D.S.O., bay gelding, aged .... Bob.
Major G. A. Duncan's, M.C., brown mare, 7 yrs.... Molly.
Lt.-Col. W. Coape-Oates' black gelding, aged ...... Jack.
Lieut. W. Imison's bay gelding, 6 yrs. .... Curragh.
Capt. R. Staniforth's black mare, aged .... Bessy.

3.30 p.m. II.—THE MEYNELL STAKES. Distance about 5 furlongs. Catch weights over 12 stones. Winner of any race 21-lbs. extra. For bona-fide Pack Ponies in 178th Brigade. Entrance, 5 francs.

First, 75 francs; Second, 25 francs; Third, Saves Entrance.

Riders: Any Officer in same Unit as ponies.

Lieut.-Col. H. S. Hodgkin's, D.S.O., bay gelding, aged .... Broncho.
Capt. Davis' brown gelding, aged .... Tonk.
Lieut. B. H. Brewill's black mare, 7 yrs. .... Bess.
Sec.-Lieut. S. Sheppard's brown mare, aged......... Mousie.
Sec.-Lieut. J. Williamson's grey gelding, 7 yrs. ... Greyback.
Lieut.-Col. M. C. Martyn's, M.C., brown gelding, aged .... Ben.
Sec.-Lieut. C. F. Parry's roan mare, aged............ Strawberry.
Lieut. T. Nadin's chestnut mare, aged .... The Cat (21-lbs.)
Lieut. J. M. Jordan's chestnut mare, aged .... Lucy Glitters.
Lieut. F. W. Smith's chestnut gelding, aged .... Iron Cross.
Lieut. G. Glessep's brown gelding, aged .... Success.
Lieut. W. H. Brierley's grey gelding, 7 yrs.......... Snowball.
Capt. W. E. V. Tompkin's brown gelding, aged ... Paddy.
Capt. H. W. Kerrigan's bay mare, 8 yrs. .... Queenie.
Lieut. G. E. Titchener's brown gelding, aged ...... Nobby.
Capt. W. N. Wright's bay mare, 8 yrs. .... Lady Angelina.
Lieut. W. Imison's chestnut gelding, aged .... The Rat.

4 p.m. III.—THE CURRAGH PLATE. Distance about 1 mile. Catch weights 12 stones 7 lbs. Open to 59th Division. Riders any Officers or other ranks in the Division. Entrance, 5 francs and 5 francs extra for starters.

Capt. M. T. Chapman's chestnut gelding, 7 yrs. ... Sandy.
Major Fisher's bay gelding, aged .... Dicky.
Lieut. Salmon's chestnut gelding, aged .... Bill.
Lieut.-Col. H. S. Hodgkin's, D.S.O., brown gelding, aged .... Okeover.
Brig.-Gen. T. Stansfeld's, D.S.O., brown gelding, aged .... Huntsman.
Lieut. W. Bullivant's brown gelding, aged .... Don.

Lieut.-Col. M. C. Martyn's, M.C., brown gelding, aged .... Alex.
Lieut. J. Williamson's, brown gelding, aged .... Broncho.
Lieut. J. M. Jordan's chestnut gelding, 7 yrs. .... Dandy Dick.
Lieut. T. Nadin's bay gelding, aged .... Pioneer.
Capt. M. A. Boswell's roan gelding, aged.......... Strawberry.
Lieut. J. A. Smith's bay gelding, aged .... Sam.
Lieut. J. Bryce's grey gelding, aged .... Robby.
Capt. R. J. Greene's chestnut mare, aged .... Marjorie.
Capt. Henderson's black gelding, aged .... Nigger.
Major H. Welch's bay mare, 7 yrs. .... Ivy.
Lieut. E. J. Friend's bay gelding, aged .... Major.
Capt. W. H. Wright's brown gelding, 5 yrs. .... Templecombe.
Sec.-Lieut. Hon. H. N. Douglas Pennant's bay mare, 5 yrs. .... Nameless.
Sec.-Lieut. Hon. H. N. Douglas Pennant's brown gelding, aged .... Tabs.
Capt. Macmillan's chestnut mare, aged .... Bess.

4.30 p.m. IV.—MULE RACE. Distance about 3 furlongs. Catch weights. Open to 178th Brigade. Entrance, Free.

First, 25 francs; Second, 15 francs; Third, 10 francs; Fourth, 5 francs.

Pte. E. A. Smith's black mule .... Lizzie.
„ S. Salt's black mule .... Mustard.
„ H. Lomas' brown mule.......... Dick.
„ H. Freeman's bay mule .... Rodger.
„ A. L. Harrison's black mule .... Buller.
Drv. Kerr's black mule .... Scroonger.
„ Weston's bay mule .... Bill.
„ Purchase's black mule .... Darkie.
„ Grey's black mule .... Giraffe.
Cpl. Mason's brown mule .... Dick.
Drv. Shield's brindled mule .... Windy.
Pte. J. Wright's bay mule.......... Joe.
„ Palmer's mouse mule .... Chocolate.
„ Merry's black mule.......... Paddy.
„ Banham's black mule .... Charlie.
„ Taylor's dark bay mule .... Alec.
„ Banlor's black mule .... Katy.
Drv. Malkin's black mule .... Diamond.
Cpl. Elden's black mule .... Joey.
Drv. Mason's bay mule .... Wallace.
„ Ratcliffe's bay mule.......... Georgina.
„ Lardner's bay mule.......... Nameless.
Sgt. Duckering's dark brown mule.......... Tony.
Cpl. Cauldwell's brown mule .... Susie.
L.-Cpl. Smith's black mule .... Boscoe.
Pte. Blood's brown mule .... Joey.
„ Fisher's dark brown mule .... Jerry.

5.15 p.m. V.—THE SOUTH NOTTS. PLATE. A Steeplechase. Distance about 5 furlongs. Catch weights 12. Open to any Horse in 178th Brigade not entered in the Rufford Plate. Riders any Officers in same Unit as Horses. Entrance, 5 francs.

First, 75 francs; Second, 25 francs; Third, Saves Entrance.

Capt. Robinson's black gelding, aged.................. Darky.
Lieut. Hulse's brown mare, aged .... Minnie.
Lieut. B. H. Brewill's bay mare, 7 yrs. .... Kitty.
Sec.-Lieut. W. Bullivant's brown gelding, aged...... Lion
Lieut.-Col. M. C. Martyn's, M.C., brown gelding, aged .... Alex.
Lieut. T. Nadin's bay mare, 7 yrs. .... Captive Princess.
Lieut. J. M. Jordan's bay gelding, aged .... Red Quill.
Lieut. H. Spendlove's bay gelding, aged .... Loughbrown.
Capt. C. P. Elliott's bay mare, 7 yrs. .... The Nun.
Major G. C. S. Hodgson's, M.C., grey gelding, aged Grey Legs.
Lieut. G. J. D. Schumach's bay gelding, aged ...... Bob.
Capt. W. N. Wright's bay mare, 8 yrs. .... Lady Angelina.
Lieut. M. B. Drysdale's brown mare, aged .... Galloping Sarah.
Lieut. R. A. C. Edkin's brown gelding, aged ...... Mouse.

5.45 p.m. VI.—THE HIGH PEAK STEEPLECHASE. Distance about 5 furlongs. Catch weights, 12-st. Open to 59th Division. Riders any Officers or O.R. in Division. Entrance, 5 francs and 5 francs extra for starters.

First, 150 francs; Second, 50 francs; Third, 25 francs. (Given by the ring.)

Major P. Coe's chestnut gelding, aged .... Tramp.
Capt. M. T. Chapman's grey gelding, 7 yrs. ...... Johnnie.
Sec.-Lieut. Hon. Douglas Pennant's grey gelding, 6 yrs. .... James.
Capt. Davis's brown gelding, aged .... Tommy.
Lt.-Col. M. C. Martyn's, M.C., bay gelding, 8 yrs. Tango.
Lieut. J. M. Jordan's bay mare, 8 yrs. .... Elton.
Lieut. T. Nadin's bay gelding, 8 yrs. .... Pioneer.
Capt. V. C. de Crespigny's bay gelding, aged ...... Big Benny.
Lieut.-Col. H. S. Hodgkin's brown gelding, aged... Okeover.
Lieut. E. C. Steel's chestnut gelding, 7 yrs. .... Tommy.
Capt. R. J. Green's chestnut mare, aged .... Marjorie.
Capt. Guy G. Sooby's bay gelding, aged .... Outlan.
Capt. A. N. Peach's chestnut gelding, aged .... Sandy.
Capt. W. E. V. Tompkins' brown mare, aged...... Joan.
Brig.-Gen. T. Stansfeld's, D.S.O., brown gelding, aged .... Huntsman.
Lieut. J. Wither's bay gelding, aged .... Mac.

PROGRAMME.

177th Infantry Brigade.

RACE MEETING,
Saturday, August 18th, 1917,
at
Cross Roads, O.17. b.6.8. (Ref.) 57.c.S.W.

Price ... One Franc.

All horses to parade in paddock half-an-hour before the race.

Patrons:
Major-General C. F. Romer, C.B., C.M.G., A.D.C.
Brigadier-General C. H. L. James, C.B.

Stewards:
Brig.-Genl. C. H. L. James, C.B., Lieut.-Col. A. B. Johnson, Lieut.-Col. H. B. Roffey, Lieut.-Col. G. B. G. Wood, D.S.O., Lieut.-Col. Sir Ian Colquhoun, Bt., D.S.O.

Committee:
Lieut.-Col. G. B. G. Wood, D.S.O., Capt. R. V. Hart-Davis, Capt. M. A. Boswell, Capt. R. J. Green, Sec.-Lieut. M. S. Payne, Sec.-Lieut. R. J. Brooke, Sec.-Lieut. W. R. Sowter.

Clerks of the Course:
Lieut.-Col. G. German, Capt. R. V. Hart-Davis.

Judges:
Lieut.-Col. Sir Ian Colquhoun, Bt., D.S.O., Major G. E. Tallents, D.S.O., Capt. R. J. Green.

Starters:
Capt. W. N. Wright, Lieut. A. J. Liddiard.

Clerks of the Scales:
Lieut.-Qr.-Mr. H. Wright, Lieut.-Qr.-Mr. E. H. Thomas.

Hon. Secretary and Stakeholder:
Sec.-Lieut. R. J. Brooke.

3.30 p.m. 1.—MELTON PLATE. Open to 177th Inf. Brigade. Distance about 5 furlongs. Catch weights over 12st. 7lbs. Riders, Owners or other Officers in the same Unit. Entrance, 5 francs and 5 francs extra for starters.

First, Cup; Second, 30 francs; Third, Save Entrance.

Lieut. J. A. Smith's bay gelding, aged............... Sam.
Capt. M. A. Boswell's black mare, aged .... Bess.

Major W. R. James's bay gelding, 7 yrs. .... Bob.
Capt. R. J. Green's chestnut mare, 6 yrs............ Marjorie.
Sec.-Lieut. R. J. Brooke's bay mare, aged .... Norah.
Sec.-Lieut. E. S. Ainton's brown mare, aged ...... Molly.
Lieut. A. A. F. Stubb's chestnut gelding, aged ... Dante.
Lieut.-Col. H. B. Roffey's bay gelding, aged ...... Jack.
Sec.-Lieut. J. H. Goulby's bay mare, aged .... Fanny.
Lieut.-Q.M. R. H. Lewis's bay mare, aged .... Rissoles.
Major G. E. Tallent's, D.S.O., brown gelding, aged The Gunner.
Capt. Vincent's bay gelding, aged .... Got your Rations.
Capt. O. Fielden's brown mare, aged .... Hermingarde.
Lieut. M. S. Payne's chestnut mare, 5 yrs. .... Peggy.
Capt. Ward's bay mare, aged.......................... Sally.
Capt. Clarke's bay mare, 7 yrs........................ Kitty.
Capt. R. Hart Davis's chestnut mare, aged .... Phyllis.
Lieut. R. S. Davis's black gelding, aged .... Ar Beer.
Lieut. Q.M. J. Withers's black gelding, 7 yrs....... Mac.
Sec.-Lieut. Heywood's chestnut mare, aged......... Dolly.

4.0 p.m. II.—HINCKLEY PLATE. Open to the 177th Inf. Brigade. Distance about 5 furlongs. Catch weights. For *bona fide* Pack Ponies, to be ridden by their leaders. Entrance, Free.

First, 25 francs; Second, 20 francs; Third, 15 francs.

Drv. E. Dean's bay gelding, aged..................... No. 17.
„ W. Kemp's bay mare, aged .... No. 76.
„ H. Cobb's bay gelding, aged .... No. 72.
Pte. A. Marshall's bay mare, aged .... Jennie.
„ P. Kirk's roan mare, aged....................... Dolly.
„ Lane's bay gelding, aged .... Billy.
„ Crowfoot's roan gelding, aged .... Bluestone.
„ Mill's bay gelding, aged .... Nobby.
„ Cough's bay mare, aged......................... Teacake.
„ Fox's chestnut gelding, aged .... Jim.
„ Parker's chestnut gelding, aged .... Tick.
„ Roscoe's chestnut gelding, aged................ Tim.
„ Goodhand's chestnut mare, aged .... Nutty.

4.30 p.m. III.—OFFA STEEPLECHASE. Open to 59th Division. Distance about 5 furlongs. Catch weights, over 12st. 7lbs. Riders, any Officers in the Division. Entrance, 5 francs and 5 francs extra for starters.

First, Cup; Second, 30 francs; Third, Save Entrance.

Capt. Guy Sooby's bay gelding, aged .... Outlaw.
Capt. W. N. Wright's brown gelding, 5 yrs......... Templecombe.
Capt. W. N. Wright's bay mare, 7 yrs................ The Nun.
Capt. R. J. Green's chestnut mare, 6 yrs............ Marjorie.

Major J. W. Coe's chestnut gelding, aged .... Tramp.
Brig.-Gen. T. O. Cope's chestnut gelding, aged ... Charlie.
Major J. H. Thursfield's .... Smooker.
Sec.-Lieut. B. W. Talton's .... Tich.
Sec.-Lieut. Hon. H. Douglas Pennant's brown gelding, aged .... Tabs.
Lieut.-Col. H. S. Hodgkin's black gelding, aged... Okeover.

5.0 p.m. IV.—BOSTON STUMP PLATE. Open to 177th Inf. Brigade. Distance about 5 furlongs. Catch weights for horses other than Officers' Chargers and Pack Ponies. Riders, N.C.O.'s. Entrance, Free.

First, 25 francs; Second, 20 francs; Third, 15 francs.

Sgt. G. Hammond's black gelding, aged ....
Sergt. A. G. Lawson's black gelding, 6 yrs. .... No. 11.
Far.-Sgt. J. P. Steven's bay gelding, aged .... No. 10.
Cpl. J. Horton's bay mare, 5 yrs. .... No. 13.
L.-Cpl. A. Bownes's brown gelding, aged .... Jack.
L.-Cpl. Crompton's chestnut gelding, aged .... Ralph.
L.-Cpl. Blanchard's black mare, aged .... Dolly.
A.S.C.'s bay gelding, aged .... Lance.
Cpl. Clement's bay mare, aged .... Polly.
Sgt. Lightfoot's brown mare, aged .... Molly.

5.30 p.m. V.—QUORN STEEPLECHASE. Open to 177th Inf. Brigade. Distance, about 5 furlongs. Catch weights, over 12st. 7lbs. Riders, Owners or other Officers in same Unit. Entrance, 5 francs and 5 francs extra for starters.

First, Cup; Second, 30 Francs; Third, Save Entrance.

Major G. E. Tallent's, D.S.O., bay gelding, 7 yrs. Rebel.
Lieut. J. A. Smith's bay gelding, aged .... Sam.
Major W. R. James's bay gelding, 7 yrs. .... Bob.
Capt. R. J. Green's chestnut mare, 6 yrs. .... Marjorie.
Lieut. A. A. F. Stubb's chestnut gelding, aged ... Dante.
Lieut.-Col. A. B. Roffey's bay gelding, aged......... Jack.
Sec.-Lieut. J. H. Goulby's bay mare, aged .... Fanny.
Capt. Oliver's black mare, aged .... The Flapper.
Lieut.-Col. G. German's black mare, aged .... Betty.
Lieut. Hawley's brown mare, aged .... Daisie.
Capt. Clarke's bay mare, 7 yrs. .... Kitty.
Capt. R. Hart Davis's grey mare, 7 yrs. .... Violet.
Capt. R. Hart Davis's chestnut mare, aged .... Phyllis.
Lieut. Clower's bay gelding, aged .... Jackie.

6.0 p.m. VI.—CARHOLME PLATE. Open to 59th Division. Distance about 1 mile. Catch weights, over 12st. 7lbs. Riders, Any Officer in the Division. Entrance, 5 francs and 5 francs extra for starters.

First, Cup; Second, 30 francs; Third, Save Entrance.

Capt. Guy G. Sooby's bay gelding, aged .... Outlaw.
Capt. W. N. Wright's brown gelding, 5 yrs.......... Templecombe.
Capt. W. N. Wright's bay mare, 7 yrs. .... The Nun.
Major G. E. Tallent's, D.S.O., brown gelding, aged The Gunner.
Capt. M. A. Boswell's roan gelding, 6 yrs. .... Strawberry.
Capt. A. M. Peach's chestnut gelding, aged......... Sandy.
Brig.-Gen. T. W. Stansfeld's brown gelding, aged Huntsman.
Capt. Bodley's brown gelding, aged .... The Fly.
Sec.-Lieut. S. C. Knott's............................... Pet.
Sec.-Lieut. B. W. Talton's .... Tich.
Lieut. M. S. Payne's chestnut mare, 5 yrs. .... Peggy.
Lieut.-Q.M. J. Wither's black gelding, 7 yrs. ...... Mac.
Lieut. A. E. Swain's brown gelding, aged............ Tommy.
Lt.-Col. Sir Ian Colquhoun's, Bt., D.S.O., bay mare, 6 yrs. .... Lady.
Sec.-Lieut. Hon. H. Douglas Pennant's brown gelding, aged .... Tabs.
Lieut.-Col. J. H. Porter's chestnut gelding, aged... Jimmy.
Major O. C. Bladen's bay mare, aged .... Tweenie.
Lieut.-Col. H. S. Hodgkin's black gelding, aged... Okeover.
Lieut.-Col. R. St. G. Gorton's bay mare, aged...... Mog.

59th DIVISION.

TRANSPORT COMPETITIONS

to be held on 19th July, 1917, on ground between 177th Brigade Camp and Barastre.

With reference to 59th Divisional Circular, No. 518/6.G., dated July 7th, 1917 (Competitions), the following will be the Transport Competitions to be held on the 19th instant.

For the purposes of these Competitions the following will be considered " Units ":—

Divisional Headquarters to include H.Q.'s, R.A., R.E., and Train 1. Each Brigade Headquarters, 1; Each Infantry Battalion, 1; Machine Gun Companies, 1; Divisional Engineers, 3; Divisional Signal Company, 1; Divisional Train, 4; The Divisional Artillery in Reserve Area, 1; Divisional Field Ambulance, 3; and Divisional Mobile Veterinary Section, 1.

Committee:
Lt.-Col. E. U. Bradbridge, A.A. & Q.M.G.
Lt.-Col. T. Hazlerigg, O.C. 59th Div. Train.
Major J. W. Coe, A.D.V.S.
Captain M. T. Chapman, D.A.Q.M.G.

Ring Master -	Capt. M. T. Chapman, D.A.Q.M.G.
Assistant Ring Masters -	Sgt.-Maj. C. O. Coombes, A.S.C. Sgt.-Major B. A. E. Heileig, A.S.C. S.-Sgt. Scott, D.H.Q.
Recorder - -	Cpl. A. E. Barrett, D.H.Q.

COMPETITIONS:—

ARENA 1.

No. 1. 11.15 a.m.—
LIMBERED WAGON TURNOUT. PAIRS MULES.
1 entry per Unit except M.G. Coys. and D.A.C.
Prizes: 1st, 20 francs; 2nd, 10 francs; 3rd, 5 francs.

No. 3. 12.15 p.m.—
PACK ANIMALS. MULES.
1 entry per Unit. Mule to be loaded with pack he usually carries.
Prizes: 1st, 15 francs; 2nd, 7 francs; 3rd, 5 francs.

No. 5. 2.15 p.m.—
FIELD KITCHEN TURNOUT. PAIRS H.D.
1 entry per Battalion.
Prizes: 1st, 20 francs; 2nd, 10 francs; 3rd, 5 francs.

No. 7. 2.45 p.m.—
LIMBERED WAGON TURNOUT and DRIVE. M.G. Coys.
Teams of 4. One entry per Company.
Prizes: 1st, 20 francs; 2nd, 10 francs.

Judges for above Competitions:
Lt.-Col. T. Hazlerigg, O.C. 59 Div. Train.
Major J. W. Coe, A.D.V.S.
Major H. V. Heather, Bde.-Major R.A.

No. 9. 3.15 p.m.—
A.V.C. JUMPING.

Judges:
Brig.-Gen. J. W. Stirling, Cmdg. 59 R.A.
Capt. C. V. C. De Crespigny, A.P.M.
Capt. N. G. P. De C. Tronson, 2/6 N. Staffs.
Prizes: 1st, 20 francs; 2nd, 10 francs.

No. 11. 3.45 p.m.—

TURNOUTS & DRIVE FOR DIV. TRAIN & FIELD AMBS.

Long rein driving. 1 entry per unit.

Judges:

Brig.-Gen. C. H. L. James, Cmdg. 177th Inf. Bde.
Lt.-Col. T. H. B. Thorne, Cmdg. 2/6 N. Staffs.
Major C. C. S. Hodgson, B.M., 178th Inf. Bde.

Prizes: 1st, 20 francs; 2nd, 10 francs; 3rd, 5 francs.

No. 13. 4.15 p.m.—

LIMBERED WAGON TURNOUTS & DRIVE, D.A.C.

Teams of 6. Four entries.

Judges:

Lt.-Col. R. St. G. Gorton, G.S.O. (1).
Lt.-Col. T. B. H. Thorne, Cmdg. 2/6 N. Staffs.
Major C. C. S. Hodgson, Bde. Major 178th Inf. Bde.

Prizes: 1st, 30 francs; 2nd, 15 francs.

No. 15. 4.45 p.m.—

OFFICERS' JUMPING. Open.

Chargers and riders, owners up.

Judges:

Brig.-Gen. J. W. Stirling, Cmdg. 59th R.A.
Lt.-Col. Heyworth-Savage, Cmdg. 48 Lab. Group.
Major J. W. Coe, A.D.V.S.

Prize: Will be communicated "confidentially" to Winner.

ARENA 2.

No. 2. 11 a.m.—

LIMBERED WAGON TURNOUT. PAIRS L.D.

1 entry per Unit except M.G. Coys. and D.A.C.

Prizes: 1st, 20 francs; 2nd, 10 francs; 3rd, 5 francs.

No. 4. 12 noon—

PACK ANIMALS. PONIES.

I entry per Unit. Animal to be loaded with pack he usually carries.

Prizes: 1st, 15 francs; 2nd, 7 francs; 3rd, 5 francs.

No. 6. 2 p.m.—

WATER CART TURNOUT.

I entry per Unit.

Prizes: 1st, 20 francs; 2nd, 10 francs; 3rd, 5 francs.

Judges for above Competitions:

Captain R. W. S. Stanton, D.A.A.G.
Captain H. M. Whitehead, A.D.C. & C.C.
Captain H. W. Dawes, A.V.C.
(For Competition 6 add Col. H. H. C. Dent, A.D.M.S.)

No. 8. 3 p.m.—

SIGNAL COY. COMPETITION.

1 entry per Bde. Section and No. 1 Section.

Conditions.

Establish Base office. Wagon will move off at the trot and lay a line about half-mile in length to include a road crossing. Forward office will be established and a telegram of 20 words handed in and transmitted to the Base Office.

Points will be given for turnout of personnel, horses and vehicles, time, correct laying out of wire and correctness of message.

Judges:

Capt. W. Allard, Bde. Major 176th Inf. Bde.
Capt. R. Staniforth, Staff Capt. 178th Inf. Bde.
Capt. R. V. Hart-Davis, Staff Capt. 177th Inf. Bde.

Prizes: 1st, 20 francs; 2nd, 10 francs.

No. 10. 3.30 p.m.—

R.E. TURNOUTS. 1 Pontoon and 1 G.S. Wagon.

1 entry per Field Company.

Judges:

Lt.-Col. E. U. Bradbridge, A.A. & Q.M.G.
Captain W. Allard, Bde. Major 176th Inf. Bde.
Capt. W. A. Wright, T.O., 2/8th Sher. Fors.

Prizes: 1st, 20 francs; 2nd, 10 francs.

No. 12. 4 p.m.—

OFFICERS' CHARGERS TURNOUT. Open to D.H.Q. only (to include H.Q.'s., R.A., R.E. and Train).

To be ridden by grooms. Points will be given for condition and turnout and not for breeding. Grooms in drill order, horses marching order.

Judges:

Lt.-Col. Heyworth-Savage, Cmdg. 48 Lab. Group.
Lt.-Col. H. S. Hodgkin, Cmdg. 2/6 Sher. Fors.
Lt.-Col. Sir Ian Colquhoun, Cmdg. 4th Leicesters.

Prizes: 1st, 20 francs; 2nd, 10 francs; 3rd, 5 francs.
(To Grooms.)

No. 14. 4.30 p.m.—

OFFICERS' RIDING HORSES (except D.H.Q. & M.G., R.A., R.E. & Train).

Points will be given for condition and turnout and not for breeding. Horses will be ridden by grooms. Grooms in drill order, horses marching order.

Judges:

Lt.-Col. R. St. G. Gorton, G.S.O. (1).
Lt.-Col. K. C. Brazier-Creagh, Cmdg. 59th D.A.C.
Major J. W. Coe, A.D.V.S.

Prizes: 1st, 20 francs; 2nd, 10 francs; 3rd, 5 francs.
(To Grooms.)

ARENAS 1 & 2.

No. 16. 5.45 p.m.—

BOOT and SADDLE COMPETITION.

1 entry per unit for Mounted N.C.O.'s. Mount to be the Riding Horse issued to N.C.O.'s concerned.

Conditions.

N.C.O.'s will picquet their horses, tied by the head only, to a previously prepared line. Saddlery to be on the ground in rear of the animal. N.C.O.'s to take off their equipment and put on their greatcoats and lie on the ground with their heads on their saddles. On the last sound of the Reveille N.C.O.'s will rouse, get dressed, roll greatcoat and put it on the saddle, saddle up, unpicquet and ride about 2 furlongs to a marked line, dismount and first put on their own and then their horses' respirators and lead their horses to a second marked line (the winning post) about 100 yards.

Judges:

Lt.-Col. K. C. Brazier-Creagh, D.A.C.
Sec.-Lt. Thornbery, R.F.A., a/D.G.O.
Capt. W. A. Wright, 2/8 Sher. Fors.
Prizes: 1st, 20 francs; 2nd, 10 francs; 3rd, 5 francs.

No. 17. 6.15 p.m.—

BENDING RACE FOR OFFICERS. Open.

Judges:

Brig.-Gen. R. A. M. Currie, Cmdg. 176th Inf. Bde.
Captain C. V. C. De Crespigny, A.P.M.
Lt. the Hon. H. N. Douglas-Pennant, A.D.C.
Prize: Will be notified "Secretly" to the Officer selected.

Conditions.

All turnouts except where otherwise stated are to be in marching order, steel helmets to be worn and box respirators carried by personnel; respirators to be carried for horses except for jumping competitions.

Wagons are to be without loads, but with complete wagon equipment.

Driving Competitions will be over a figure of eight course through one gate and four pairs of blocks. Pace—Trot.

Officers or soldiers equipped with a pack will wear the pack when competing in mounted competitions, except Jumping, Bending Race and Best Turned Out Charger.

Points.

For Turn-out Competitions—

4 for condition and cleanliness of animal.
4 for harness.
4 for vehicles.
2 for men.

For Turn-out of Chargers, Riders and Pack Animals—

4 for condition and cleanliness of animal.
4 for saddlery.
4 for pack.
2 for turn-out of soldier.

In Driving competitions deduct 2 points for each obstacle knocked down and 1 for each obstacle grazed.

All entries " Post entries."

A place of assembly is marked for each Arena. A.P.M. will arrange to marshal the competitors in to these places of assembly.

It is to be arranged that vehicles and horses do not arrive at these assembly places until the time fixed for the event before that for which they are entering.

E. U. BRADBRIDGE, Lt.-Colonel,
A.A. & Q.M.G., 59th Division.

17th July, 1917. 6.30 p.m.

59th Div. No. A2605/58.

All Units.

The G.O.C. wishes all reinforcements to be told of the many occasions on which the Division has won distinction during the War, and of the gallant deeds performed by N.C.O.'s and men of the Division since its arrival in France.

They should be reminded that it is their duty to maintain the reputation won for it by the gallant conduct and soldierly spirit of units which are no longer in the Division.

In addition to being taught the names of their own Regimental Officers, the G.O.C. wishes all ranks to know the names of the Divisional and Brigade Commanders and something about the staff of formations.

The attached notes have been compiled with a view to assisting Regimental Officers in lecturing drafts on arrival.

The composition of the Division, and more particularly of the units of the Brigade, should be made known to all troops on joining, and the functions of the various arms briefly explained.

J. H. WESTLEY, Lieut.-Col.,
A.A. & Q.M.G., 59th Division.

17th September, 1918.

59th DIVISION.

NOTES.

Names of General Officers.

The 59th Division is commanded by Major-General N. M. Smyth, V.C., C.B.

Under him are four Brigadier-Generals:—

Brigadier-General J. F. Laycock, C.M.G., D.S.O., Commanding Royal Artillery.
Brigadier-General T. G. Cope, D.S.O., Commanding 176th Infantry Brigade.
Brigadier-General C. H. L. James, C.B., C.M.G., Commanding 177th Infantry Brigade.
Brigadier-General T. W. Stansfeld, C.M.G., D.S.O., Commanding 178th Infantry Brigade.

Staff.

The Divisional Commander is assisted by a Staff whose duty it is to convey his orders to those who have to act on them and to help the troops in every possible way to carry them out according to the wishes of the Major-General.

Staff Officers wear red patches on their tunics and a red band round their hats. Divisional Staff Officers wear a red band round their right arm, with the Divisional sign embroidered on it. Brigade Staff wear a blue band, also with the Divisional sign.

The Staff is divided into two branches—
The General Staff,
The Adjutant and Quartermaster General's Staff.

The General Staff deal with fighting and plans for fighting.

The Adjutant and Quartermaster General's Staff, or "Q" Branch as it is called, deal with the provision of men and things necessary for fighting, and discipline. By things I mean food, water, ammunition, clothes, guns, lorries, wagons, horses, and all the hundred and one things that go to help the soldier beat the enemy.

The General Staff, or "G" Branch as it is generally called, has a Lieut.-Colonel at the head of it known as the G.S.O.1.—

Lieut.-Col. R. S. Follett, D.S.O.

The Adjutant and Quartermaster General's Staff, generally known as "A. & Q.," has also a Lieut.-Colonel at the head of it, known as the A.A. & Q.M.G.—

Lieut.-Col. J. H. S. Westley, D.S.O.

Each Brigadier-General is assisted by two Staff Officers, a Brigade Major and a Staff Captain.

Divisional Sign.

The Divisional Sign is the Cross of Offa, King of Mercia. This was selected on account of the Division being originally raised in that part of the Midland Counties over which this King reigned before the Normans came to England.

Each of the Infantry Brigades has distinctive colours—

Red,
Yellow,
Green.

This colour is worn on both sleeves just below the shoulder, a different shaped patch being worn by each of the three battalions of the Brigade.

The Divisional Sign is painted on all vehicles in the Division.

The 59th Division, originally known as the 2/1st North Midland Division, commenced to mobilise at Luton in January, 1915, and by the end of the year was prepared for service overseas.

On the 24th April, 1916, orders were suddenly received for one Infantry Brigade to proceed at once to Ireland to assist in the suppression of the Sinn Fein rebellion which had broken out in Dublin.

The 178th Infantry Brigade proceeded on the 25th, and by the 27th April the whole of the Division, less Artillery, had disembarked at Kingstown.

The Sinn Feiners were holding a portion of Dublin in some strength, and the Division encountered considerable opposition before they succeeded in entering Dublin. The bulk of the fighting fell to the 178th Infantry Brigade, who were held up near Balls Bridge by the Sinn Feiners, who were holding a house commanding the bridge over the Dodder and the roads along which the Brigade had to advance.

After some stiff fighting the 7th and 8th Bns. Sherwood Foresters succeeded in rushing the house, but not until they had lost in casualties approximately five officers and 150 other ranks, about 70 of whom were killed.

A good deal of irregular fighting went on for some days, but a cordon was drawn round each part of Dublin held by the Sinn Feiners and gradually tightened until all the rebels were captured or surrendered.

Flying columns were subsequently sent to various parts of Ireland, but little or no opposition was encountered, and in a very short time the whole rebellion had been suppressed.

The Division remained in Ireland until the end of 1916, when they proceeded to Fovant for final training before proceeding to France.

The Division proceeded to France in February, 1917, and proceeded to join III. Corps, relieving the 50th Division in the line near Foucaucourt on the 5th March.

On the 17th March the Germans commenced their retirement on the Somme, and the Division proceeded to follow them up and crossed the Somme after little or no opposition on the 19th.

Owing to the exceptional bad weather and the complete lack of accommodation (all buildings, dug-outs, etc., having been destroyed by the Germans), the troops of the Division suffered considerably from exposure during their advance.

On the 31st March, 177th and 178th Infantry Brigades were engaged with the enemy and captured the villages of Vendelles, Hervilly, Hesbecourt and Jeancourt, and some prisoners.

On the 3rd April some heavy fighting occurred near Le Verguier, where the 7th Sherwood Foresters were engaged.

On the 27th April the 176th Infantry Brigade were heavily engaged in the attack on the Hargicourt Quarries.

On the 3rd May the 178th Infantry Brigade attacked Malakoff and Cologne Farms, capturing the former after a hard fight.

On the 24th May the Division was relieved in the line by the 4th Cavalry Division and were withdrawn into camps in the neighbourhood of Bouvincourt, subsequently taking another sector of the line near Havrincourt Wood, with Headquarters at Equancourt.

On the 10th July the Division was withdrawn from the line and proceeded to Barastre for training.

After about one month's training at Barastre, the Division proceeded north to take part in the battle for Passchendaele, which was then raging near Ypres. They were first accommodated near Winnezeele, where training continued for about a fortnight, and on the 20th September marched into the Ypres sector to relieve the 55th Division in the St. Julien-Wieltje area.

On the morning of the 26th the Division attacked and took all its objectives.

The casualties in the actual advance were not heavy, but the troops holding and consolidating the positions won suffered heavily, and on the 28th the Division was withdrawn into rest.

They then proceeded to Steenbecque and subsequently to Bomy, from which place they relieved the 4th Canadian Division in front of Lens, with Headquarters at the Chateau-de-la-Haie.

The Division remained in the line at Lens for about one month, when they were again withdrawn to take part in the Cambrai battle, which was then being prepared. They were transferred to the III. Corps, but subsequently joined the IV. Corps and relieved the Guards Division in the Bourlon Wood area after the successful advance on Cambrai.

The 2/6th South and the 2/6th North Staffs. Regiments successfully held Bourlon Wood for two days, in spite of the continued stream of gas shells which were poured into it by the Germans. The gas clung to the thick undergrowth in the wood, with the result that after wearing their respirators for hours nearly every individual in the two regiments was more or less badly gassed before they could be relieved. When these two battalions were finally withdrawn they were found to be in such a bad state that they both had to be sent to Rue, on the coast, to recuperate from the effects of the gas.

The Division took part in the retirement from Bourlon Wood, and also in repulsing the sudden German attack on Gouzeacourt.

On this occasion the Germans had penetrated the line and were nearly 1,000 yards west of Gouzeacourt.

The 470th Field Company R.E., marching up to join its Brigade Group, were hurriedly thrust in to fill up the gap, and with great gallantry succeeded in holding up the Germans until the arrival of the Guards, when they assisted in driving the Germans back and recapturing Gouzeacourt. Amongst other decorations earned on this occasion, Major Robinson, commanding 470th Field Company R.E., received the D.S.O., as did also Major Conlan, A.S.C., the S.S.O. of the Division, who, happening to be on the spot, fetched ammunition in his car and took it up to the 470th Field Company, remaining with Major Robinson and assisting him until the Germans had been driven out of Gouzeacourt.

The Division remained in this sector until 22nd of December, when they were withdrawn into rest and spent Christmas in the Le Cauroy area.

After about one month's rest the Division again went into the line, this time under the VI. Corps, in the Bullecourt area, with Headquarters at Behagnies. They were in this sector when the great German offensive of the 21st March commenced, when they again gallantly upheld the fine fighting tradition of North Midland troops.

After desperate fighting round Bullecourt and Ecoust, the Germans only succeeded in driving them back a few miles and entirely failed to cross the Arras-Bapaume Road, which was one of their objectives. In this defence the 176th and 178th Infantry Brigades were partly wiped out, but gallantly held on until finally relieved on the morning of the 22nd. The 177th Infantry Brigade remained in the line under the 40th Division and did splendid work, while the remainder of the Division was withdrawn to be refitted. After several changes of Headquarters the Division was transferred to the First Army and went into the Villers Chatel area, where the 177th Infantry Brigade rejoined it. During this short rest H.M. the King visited all the Brigades and went round several billets in each group, personally thanking officers and men for the gallant fight they had put up at Bullecourt.

After a very few days' rest the Division was transferred to the Second Army and proceeded once more to the Ypres salient, where they relieved the 33rd Division in the line with Headquarters in the Ramparts. While holding this part of the line the second German offensive commenced, which necessitated the withdrawal from Passchendaele. The Division was relieved by the 41st Division and was hurriedly put into the fight round Bailleul, where they again experienced heavy fighting, having casualties amounting to 2,362 all ranks.

On the 19th April they were again withdrawn and proceeded to the St. Janster-Biezen area, where they were employed under the VIII. Corps in preparing defences in the neighbourhood of Poperinghe.

On the 6th May they proceeded to St. Omer, where, to the great distress of all ranks, the orders were received for the Division to be reduced to a Training Cadre Establishment, by which arrangement all Infantry, except 10 officers and 43 other ranks per battalion, were taken away and put into the pool to form reinforcements for other Divisions.

On June 14th it was decided to make up the Division with Category " B " men, and very soon the Infantry of the Division consisted of the following units, which are now still with it, grouped in the following order:—

176th Infantry Brigade:

- 25th Bn. Liverpool Regiment.
- 26th Bn. Royal Welsh Fusiliers.
- 17th Bn. Royal Sussex Regt.

177th Infantry Brigade:
- 11th Bn. Somerset Light Infantry.
- 15th Bn. Essex Regt.
- 2/6th Bn. Durham Light Infantry.

178th Infantry Brigade:
- 36th Bn. Northumberland Fusiliers.
- 11th Bn. Royal Scots Fusiliers.
- 13th Bn. West Riding Regt.

25th Bn. King's Royal Rifle Corps (Pioneers).

The 23rd Bn. Cheshire Regt., 17th Bn. Worcestershire Regt., 23rd Bn. Lancashire Fusiliers, and the 2nd Royal Irish Regt. were also with the Division for a short time, but were subsequently transferred to the 40th Division.

Since then the Division, as a "B" Division, has taken its share in the line, relieving the 2nd Canadian Division in the Mercatel sector, with Headquarters at Basseux, and thus enabling it to take part in the successful operations east of Amiens, and again in the Merville sector, where they relieved the 74th Division on the 27th August.

The following are a few examples of gallant deeds performed by officers and men of the 59th Division:—

No. 50842, Cpl. John Frederick Thomas, 2/5th North Staffs. Regiment.

Showed most conspicuous bravery, coolness and resource in action.

He saw the enemy making preparations for the counter-attack, and, together with a comrade, on his own initiative, decided to make a close reconnaissance. They proceeded out in broad daylight, in full view of the enemy, under heavy machine gun fire.

His comrade was hit within a few yards of the trench, but undeterred he proceeded alone; working round a small copse he shot three enemy snipers, and then pushed on until he reached a building which the enemy used as a night post. From here he saw whence the enemy were bringing up their troops and where they were congregating.

He stayed in this position for an hour, sniping the enemy the whole time and doing great execution.

He returned to our lines after being away three hours, with information of the utmost value respecting the enemy's dispositions, thus enabling definite plans to be made and artillery fire to be brought on their concentration, so that when the attack took place it was broken up.

For this gallant act Corporal Thomas was awarded the Victoria Cross by His Majesty the King.

Sergt. Alfred Herbert Grooms, 2/4th Leicester Regt.

On the evening of the 25th March, in front of Ervillers, during a counter-attack by his Company on the enemy, who had penetrated the front posts, showed a splendid example of coolness and gallantry.

On reaching the objective he barricaded the road, and going back, under heavy machine gun fire, brought up reinforcements.

During the night he evacuated all his wounded.

Awarded the Military Medal.

No. 283226, Pte. Samuel Thomas Ottey, 4th Lincoln Regiment.

At Vraucourt, on March 22nd, 1918, he showed exceptional courage and fearlessness.

On his own initiative he carried barbed wire obstacles over the open and successfully blocked a communication trench leading to a trench which was in the hands of the enemy.

This difficult feat was carried out over ground swept by machine gun fire and covered by enemy snipers, and it was only by dogged pluck and determination that he was able to complete this most valuable and difficult piece of work which he had set himself to do.

Awarded the Military Medal.

No. 240790, Sergt. H. A. Brown, 2/6th Notts and Derby Regiment.

At Hargicourt Quarries on 27th April.

After his Platoon Commander had been wounded he took command and led it with great dash. He personally bombed the gunners and captured their machine gun. Throughout the operations his conduct and bearing was an example to his command.

Awarded the Distinguished Conduct Medal.

No. 200667, Pte. William Oakland, 4th Bn. Lincoln Regiment.

During the operations between Ecoust and Gomiecourt from March 21st to 26th, this stretcher bearer displayed the greatest courage and devotion to duty. Time after time he brought in and dressed wounded under intense fire and in full view of the enemy. Subsequently he was wounded himself, but the Medical Officer being busy at the time he managed to dress his own wounds, and continued his care for others without even mentioning his own case until the battalion was withdrawn from the front line.

Awarded Bar to the Military Medal.

No. 201107, Pte. Harry Allen, 4th Bn. Lincoln Regt.

At Vraucourt, on March 22nd, 1918, he showed conspicuous bravery by several times taking his Lewis gun out into the open under heavy shell and machine gun fire to obtain a good view of the enemy, and was observed to inflict considerable casualties on him.

Finally, when his Company's right flank was completely turned and the Company was ordered to withdraw from the untenable position, he stayed to the last to cover the retirement and then brought back his Lewis gun over 500 yards across the open under a hail of machine gun bullets.

His care for his gun's safety rather than his own was an example of the highest order to his comrades.

Awarded the Distinguished Conduct Medal.

No. 40376, Pte. Lawrence Edward Jackson, 2/6th N. Staffs. Regt.

On the 21st March, 1918, at Bullecourt, during the enemy attack, this man was sent forward to reconnoitre, as all communication was destroyed by the very heavy barrage which preceded the attack. Owing to the mist he ran into a large party of the enemy, who were all round him, and he had to fight his way through, bringing back very useful information. After that, when the right flank had become enveloped, he assisted his officer in collecting a party of men and repulsed several enemy attacks until late in the afternoon. He then retired on to the left flank and joined up with the 3rd Division, with whom he remained in the line 15 days. Through his personal bravery and endurance he greatly assisted in preventing the enemy rolling up the right flank.

Awarded the Distinguished Conduct Medal.

2nd Lieut. Lee Cowley Grice, 5th North Staffs. Regt.

For most conspicuous gallantry and devotion to duty on February 18th, 1918, near Bullecourt. An N.C.O. had left our front line at dawn to endeavour to locate an enemy post in Pudsey trench, and was seen to fall. At 2.30 p.m. this officer, accompanied by Capt. Wenger, left our lines in an endeavour to recover the body of the N.C.O. in order to prevent the enemy obtaining an identification. They advanced down Pudsey support trench until fired upon by an enemy from a block. Seeing the N.C.O.'s rifle lying on the edge of a shell hole, Capt. Wenger kept the enemy post under fire whilst 2nd Lieut. Grice got out of the trench and succeeded in reaching the shell hole, where he found the N.C.O. badly wounded in the leg and unable to move. Through continuous fire from two enemy posts, 2nd Lieut. Grice carried the N.C.O. back to Pudsey support and thence back into our own lines. This officer's coolness and resource undoubtedly robbed the enemy of a valuable identification, besides saving the life of the N.C.O.

2nd Lieut. Grice was recommended for the V.C., and was awarded the Military Cross.

No. 97984, Sergt. R. W. Frith, B/295th Brigade, R.F.A.

This N.C.O. was in charge of the party which went over with the officer acting as Liaison Officer with "C" and "D" Batteries in the attack on Cologne Ridge on the 26th August, 1917.

Under very heavy shell fire he repaired his lines, which were repeatedly cut in Hargicourt. He also maintained visual communications with the forward group exchange by means of a Lucas lamp, which had to be set up in the open.

Awarded Bar to the Military Medal.

Capt. (T/Major) F. Davenport, M.C., A/296th Brigade, R.F.A.

At about 1.0 a.m. until 2.0 a.m., on the 20th August, 1917, the gun position of A/296th Battery in Ronssoy Wood was for the second time during 24 hours subjected to a concentrated and accurate destructive shoot of 5.9in. and 8in.

Major Davenport superintended the withdrawal of the detachment down the mined dug-outs, but on his way back had to take refuge in the mess, which was destroyed by a direct hit, with the result that he was buried. He was extricated after the shelling ceased, and he re-organised the battery and answered two S.O.S. calls before 4 a.m., when his battery was due to take part in an offensive barrage. The data for this barrage was destroyed, but a fresh copy of orders having been sent for and obtained, he succeeded in carrying out his tasks most successfully.

It was entirely due to this officer's gallant leading and to the ever-cheerful confidence with which he inspired his men that the fire of this battery was available for two most important S.O.S. calls on the Knoll and for the barrage covering the successful "Ossus Raid."

Awarded the Distinguished Service Order.

Lieut. (T/Capt.) J. S. C. Oates, M.C., 2/8th Sherwood Foresters.

On 27th April, at Cologne Farm.

On the death of Capt. Woolley, this officer was left in command of the Battalion in front of Battalion Battle Headquarters.

An urgent request for help was sent to him from the front line, and at the same moment the platoon holding the switch trench guarding the left flank of the Battalion was driven out by counter-attack. He had only three platoons in reserve. One he sent to retake the switch trench and a second to reinforce the front line. Capt. Oates then coolly proceeded across the open under heavy fire, as there was no other way, first to the switch trench and then to the front line to see for himself the state of affairs. This process he repeated several times during the day, although heavily sniped at. The distance he had to travel across the open was 500 yards. Later he ordered a bombing offensive, successfully blocking vital points in advance of our lines, capturing a M.G. and eventually raided an enemy post during the succeeding night, completely establishing our ascendency over the enemy.

Awarded the Distinguished Service Order.

No. 417360, Pte. Ernest Roberts, 2/1st N.M. Field Ambulance.

On March 21st, east of Mory, this man brought away four wounded men from dug-outs at a heavy battery position near to Ecoust, under very heavy shell fire. He was assisted by a man of the 2/3rd North Midland Field Ambulance, and they carried the wounded a distance of about 800 yards through the enemy barrage. He showed the greatest courage and bravery and utter disregard of danger, and thus was enabled to save the lives of these four men.

Awarded the Military Medal.

Lieut. (T/Capt., A/Major) L. Robinson, 470th Field Company, R.E.

For conspicuous service rendered at a most critical moment before Gouzeaucourt on November 30th, 1917. This officer's company (on the march) was nearing Gouzeaucourt at the moment the German advance was topping Quentin Ridge. Major Robinson sent back his transport, led his company forward and arrived when remnants of the Infantry were being driven right in by the Germans. One section was immediately thrown forward to reinforce the Infantry, and the remaining three sections took up a defensive line on the eastern side of the village, in immediate support. The gallant bearing and fine defence put up by Major Robinson under circumstances of the greatest difficulty materially checked the German onrush, and was of the greatest importance in facilitating the re-capture of the village later on in the day; the possession of it being a vital point in our line.

Awarded the Distinguished Service Order.

Lieut. (T/Major) Vernon Douglas Robert Conlan, A.S.C.

Major Conlan, hearing that Gouzeaucourt was being held, came up in his car to see if he could be of any assistance. Ammunition had run out, and he proceeded to Fins dump to fetch some. He brought some up to the firing line in his car, the road at the time being swept by machine gun fire. He returned to Fins dump to try to get machine guns. He failed in this, but brought up drums of Lewis gun ammunition. In the meantime two Lewis guns had been obtained, and the ammunition he brought up kept the enemy out of the wire. He took part in the attack on Gouzeaucourt. There he sprained his knee and he was ordered to return. But for his timely aid in bringing up supplies of S.A.A. at great personal risk to himself, the men holding the line would have been routed.

Awarded the Distinguished Service Order.

No. 492378, Spr. (L/Cpl.) S. Meddings, 59th Divisional Signal Company.

For great gallantry and devotion to duty near Bourlon Wood. At one period he remained on duty continuously for more than 48 hours repairing telephone cables under heavy shell fire. On the night of the 30th November, 1917, he remained in the zone of the enemy's barrage and repaired the wire in 14 different places. This N.C.O.'s extreme disregard of danger enabled forward communication to be kept through. He had done fine work previously.

Awarded the Military Medal.

No. 307122, Pte. S. J. Delight, 2/8th Notts. and Derby Regiment.

On 27th April, in front of Cologne Farm, this stretcher bearer was wounded in the arm and back by a shell. He went forward and dressed some other wounded men under fire, thus being the means of saving their lives. He carried away on his back Pte. Hickmott to a place of safety, fetched a stretcher bearer party, saw he was taken to a dressing station, and then assisted two walking cases back to the Regimental Aid Post, handed them over to a doctor, saw them dressed, and then said that he himself was wounded and could they dress him.

He was afterwards admitted to hospital.

Awarded the Distinguished Conduct Medal.

No. 205892, L/Sergt. E. Bilton, 2/8th Notts. and Derby Regiment.

On April 3rd an aeroplane dropped a message the other side of some thick (old German) wire. This N.C.O. immediately jumped out of the trench and went to get the message. He found the wire impassable, and returned for wire cutters. He then went back and succeeded in getting through the wire, bringing back the message. All this time he was subject to fire from enemy's sniper, under 100 yards away.

Awarded the Military Medal.

No. 417330, Pte Sidney Pountain, and No. 417491, Pte. William Hardy, 2/1st (N.M.) Field Ambulance.

For cool courage and gallantry on the night of August 21st, at Le Fermont, when the unit was repeatedly bombed by hostile aircraft.

There were a number of casualties amongst the patients and men of the unit, and Ptes. Pountain and Hardy worked incessantly, with utter disregard of danger, removing the wounded from the wreckage and carrying them to a place of safety. A little later, when bombs began to fall in a neighbouring Artillery camp, these two privates, on their own initiative and without hesitation, ran across with a stretcher and worked there until all the wounded had been removed. I consider that these men, by their coolness, promptitude and fine example, were largely responsible for the rapid collection of the wounded.

Awarded the Military Medal.

No. 486706, Cpl. Frank Darby, 470th Field Company R.E.

On the night of August 21st, 1918, this N.C.O. was one of a party detailed to bridge the River Cojeul at Boisleux St. Mare, close to the front line. For over six hours he was indefatigable in helping and encouraging the men to get on with the work, during which time the enemy were shelling heavily with H.E. and gas shells, and gas masks had to be worn nearly the whole time. He was of the greatest assistance to his officers, and it was largely owing to his pluck that the job was completed in time. He had previously done good work.

Awarded the Military Medal.

The Division has taken part in most of the big battles on the British front since February, 1917, and has won distinction by the gallant deeds performed by the officers, N.C.O.'s and men who have served in it.

It is the duty of all soldiers serving with the Division to maintain and, if possible, add to the reputation won for it in the past.

The attached extracts from a captured enemy document must also be brought to the notice of all officers and men joining the Division :—

Enemy difficulty in obtaining information from British Prisoners of War.

Extract from an Enemy Divisional Summary:

> "The examination (of the prisoners) presented great difficulties, as the prisoners, especially those of the 23rd London Regiment, were apparently excellently schooled in the way they should behave if taken prisoner, and gave very clever evasive answers. The captured sergeant refused absolutely any information."

NOTE.—This refers to British prisoners captured by the enemy on 23rd August, and constitutes further evidence that the enemy appreciates and respects soldierly behaviour on the part of prisoners.

59th Division.

The Corps Commander wishes to express his appreciation to the G.O.C. and all ranks of the 59th Division for the work so cheerfully done by them, frequently under very trying circumstances, during the last two months. The advance and close pursuit of the enemy from Lestrem to L'Escaut has been a very fine achievement, and the fact that constant touch with the enemy has been maintained reflects the greatest credit on the Infantry Brigades and Battalions, and on the XI. Corps Mounted Troops which have been attached to the Advanced Guards of the Division. The difficulties of crossing the Rivers Lawe, Deule, Marque and L'Escaut, and in making practicable the roads so skilfully destroyed by the enemy, have been successfully overcome by the Royal Engineers and the Pioneers. The Field Artillery Brigades have pushed forward with the greatest energy, and in spite of every obstacle they have been well forward and have afforded the closest support to their Infantry. All ranks of all arms have co-operated to bring about this success.

A Division which has shown such energy and determination cannot be described as a " B " Division, and the Corps Commander directs that henceforward, in the XI. Corps, the 59th Division shall never be referred to in that manner.

A representation to the same effect has also been forwarded to the Army.

(Sd.) J. BRIND,
B.G., G.S.

XI. Corps,
23-10-18.

The Fighting at Cambria, 1917.

During the fighting following the British tank attack at Bourlon Wood, the 2/6th Sherwood Foresters was out at rest near La Vacquerie. When the German counter-attack was launched the 2/6th Battalion was rushed up to fill a gap in the line and was temporarily attached to the 60th Infantry Brigade, 20th Division. Their soldierly conduct on that occasion is shown in the following official correspondence:—

Subject: 2/6th Bn. The Sherwood Foresters.

H.Q.,
59th (N.M.) Division.
Date: 19/12/17.

No. A51/47/116.

H.Q.,

178th Infantry Brigade.

The Divisional Commander has much pleasure in forwarding you the attached letter, the contents of which should be conveyed to Lieut.-Col. Clarke and the 2/6th Bn. The Sherwood Foresters.

(Signed) R. W. STANTON, Major,

For Lieut.-Col,, A.A. & Q.M.G.,

59th Division.

No. 1444/16. H.Q.,
178th Infantry Brigade.
Date: 23/12/17.

To the O.C. 6th Bn. The Sherwood
Foresters.

The G.O.C. Brigade directs me to say that he has the very greatest pleasure in passing you the attached letter, and wishes his congratulations to be conveyed to you, to your officers, N.C.O.'s and men.

Please return letters after taking copies.

(Signed) B. DARBYSHIRE, Capt.,
A/Staff Captain, 178th Infantry
Brigade.

60th Infantry Brigade, No. 456/R.3.
10/12/17.

Headquarters,
20th Division.

I have the honour to bring to the notice of the Divisional Commander the splendid services rendered by the 6th Bn. Sherwood Foresters during the recent fighting at Cambrai.

While separated from my own Brigade, I found myself in command of the 59th Brigade. This Brigade was hard pressed, and the 6th Sherwood Foresters were lent from the 6th Division. Under most trying and difficult circumstances the Battalion came over and joined the fighting line with the 59th Brigade and fought hard for two days, suffering heavy casualties.

All who saw the 6th Sherwood Foresters have spoken to me in the highest terms of their splendid soldierly qualities. I consider that it is very largely due to their dogged determination and fine spirit that the enemy was held back so long.

I should like particularly to bring to notice the name of Lieut.-Col. Clarke, Commanding 6th Bn. Sherwood Foresters. He gave me every assistance and did everything he possibly could without any hesitation or difficulty whatever.

I should be very glad if the warm thanks and admiration both of myself and those officers and men who were with me could be conveyed to Lieut.-Col. Clarke, his officers, N.C.O.'s and men.

(Signed) F. J. DUNCAN, Brig.-General,
Commanding 60th (L.) Infantry Brigade.

20th Division, No. A/6960.

Headquarters,
59th Division.

I have much pleasure in forwarding the above report.

(Signed) F. J. DUNCAN, Brig.-General,
Commanding 20th Division.

14/12/17.

"A" Form.

MESSAGES AND SIGNALS.

To 59th Division.

Sender's Number G.A.542. Day of month 11th.

Following received from 5th Army begins. Hostilities will cease at 11.00 hours to-day, Nov. 11th. Troops will stand fast at positions reached at hour named. Line of outposts will be established and reported to Army H.Q. Remainder of troops will be collected and organised and ready to meet any demand. All military precautions will be preserved, and there will be no communication with the enemy. Further instructions will be issued.

11 Corps.
0800.

Issued to All Units of the 59th Division.

"A" Form.

MESSAGES AND SIGNALS.

Sender's Number G.296 Day of month 11

Hostilities will cease at 11.00 to-day, Nov. 11th aaa Troops will stand fast in present positions aaa 178 Bde. will continue to hold outpost position until units of 74th Div. have established a line further East and in front of them aaa Touch will be gained with flanking formations aaa Line to be reported to D.H.Q aaa Precautions will be preserved and there will be no communication with the enemy aaa Bdes. C.R.A. will report location of all units aaa Addressed 3 Bdes. C.R.A., C.R.E., D.M.G.C., C.M. Troops, Q.

From 59th Division.

Time 09.00.

(Sd.) GEORGE CROSSMAN,
Lt.-Col., G.S.

Copy of a letter given to every Soldier of the 59th Division on Demobilisation.

Headquarters,
59th Division,
B.E.F.,
France.

Now that the time has come for you to leave the Army and go back to civil life, I wish, both personally and officially, to thank you for the service which you have given.

You take away with you the priceless knowledge that you have played a man's part in this great War for freedom and fair play. You will take away with you also your remembrances of your comrades, your pride in your Regiment, and your love for your Country.

You have played the game; go on playing it, and all will be well with the great Empire which you have helped to save.

I wish you every prosperity and happiness.

W. S. KNOX-GORE,
Lt.-Col., G.S.,
for Major-General
Commanding 59th Division.

59th DIVISION

1915 - 1918

FURTHER NARRATIVES.

THE 59TH DIVISIONAL ROYAL ENGINEERS—HEADQUARTERS—
BY CAPTAIN K. NEVILLE MOSS.

THE 467TH FIELD COMPANY, R.E.—
BY CAPTAIN B. C. DEACON, SECOND-IN-COMMAND.

THE 469TH FIELD COMPANY, R.E.—
BY MAJOR W. R. JAMES, M.C., O.C. OF THE COMPANY.

THE 470TH FIELD COMPANY, R.E.—
BY CAPTAIN F. C. SALMON, SECOND-IN-COMMAND.

THE 176TH INFANTRY BRIGADE—
BY COLONEL SIR T. G. COPE, BART., C.M.G., D.S.O.

THE 515TH COMPANY R.A.S.C., 59TH DIVISION, AND REMINISCENCES—
BY CAPTAIN R. J. GREEN, T.D.

Market Road,

Chelmsford,

August, 1931.

My dear Sir,

I am glad that at "long last" I am able to send to you the Supplement of the 59th Divisional Record and also a Notice of the Record of the 177th Infantry Brigade which has been compiled by Lieut.-Col. J. P. W. Jamie, M.C.

I am sure you will agree that it is satisfactory that these two publications have the effect of preserving the record of the gallant services rendered by the personnel of the units mentioned.

Our sincere thanks are due to the Authors, Colonel Sir T. G. Cope, Bart., Captain K. Neville Moss, Captain B. C. Deacon, Major W. R. James, Captain F. C. Salmon and Captain R. J. Green; also to Captain G. J. Edmunds, of "The Derbyshire Times," Chesterfield, whose generous and efficient assistance has enabled the printing to be carried out.

Very sincerely yours,

E. U. BRADBRIDGE, Lieut.-Col. (Rtd.),

late A.A. & Q.M.G., 59th Division.

FIFTY-NINTH DIVISION.

1915—1918.

The 59th Divisional Royal Engineers.

Headquarters.

By Captain K. Neville Moss.

The Headquarters were formed at Luton, in the early part of 1915. The R.E. at the time was composed of two Field Companies, afterwards known as the 469th and 470th.

Headquarters staff then consisted of the C.R.E., Lieut.-Col. W. E. Harrison; Capt. D. B. Frew, Adjutant; R.S.M. Tidnam, and Sergt. R. J. Morris. In July, 1915, Headquarters moved to Radlett, and whilst there two staff changes took place. In November Capt. Frew was appointed O.C. of the newly-formed 467th Field Company and Lieut. (afterwards Capt.) K. Neville Moss succeeded him as Adjutant. In the following March Lieut.-Col. G. B. Roberts, R.E., succeeded Col. Harrison on account of the latter's physical unfitness for service overseas.

Headquarters moved to Ireland in April, 1916, and to France in February, 1917, leaving R.S.M. Tidnam behind to continue the good work of training raw recruits at home.

In France, the Headquarters of the R.E., though attached to Divisional Headquarters, kept in the closest touch with each of the three Field Companies.

In January, 1918, the C.R.E., Col. Roberts, was unfortunately invalided home, his place being taken by Lieut.-Col. A. C. Howard, who left after five months' good work to take over another Divisional R.E., and was succeeded by Lieut.-Col. L. J. Coussmaker. Capt. Moss was demobilised in January, 1919, after handing over the office of Adjutant to Lieut. H. Taylor. Lieut.-Col. Coussmaker and Sergt. Morris remained with the Divisional R.E. until it was disbanded.

The work of the R.E. was carried out loyally and efficiently by its Field Companies, and it is left for an officer of each Company to record its history.

The 467th Field Company, R.E., by Capt. B. C. Deacon, Second-in-Command.

The 467th Field Company, R.E., was recruited in November, 1915, from the North Midland towns of Nottingham, Derby, Mansfield, Birmingham, and Leicester. It carried out its early training at Shenley, in Hertfordshire, under the command of Major D. B. Frew, M.C., R.E., who had previously been Adjutant of the 59th (N.M.) Divisional Engineers.

On the outbreak of the Rebellion in Ireland, during Easter of 1916, the Company was drafted to Dublin with the remainder of the Division, and took part in restoring peace in the capital. On the completion of their training at the Curragh, they were transferred to Salisbury Plain, and in February, 1917, embarked at Southampton for Le Havre. From this port they immediately entrained for the Somme area and moved into the line at Belloy on March 6th, in front of the retiring 6th German Army. Here the Company had their first baptism of fire, and suffered several casualties while engaged on trench improvements behind the front line.

Moving eastward in pursuit of the retiring German Army, the Company spent the night of March 26th in assisting to complete the bridge over the Somme at Brie, thence proceeding to Estrie-en-Somme, where they were accommodated in water-logged shelters, which had been used as a German bombing school.

While in this area the Company went into the line at Fléçhin and took part in the disastrous counter-attacks of the enemy, and still moving eastward in their wake, their time was fully occupied in repairing roads, bridges and water supplies, and searching for " booby traps " which had been freely set by the Germans.

Halting at Bernes, on April 10th, 1917, the Company went into a well-earned rest, and employed the time in the reconstruction of roads, preparing shelters and billets for the Infantry, and training for the sterner duties to come.

wide front, capturing many thousands of prisoners and large numbers of guns. Withdrawing from this position, the Company was forced back, with the whole of General Gough's Army, to the neighbourhood of Albert, from whence they again moved into the line at Gaucourt, and from there on to Ypres once more. The Company was billeted in shelters and shacks outside the Menin Gate, and on the 8th March took part in one of the terrible battles over that area. The shell fire was most intense, and the casualties, in consequence, were many. The Company worked throughout the day in constructing roads and tracks for the passage of guns and stores and in repairing and strengthening German pill boxes, which were in use as forward dressing stations.

Several nights of intense bombardment rendered the shelters outside the Menin Gate untenable, and the Company was then withdrawn to Vlamertinghe for a few hours rest. Two days later they arrived at Locre in a dense fog, and after settling down to a few hours' well-earned rest in this apparently peaceful village, they were suddenly called into activity again by the raising of the fog and heavy shelling from enemy lines.

The horses were got out under the greatest difficulty, many of them being wounded and in a state of panic, and, by the time darkness had set in the once-smiling village of Locre was a smoking ruin.

On the same night the Company entered Bailleul, which the remaining populace had just evacuated. Here, well-stocked shops (which had supplied the various Army schools in the district) and comfortable well-furnished billets were left at a moment's notice, only to be destroyed and looted by the advancing hosts of the German Army. With heavy casualties and loss of stores, the Company moved back to refit, and at length found themselves, on May 11th, 1918, at Auchell, where they were employed, first with the Chinese Corps and afterwards with the Portuguese, in digging a part of the great Army reserve line for the protection of the Channel ports. At Auchell the Company enjoyed, for the first time, the proximity of a civilian population and the advantages of shops, hot baths at the mines, and other almost forgotten luxuries.

From there, by stages, the Company moved North, still carrying out road and bridge repairs, water supplies, etc., eventually going into the line in front of Gouzeaucourt Wood. Several weeks were occupied in repairing the trenches and in the construction of forward posts in front of the existing front line, for an attack to be carried out later. In spite of continued gun fire and shelling by trench mortars, the work was successfully carried out with but few casualties. On September 4th the Company arrived at Ypres and went into shelters in the Ramparts. For three weeks they assisted in building tracks and consolidating the positions east of the city. Owing to the nature of the country, combined with the exposed position of the sector, which was fully under observation from Passchendaele Ridge, work carried out here was somewhat unremunerative; no sooner was a track laid down or a trench consolidated than it was blown to pieces by shelling, and had to be reconstructed. Gas shells were a particular source of annoyance, and caused many casualties.

Moving from Ypres on September 30th, the Company next went into the line at Lievin, opposite Lens, which was then occupied by the enemy, and worked day and night in restoring and draining the water-logged trenches and cellars in the front line. Cellars in the hands of the enemy actually abutted against those occupied by our Infantry, and many were the tales of mines and "booby traps," which the Sappers had to investigate. This was followed by a period of action around Flesquières, in which the Company assisted in resisting the enemy push at this point. From here, the Company moved back to rest at Denier, where they spent the Christmas of 1917, in special training for the Spring campaign.

Moving South again, the Company reached Ervillers on the 30th January, 1918, and went into the line at Noreuil (Bullecourt area) with the Third Army, where the work consisted mainly of consolidating front line trenches, water supplies and the laying of mine fields. After intense preliminary bombardment, followed by hand-to-hand fighting, the enemy retook the line on March 21st, and continuing their pressure, drove forward with irresistible force over a

Moving from this neighbourhood and passing through the towns of Cauchy a la Tour, Warluzie, Frévent, and Anvin, at which places various works were carried out, the Company at length reached St. Venant, from whence three sections were despatched to Lestrem, in order to reconstruct three of the bridges over the river, which had been destroyed by the enemy on their retirement. Owing to delay in receiving materials for this purpose, darkness had set in before a start could be made, but under the greatest difficulties, owing to the debris in the river bed, the darkness and the enemy shell fire, a first line transport bridge was completed before dawn, which enabled the field guns to pass over and take up their positions in full view of the retiring army. This bridge, having served its purpose, was replaced the following day by one of greater strength to carry the heaviest motor transport. The bridge, 70 feet long and standing about 20 feet above the river bed, was constructed of timber obtained from the ruins of the village, and the work of removing the old bridge, clearing the site and constructing the new one was completed successfully, in spite of shell fire, in one day.

The enemy were now in hurried retirement, and the Company participated in the general advance.

A temporary check was made by the enemy near Templeuve, and the River Escaut had to be bridged in face of machine gunning and trench mortar fire, before the advance could proceed. Several foot bridges were thrown over during the night, under most difficult circumstances, in some cases the enemy requiring to be dislodged from the other bank by bombing before an anchorage could be made for the bridge. Actually it was thought that before the enemy was finally dislodged, they made as much use of the bridges constructed by the Company as our own Infantry.

Soon after crossing the river and while the Company was still in rapid movement after the Germans, the Armistice was proclaimed. This came as a surprise to the whole Company, as it had been completely cut off from all outside news for some time. However, necessary action was taken and sufficient stores of approved quality were requisitioned to duly celebrate the event.

From this time until demobilisation, the Company was first of all occupied in removing explosives from undermined road junctions, and later upon the erection of demobilisation camps at various centres. Finally, the company arrived at Dunkirk, where demobilisation of personnel and horses was completed and where innumerable courts of enquiry were set up for the accounting of stores, and when the last "compass, prismatic officers for the use of," was eventually disposed of, the Company was demobilised.

The 469th Field Company R.E., by Major W. R. James, M.C., O.C. of the Company.

The 469th Field Company R.E. was recruited principally from the engineering trades and mines of the Cannock Chase district of Staffordshire, and became a company of R.E. in November, 1914. Training commenced at the Smethwick R.E. Depot, and was continued as a unit of the 2nd line North Midland Division at Luton and Radlett.

Very few of the officers or men had received previous military training, but under the able guidance of Lieut.-Col. W. E. Harrison, the Company commenced intensive training in field work, bridging, demolitions and tunnelling, and quickly formed a sound and efficient unit.

The Division was under orders to proceed to France, but owing to the Irish Rebellion in March, 1916, it was ordered to Dublin. After the outbreak had subsided, the Field Company continued its training with the other Field Companies of the Division at the Curragh Camp, until the Division was ordered to France.

On arrival in France in January, 1917, the Division took over a section of the front line, the Field Companies being attached to various Infantry brigades, with whom they were always in close touch. The principal operations of the sappers were directing, instructing, and assisting working parties of Infantry in wiring and fortifying the front line, improving conditions in the trenches, making shelters, strong points, dug-outs, and machine gun emplacements. Sections of sappers were employed almost nightly in this way. They were also utilised by the Division for special work requiring technical knowledge, and occasionally did work for the Artillery.

The Company rarely remained in one place for more than two or three weeks at a time, being constantly moved to various parts of the line between the Somme and Ypres.

The operations of the Company which stand out prominently are:—

1. The bridging of the River Somme near Brie. The river at this point was 110 yards wide.

2. The Battle of Passchendaele, when the Company was utilised for wiring and consolidating the captured positions. During this battle over 30 officers and men became casualties.

3. Fortifying and wiring the village of Flesquières. Sappers had not completed this work before the Germans attacked, and at night-time were in such close proximity that Very-lights revealed parties of engineers and Germans all mixed up together.

4. Constructing strong points, wiring, and duck-boarding communication trenches to the front line in front of Zonnebeke.

5. Constructing strong points, mine fields, and wiring front line in front of Bullecourt, for six weeks immediately preceding the German offensive of March, 1918.

6. Attached to Scottish Fusiliers to form a counter-attack battalion near Kemmel, when a considerable number of casualties occurred.

7. The bridging of Haute Deul canal and river near Lille.

In one night the Company constructed two good bridges, which carried the whole of the Corps guns and transport over before daybreak. The officers and men were heartily congratulated for this work by the Corps General and the C.E. Corps. This bridge was used for some time, being strengthened next night to carry a load of eight tons.

A heavy toll was exacted during the two years prior to the armistice; 1,000 all ranks had to be drafted into the unit to keep it up to strength.

The Company was most loyally served by officers, non-commissioned officers and men. A true spirit of comradeship always existed right up to the end, at times under most adverse and trying conditions.

It is unfair to individualise on the merits of either officers or men. Many brave deeds were performed; some paid the extreme penalty, others were wounded, and all rendered true and valuable service.

The 470th Field Company R.E., by Capt. F. C. Salmon, Second-in-Command.

The Company, originally known as 3/1 North Midland Field Company, was recruited chiefly from North Staffordshire (Stoke-on-Trent) and the Smethwick area.

Training was commenced at Luton, the Company being in camp at Roundgreen until July, 1915, when a move was made to Radlett, Herts.

In July, 1915, Major C. J. Stewart relinquished command of the Company on being appointed Commandant of the S.M.E. at Brightlingsea, and was succeeded by Capt. (later Major) Fisher.

The days of training were chiefly notable for the lack of equipment and materials with which to practice.

For many months the total "armaments" of the Company was three .22 rifles, and a special drill was evolved for the ceremony of mounting the Guard, whereby the old Guard, after "presenting arms," handed over rifles to the new Guard, and the ceremony proceeded. Rifles were not issued until the Spring of 1916.

Wagons, harness and equipments came along by degrees. The early voyages of the pontoon wagons, complete with six horse teams, were not devoid of excitement. The teams "formed fours" with almost military precision, and the toll of gate posts removed en route made serious inroads into "Regimental funds."

In October, 1915, home service details left us, and were replaced by drafts from Redmires.

Our stay at Radlett came to an abrupt termination in Easter week, 1916, when we proceeded to Ireland with the Division. The only duties falling to our lot in connection with the Irish Rebellion was the construction of strong points during a "comb out" of a rebel infested district known as Irishtown.

Work in Phœnix Park on sewers, water supply and camp construction was ended on our removal to the Curragh on June 1st.

There we soon settled down to serious training, and the Company went through its musketry course. The period spent here was comparatively pleasant, and ended on our removal to Salisbury Plain in January, 1917, preparatory to proceeding overseas.

We arrived in France (Le Havre) on February 26th, and entered the line for the first time at Foucaucourt on March 8th. We had not been in the line many days when the enemy retreated to the Hindenburg Line, and we were soon busily engaged on bridging the River Somme at St. Christ and the River Omignon at Athies.

Then followed many dreary weeks in bitterly cold weather erecting huts, filling in road craters, and making road diversions in the devastated area.

On May 2nd we moved to Metz-en-Conture. There we had our first experience of Infantry working parties and task work. For over two months we were engaged in digging new C.T.'s and improving trenches in the sector near Havrincourt Wood, with working parties of 500 to 600 each night. I am afraid we were not very popular with the Infantry at this time.

On July 9th we moved to the Rocquigny area, and for over two months were training with the Division for the Ypres battle in September.

We arrived at Ypres on September 23rd, and were quartered in dugouts in the Canal Bank. The Company was attached to the 178th Brigade for the attack on the 26th, and its principal job was the construction of strong points in the captured territory. This work was successfully carried out. The Company sustained many casualties, including our greatly esteemed O.C., Major Fisher, who was killed on the Wieltje road on the morning of the attack. His loss cast a gloom over the whole Company. Capt. L. Robinson, Second-in-Command of the Company, was appointed his successor. After a week at Ypres we had a spell in the Lens sector, which at that time was fairly quiet, and our work chiefly consisted in improving the trenches.

On November 19th began a long trek by night marches to the Cambrai area, and from dugouts at Flesquières, work on consolidation of the ground captured in the battle was carried out.

On November 30th the Company played a memorable part in holding up an enemy counter attack. The whole Company, with transport, were marching to take up quarters at Gouzeaucourt, when it was found that the enemy were almost in the village. The Company took up a position, and, although short of ammunition and unused to the use of rifles, were successful in holding up the enemy until relieved by the Guards later in the day. The Company sustained many casualties. For this exploit the O.C. was awarded the D.S.O. and three sappers gained the D.C.M.

We left the line on December 22nd for a period of rest and comparative comfort near St. Pol.

The Company entered the line again on February 11th near Bullecourt, forward H.Q. being at Noreuil, and was here when the enemy attack was launched on March 21st. The forward sections took up a position in a sunken road and fought until surrounded. Its losses that day were three officers and nearly 80 other ranks.

The remains of the Company were withdrawn in the afternoon of 21st, and then began a wearisome trek for over a fortnight until we found ourselves again in the Ypres sector. During the trek we had received reinforcements, and were now actually stronger than at any time since leaving England.

After a few days' work on Passchendaele ridge, we moved with the Division to Kemmel and remained there until relieved by the French Cavalry Division.

Soon after this came the break up of the 59th Division. Although we remained as part of the re-organised Division, it was with great regret that we parted from our Infantry friends, with whom we had worked so long.

For some months we were detached from the Division and worked with Chinese working parties on the construction of rear defence lines in the neighbourhood of Houdain. Although many miles from the line and in comparative comfort, we were greatly annoyed by aerial bombing, and on one night lost 30 horses.

We returned to the line in the Armentières area on August 27th.

The final advance having by this time begun, we had a very strenuous time until the day of the Armistice, building bridges and making road diversions. In one period of 31 days 19 bridges were built, many of them heavy bridges for guns.

Armistice Day found us at a place called Obigies, North of Tournai, with only about a gill of brandy between six with which to celebrate.

Demobilisation took place very rapidly, as many of our men were in special trades, the Company being finally disbanded at Etaples.

Appended is a list of places occupied by Company H.Q. It will be seen that the Company, at any rate, did its share of travelling. During 1918 the transport covered over 600 miles in moving from place to place.

1915.		1917.	
	Luton	Mar. 19	St. Christ
July 26	Radlett	April 2	Eterpigny
1916.		„ 6	Bouvincourt
April 26	Liverpool	May 2	Metz-en-Conture
„ 29	Ballsbridge	July 9	Rocquigny
May 6	Phœnix Park	Sept. 1	Winnezeele
„ 31	Naas	„ 20	Watou
June 1	Curragh	„ 23	Ypres
1917.		„ 30	Watou
Jan. 4	Salisbury Plain	Oct. 2	St. Sixte
Feb. 26	Le Havre	„ 11	Carency
„ 28	Blangy Tronville	Nov. 19	Gouy-en-Artois
Mar. 1	Warfusee	„ 20	Blairville
„ 8	Foucaucourt	„ 21	Gomiecourt

1917.

Nov. 23 Equancourt
„ 30 Gouzeaucourt
Dec. 1 Lechelle
„ 3 Trescault
„ 22 Beaulencourt
„ 25 Moncheaux

1918.

Feb. 8 Barly
„ 9 Mercatel
„ 11 St. Leger
Mar. 7 Mory
„ 11 Noreuil
„ 21 Ayette
„ 23 Bouzincourt
Mar. 25 Pont Noyelles
„ 26 Montrelet
„ 28 Maisnil St. Pol
„ 29 Hermin
„ 31 Ecquebecque
April 1 Le Romarin
„ 2 St. Jan-ter-Beizin
„ 4 Ypres—St. Jean
„ 12 Locre
„ 13 Kemmel
„ 20 Elvertinghe
„ 21 Houtkerque
„ 27 St. Jan-ter-Beizin
May 6 Houtkerque
„ 7 Rubrouck

1918.

May 8 Nieurlet
„ 9 Rebecq
„ 10 Bours
„ 11 Dieval
„ 13 Maisnil-le-Ruitz
July 10 Houdain
„ 24 Predefin
„ 25 Avesnes-le-Comte
„ 26 Bellacourt
Aug. 3 Roziere
„ 24 Wavrans
„ 25 Manqueville
„ 27 Robecq
„ 30 Callone-sur-la-Lys
Sept. 4 Lestrem
Oct. 4 Fleurbaix
„ 17 La Vesee
„ 17 St. Andre, Lille
„ 19 l'Hemponpoint
„ 20 Templeuve
„ 31 Toufflers
Nov. 9 Obigies
„ 12 Leuze
„ 20 Petit Ronchin
Dec. 14 Vaudricourt

1919.

Feb. 1 Etaples

The 176th Infantry Brigade,

By Colonel Sir T. G. Cope, Bart., C.M.G., D.S.O.

My first acquaintance with the 176th Brigade was not till August 9th, 1917, where I found them at rest behind the line at Barastoe. On August 13th the Brigade held some sports, and Sergt. Pool, the well-known trainer, and Sergt. Aveluy, the jockey, who were then in the Transport of the 2/6th North Staffs, produced a good-looking chestnut named Charlie on which I won the Open Jumping Competition, but in the closed Competition for the Brigade, Charlie only got second.

On August 18th the 177th Brigade held a race meeting, which was unfortunately marred by Captain Coe, the popular Vet., falling and breaking his neck. Charlie carried me into third place in this race. Our time here, apart from these interludes, was spent in training and getting fit, as we were being "fattened" for the third battle of Ypres. The Division took part in the big attack on September 26th. The zero hour was 5.50 a.m.; the 177th Brigade attacked to the right of the Division front, the 178th on the left. The 2/5th South Staffs. were attached to the 177th and the 2/5th North Staffs. to the 178th, the other two battalions being in the old English line. At first all went well and all objectives were reported captured. At 5.15 p.m. the Hun barraged our support lines and the troops in them started to come back. I was told to send up the two reserve battalions to clear up the situation. After they had gone it was found the front line was all right, but the battalions remained up there. The following day the 2/6th North Staffs. took over a portion of the 58th Division line North of the Hannebeck, being under the 178th, the other three battalions returning to me in the old German and British lines. My headquarters were in the Wieltje dugout of evil memory. It was a long passage with little cubby holes every few yards. The water dripped incessantly and the stench was horrid. Taylor, the Brigade Major, was sitting at the door of our cubby hole, and over his head was stretched a mackintosh sheet to catch the drips. He was busy writing orders, and his temper was somewhat short after a hectic night. Presently a nose came round the corner and a voice enquired if this was H.Q. 176th Brigade. Taylor replied curtly with "Yes, who are you, and what do you want?" The reply came, "I am General Gough, and I want the Brigadier." Taylor sprang smartly to attention, his head struck the centre of the waterproof sheet, and to my horror I watched the inky stream cataract all over the 5th Army Commander. He was most extraordinarily forgiving about it all, and Taylor did not have to face a firing squad in the early dawn. Another experience from Wieltje remains in my memory. It was necessary to form a large ammunition dump outside, and all one night Clowes, the Staff Captain, was busy organising the job. About mid-night the Hun started to send over some shells, which came unpleasantly close to those busy on the dump; they burst with a faint hissing noise instead of the usual crump, and Clowes kept on saying: "Oh, a dud, a dud." and got the men to continue working. It was not till next day that he realised that these were mustard gas shells, but curiously enough, although no one troubled about gas masks, there were no casualties. We were relieved by the 2nd New Zealand Brigade on September 29th, and we moved down by easy stages till on October 13th the Brigade took over the line in front of Lens from the first Canadian Brigade. This tour was enlivened by various raids made on our lines, presumably to discover who had taken the Canadians' place, but fortunately the enemy failed to get an identity.

We stayed in this area till November 17th, when we were relieved by the 3rd Canadian Brigade, and moved South to be in reserve for the Cambrai battle, which commenced on November 20th.

On November 23rd we arrived at Heudicourt in reserve to the south portion of the salient we were now holding in front of Welsh Ridge.

On November 25th I went up to see the 6th Buffs of the 12th Division, and was shocked to see how thin the whole line was. The men had been in the line since carrying out the first attack, and had suffered 50 per cent. of casualties, and the O.C. told me all the Brigades of the Division were in like plight. This so impressed me that I determined to practice for a counter attack on Gouzeaucourt. On the supposition that the enemy had broken through, I held a tactical scheme for officers on November 26th, and on November 27th we were to have done it with the whole Brigade, but fortunately the morning dawned wet, so we stood by. At 10 a.m. we were told to march across the base of the salient to Flesquieres to relieve the Guards, who had one Brigade roughly handled at Bourlon Wood. The Brigade billeted that night round Ribecourt, and on November 28th took over from the 2nd Guards Brigade in the Bourlon Wood and Fontaine Sectors. The 2/5th Leicesters were attached to the Brigade, and were put in right support.

2/5th South Staffs. on right.
2/5th North Staffs. in centre.
2/6th North Staffs. Bourlon Wood.
2/6th South Staffs. support in Bourlon Wood.

I at once realised that no sane man would attempt to attack through Bourlon Wood, which at that time was so knocked about that it was almost impossible to get through, and I asked General Romer if I might hold the wood with two Companies and move the remainder back to a more healthy position, where they could be used if required to counter attack, as it seemed quite obvious that in case of a Hun attack, the enemy would fill the wood with gas and attack on each side.

General Romer quite agreed, and orders for this had actually gone out when a wire arrived to say that Corps did not approve as they considered Bourlon Wood a most important tactical feature, and the minimum garrison must be two Battalions. I could have cried as I knew what was coming, and if my Battalions broke on the Fontaine Sector (they were stretched like a bow-string), I had no reserves. On November 30th the storm broke, but miraculously the bow string held, but all the while gas was being pumped into Bourlon Wood. The Hun broke through the 55th Division front and captured Gouzeaucourt, threatening our rear. If only we had still been at Heudicourt we should have had the unique experience of actually carrying out in reality what we had practised in a field day, and I have always regretted that this experience was denied us. Certainly no one could have done the job better than the Guards did without any rehearsal at all, but I could not help smiling to myself when I remembered the unholy glee with which the Guards handed over to us, and departed to their well-earned rest, only to be hauled back again.

On December 1st the poor 2/6th South and 2/6th North were in a very bad state suffering from gas; the whole wood smelt like a laboratory, and these Battalions had now had 36 hours of it, so that it was almost impossible to avoid taking off your gas mask, if only to put some food in. The result, of course, was that these Battalions, with the T.M. Battery, had to be sent back to Rue on the sea coast to recover. They left on December 10th, and did not rejoin the Brigade until the end of January; practically all those who had been in the Wood had to be evacuated and took no further part in the War. The 2/5th South Staffs and 2/5th North Staffs, although stretched to their utmost, withstood the repeated attacks of the enemy. Corporal Thomas, 2/5th North Staffs, as related elsewhere in this book, gained the V.C. for his gallant conduct on this day. On December 5th the Brigade was withdrawn to Ytres and Lechelle, but on December 10th the 2/5th South Staffs and 2/5th North Staffs returned to the trenches, coming under orders of the 178th Brigade, but Christmas and the New Year was spent in the Le Cauroy area well behind the lines.

To keep our hands in at fighting, Brigade H.Q. delivered a spirited night attack on H.Q. 2/5th North Staffs with snowballs as ammunition, but were eventually driven off. Some enjoyable rides were had with the 178th Brigade hounds during this period. The 2/6th North and 2/6th South Staffs rejoined from Rue on January 23rd, but to everyones' dismay the 2/5th South Staffs were taken from the Brigade and turned into the 5th South Staffs with the 46th Division. This was in accordance with the scheme throughout the B.E.F., whereby every Brigade lost one Battalion. As a result Brigades in action were like a four-cylinder engine only sparking on three cylinders. The same work had to be done, and with only three units instead of four, constant borrowing and lending of Battalions had to take place. As the same staff was necessary to run these depleted Divisions it surely would have been more economical to have broken up Divisions, which would have released large quantities of officers and men from rearward services, who could have been put to the more useful work of killing Bosche.

On February 10th the Brigade took over the Noreuil sector from the 120th Infantry Brigade of the 40th Division; the 2/5th South were on the right, 2/6th North on the left, and 5th North in reserve. While here great activity was displayed by everyone in strengthening our defences. So much so that the reserve Division was sent up all unbeknown to me and stretched a beautiful new barbed wire apron fence across the landscape. Whilst riding back from visiting the front lines along the usual track one dark night I fell head over heels into this unpleasant obstacle. On March 6th the 5th North did a raid and captured seven prisoners and a light machine gun. The T.M. Battery joined in the fray, and did great work, but sustained a severe loss when Hempseed, their energetic Commander, was wounded in the subsequent retaliation.

On March 10th we were relieved by the 178th Brigade and went into Division Reserve at Durrow Camp, Mory. The 177th Brigade captured a deserter, who stated that the Hun was going to attack us on the morning of the 13th, so our time in reserve was spent in practising counter attacks. We were all ready for him on the 13th, but no attack developed, and we returned to Mory at 9.30 a.m. On March 19th the Brigade relieved the 177th Brigade in the Bullecourt sector after dark; 2/6th South on right, 5th North on left, and 2/6th North in support in front of Ecoust in the first battle zone. Brigade Headquarters at Mort Homme.

On March 21st, at 5 o'clock a.m., the Hun started his great offensive with high explosive and gas shells. He knocked off the gas at 6 a.m., and his Infantry advanced at 9.40. The right at Railway Reserve was quickly rolled up, the Huns having come up the Noreuil Valley, reached Ecoust. The 2/6th North made a stand at the Railway embankment. The 177th Brigade in reserve came up and occupied the front line of the third system, and later two Companies of the East Lancs. from 34th Division arrived and prolonged the 177th line, but there was a big gap on the left. Major Curtis then came up from Dysart Camp with oddments from the band, courses, etc., and filled the gap. The Hun was held up here, and at dusk the 70th Division arrived to relieve us. But alas, there was no one (apart from the few details with Major Curtis, who remained with the 177th Brigade) left to relieve. Out of those who held Bullecourt and Ecoust that morning scarce a score returned to tell the epic tale of heroism. Fortunately, owing to the system by which a proportion from each Company was always left out of the trenches, a nucleus still remained, and the Home Government, now thoroughly alarmed, were not slow in sending out reinforcements. By April 11th we were again in the line, this time at Passchendaele, and were able to look over the ridge we had gazed at for so long the previous autumn. The next day, however, we were ordered to hand the line back to 122nd Brigade and return to Brandhoek, the Battalions getting in by 5 a.m. on the 13th. At 10 a.m. we started to march to Westoutre, coming under the orders of the 49th Division. The Brigade arrived at 5.30 p.m., and at 8.30 p.m. got orders to march at once to Locre. I asked if I could arrange to arrive at 4.30 a.m. so that the men could have a few hours rest; this was agreed to. We arrived at Locre before dawn, and after various contradictory orders we were told to relieve the 147th, 101st and 74th Brigades, who were holding just south of Bailleul. The relief was complete by 7 a.m. on April 15th, 5th North being on right, 6th South in centre, and 6th North on left on Mont de Lille. At 2 p.m. the Hun commenced heavy bombardment and at 4 p.m. his Infantry advanced, broke through beyond our left flank and turning due West marched across the Aerodrome and entered Bailleul. Meanwhile the 6th North, under Colonel Porter, had carried out a brilliant counter attack, recaptured the whole of the Mont de Lille, and established posts on the Bailleul-Armentieres Road. When darkness closed in, the curious position was that while the enemy were in Bailleul, the Battalions were on the far side. The famous Alpine Corps of the German Army had carried out their attack, and as soon as it was dark they pushed out patrols. The patrols put up Verey lights, fired their machine guns, and then rushed up in V-shaped formations, which had a disconcerting effect on the mixed units which were endeavouring to dig a fresh line, and by these means over a mile of ground was gained by the enemy. Eventually the Division telephoned through to say that a fresh line had been occupied by the 147th Brigade just South of St. Jans-Cappel, and that the 176th were to return to Locre. This was easier said than done, as by this time enemy patrols were well beyond Brigade Headquarters, and it was impossible to distinguish friend from foe. Fortunately, I had two machine guns with me at my farm, and by the simple stratagem of firing two belts in the air the wind was put up the Bosche, and it kept him quiet while we got away. The 147th Brigade asked for a Battalion, so I left the 5th North and the T.M. Battery, who next day did a specially good work firing on a farm at which the enemy were concentrating preparatory to a fresh attack. April 19th found the Brigade at Jock Camp, International Corner. It was a lovely moonlight night, and presently a plane came over intent on laying eggs; it laid six well and truly right in the middle of the camp, but as all were lying flat on the ground not one man was hit, save the Brigade Headquarters cook, who, after standing five bombs, thought it time to quit, and the sixth smote him in the hinder parts. From April 26th to May 5th the Brigade occupied a reserve line known as the Ouderdom Switch, near Reninghelst, but did not come into action as all further attacks by the enemy on the Shoepenberg were beaten off. On May 9th the Brigade as then constituted paraded for the last time. General Romer presented medals and made a farewell speech. The fighting part of the Brigade was sent away in two trains to join up with its sister Brigade in the 46th Division. The cadres which were left soon after departed to train Yanks, and Brigade Headquarters moved to Avesnes-le-Comte, and six Garrison Guards Battalions now formed Battalions of the 176th Infantry Brigade. These were employed in digging what was known as the Army Line. On May 25th these Battalions were named as follows:—

17th	Garrison Battalion the		Worcestershire Regiment.
25th	do.	do.	King's Royal Rifle Corps.
13th	do.	do.	West Riding Regiment.
23rd	do.	do.	Lancashire Fusiliers.
17th	do.	do.	Royal Sussex Regiment.
26th	do.	do.	Royal Welsh Fusiliers.

These were soon reduced to three Battalions, the Brigade then consisting of 26th Battalion Royal Welsh Fusiliers, 17th Battalion Royal Sussex Regiment, 25th Battalion the King's Liverpools. Digging ceased and training commenced in good earnest. Finally, on July 25th, we were judged to be fit for the trenches, and took over the Mercatel Sector from the 7th Canadian Brigade. Here we stayed till August 23rd, when the 156th Brigade of the 52nd Division attacked through our lines and captured their objectives. We withdrew that evening to Saulty. Next day we entrained for Lillers. While waiting at St. Pol station an enemy 'plane flew over and started looking for a target. The question came to my mind: What is the correct tactical disposition to pursue. Should the men be got out and told to adopt Arty formation, or should we sit still and hope for the best. I adopted the latter course, and fortunately the Hun selected an ammunition train to bomb instead of ours; but I am still doubtful as to what is the correct procedure. On August 26th we took over from 230th Brigade 74th Division, in reserve near Guarbecque. On September 4th we took over the front line from 178th near Lestrem. On September 11th the Welsh Fusiliers repulsed a raid, capturing two prisoners and killing another. We were in and out of the line facing Aubers Ridge till October 2nd. On that date the 25th King's Liverpools attacked, at 7.30 a.m., Two-Tree Farm, under cover of an Artillery barrage, and captured nine prisoners and nine machine guns. The prisoners stated that their other companies had withdrawn seven kilos. at 4 a.m. that morning, so we all pushed forward and reached the line of the Rue Pecillion with outposts in front by dark. After dark we were relieved by a Brigade of 47th Division. On October 3rd the Brigade moved to the support area, with headquarters at Sailly, and next day relieved the 178th in the line West of Wez Macquat. On October 5th the Sussex were ordered to pass through the Welsh and capture the system of trenches East of Wez Macquat at 5 p.m. They were stopped by machine gun fire and heavy shelling, and ended by relieving the Welsh in our original front line. On October 8th the Liverpools and Sussex succeeded in occupying the old Hun lines East of Wez Macquat, in spite of much shelling; but that night the Hun raided and succeeded in ambushing one of the new posts of the Liverpools and capturing one man of the Sussex. Finally, after much desultory scrapping, this resulted in gaining about a mile of ground. On October 17th civilians came in at 9 a.m. to say the enemy had fled from Lille. The whole line advanced on to the Northern outskirts of Lille, reaching the Basse Deule Canal at 4 p.m. to find the Huns had indeed gone. We took up an outpost line for the night, and next day continued the advance, covered by King Edward's Horse. On approaching Forest Lille the Hun opened with his Artillery. Two Companies of the Sussex advanced and captured the village; the Welsh, meanwhile, had reached the Marq River, and we again put out outposts for the night. Next day, October 19th, the advance was continued at 8 a.m. The Liverpools passed through the Welsh Fusiliers and reached their objectives, the line Templeuve-Néchin, at 3.30 p.m. This was a great feat of marching, for the Liverpools had only left Wez Macquat the previous morning. They accomplished 26 miles in 31 hours, the last 10 being leading Battalion, had to be done across country, with all on at the end. This would not have disgraced an A.1. Battalion, so was especially creditable to the B category men who composed the Battalion. Sunday, October 20th, we again pushed forward, and by evening the Battalions had posts along the Escault Canal near Havron. Orders were received that night to cross at 10 a.m. next day and capture Mont de la Trinité and Mont St. Aubert, so I asked if the C.R.E. could meet me and discuss the ways and means of crossing. After describing the Canal to the C.R.E.—it had banks five feet to water edge, then six feet of water and two feet of mud, the whole being 60 feet wide—I asked if pontoons were available, but was informed these were some days marching behind. "What about it, then?" I said. After profound reflection, the C.R.E. gazed at the ceiling till a brilliant brain-wave overtook him. "Why shouldn't they wade?" But Colonel Lemcke, O.C. the King's Liverpools, solved the problem. He cut down a tall tree growing on the bank and on to the end he tied a ladder, and by this precarious bridge he passed over three companies, which formed a bridge-head, which was invaluable in keeping the enemy at bay while a proper pontoon bridge was built. This took some days, and by that time the 176th was no longer in the front, having been relieved by 177th on October 22nd, who all this time had been chafing to get into the hunt instead of following on behind like, as their Brigadier put it, the tail of a donkey. But it was not to be, for after holding the line for some days longer than strictly fell to them in the hopes of the enemy retiring, they were relieved by the 178th on November 8th, we going up into support and the 177th coming back into reserve. The very next day the Hun retired, and the 178th crossed the Escault and advanced on Mont Trinité. The 176th, after crossing by foot bridges, followed them as far as Peplanque. November 10th found us still on the march, heading straight for Waterloo, which we hoped to reach on the 12th, but the next day we were whipped off our beaten fox, experiencing the same feelings of anger which arises in the fox hunter's breast when hounds have to be stopped from entering some pheasant preserves. The inhabitants of Violaines unearthed some quaint old brass instruments and insisted on serenading Headquarters to celebrate the Armistice. Their rendering of " God Save the King " made the stoutest hearts quail, but I retaliated by a speech in French. After this the Brigade moved back by easy stages to the Lille area, where a Brigade Horse Show took place on November 23rd, and some sport was enjoyed with the 178th Brigade hounds. On December 30th the Brigade moved to Hondeghem demobilisation camp, North of Hazebrouck, and became housemaids to the camp. Our job was to look after about 2,000 men a day and dispatch them to the base posts prior to demobilisation. After a month here we moved on January 30th to Dunkirk to re-inforce the 178th Brigade, who were running the demobilisation camp there, but as they themselves were continually being demobbed, kept growing beautifully less. Here the 176th Brigade stayed to the end, gradually dwindling away to nothing. It was a trying time for the men, who were all longing to be home before all the jobs had gone, and it was everlastingly to their credit that they worked on loyally to the end, Dunkirk being the only base demobilisation camp which did not have a regrettable incident.

The 515th Company R.A.S.C., 59th Division,

by Capt. R. J. Green, T.D.

The 515th Company R.A.S.C., originally known as the 2/1st (N.M.) Divisional Transport and Supply Column, was equipped and recruited through the Leicestershire and Rutland Territorial Force Associations, Leicester, in September and October, 1914. After several weeks training it proceeded to Luton on January 21st, 1915, to join the 2/1st (N.M.) Division, afterwards known as the 59th Division, which was at the time being concentrated in the Luton area. This Division at this time consisted of the 176th, 177th and 178th Infantry Brigade Group. The 59th Divisional Train comprised of Nos. 513, 514, 515, and 516 Companies R.A.S.C., or Nos. 1, 2 3 and 4 Companies of the 59th Divisional Train, and was under the command of Lieut.-Col. T. Hazlerigg, D.S.O. (who comes of a well-known Leicestershire family, and who has been the Commanding Officer of the Formation) from June, 1916, till February, 1919, when he left France for duty at Aldershot.

The Company moved by road to St. Albans on the 5th August, 1915. At this time it was known as No. 2 Company 59th Divisional Train, and was affiliated to the 177th Infantry Brigade Group, which was comprised of the 2/4th and 2/5th Lincolnshire Regiments and the 2/4th and 2/5th Leicestershire Regiments.

Whilst at this station the Company Supply Wagons of the Brigade Group drew rations from the Divisional Supply Refilling Point, Rubber Works, St. Albans, delivering daily in detail to units of the Brigade Group.

On February 16th, 1916, orders were received to proceed to Watford, the Company then being temporarily attached to the 178th Infantry Brigade in place of No. 4 Company of the Train.

While here rations were drawn from the Brigade Supply Refilling Point and delivered to the 178th Infantry Group.

On Easter Monday night, April 25th, 1916, the Company received orders to proceed at a few hours' notice with the

178th Infantry Brigade to Ireland to assist in the suppression of the Sinn Fein Rebellion which had broken out in Dublin. The Company disembarked at Kingstown on April 26th, 1916, and proceeded to Kilmainham Hospital on the 27th.

During the trek from Kingstown to Kilmainham considerable resistance was encountered, the convoy being attacked by rebels and held up on the South Circular Road for five hours, most of the N.C.O.'s and men coming into action. Ultimately the convoy passed through the 7th and 8th Battalions Sherwood Foresters into the grounds of Kilmainham Hospital, where they remained in quarters for a fortnight.

During the period the supplies were drawn under great difficulties from Kingsbridge Station for the garrison, and in addition the Company did valuable work in supplying the Brigade with grenades and ammunition. Later the Company moved to Balls Bridge, Dublin, and rejoined the 177th Infantry Brigade.

On leaving the 178th Brigade it received from the Brigadier-General commanding the Brigade Group (Brig.-General Maconchy), through the Division, a letter of recognition for valuable services rendered.

On May 28th, 1916, the Company moved with the Brigade Group to the Old Barracks, Fermoy, in the South of Ireland, and remained there until the end of 1916. The supplies for the Brigade Group were delivered by Company Transport at such places as Tralee, Killarney, Old and New Barracks, Fermoy, Kilworth and Moore Park, in the vicinity.

In August and September, 1916, the Company was inspected by General Maxwell, G.O.C. Irish Command, and Field-Marshal Sir John French, obtaining excellent observations on its state of efficiency. In January, 1917, the Company proceeded to Fovant, Salisbury Plain, for final training before proceeding overseas. Whilst at this station it was inspected by H.M. the King. Before proceeding overseas the nomenclature of the Company was changed from No. 2 Company to 515th Company R.A.S.C., or No. 3 Company 59th Divisional Train.

The Company embarked at Southampton on February 17th, 1917, on H.M. Troopship Huntscraft, and during the sea journey the ship went on the rocks 14 miles N.W. of Havre, near Cape Antifor, at midnight, February 20th, 1917. After standing to all night the Company was transferred to torpedo boats and tugs, and landed in Havre harbour later in the day. Eventually the troopship came into harbour and transport was disembarked. The following day the Company entrained for Amiens, joining the Third Corps. The Division relieved the 50th Division in the line near Foucaucourt on the 5th March, 1917.

On the 17th March the Germans commenced their retirement on the Somme, and the Division followed them up. The Company crossed the Somme River during the night of 25th/26th March, 1917. Owing to the exceptional bad weather and the complete lack of accommodation, the Company suffered considerably from exposure during their advance, and several casualties occurred amongst the horses.

During this period considerable difficulties had to be overcome to maintain contact with units of the Brigade Group and get the supplies delivered, as supplies were being drawn and delivered on a 19 miles depth.

The Company moved to Roisel on May 7th, 1917, the Division at this time occupying a sector of the line forward of this town.

On the 24th May, 1917, the Division was relieved by the 4th Cavalry Division, and were withdrawn into camps in the neighbourhood of Bouvincourt, subsequently taking over another sector of the line near Havrincourt Wood. The Company was in camp at Ytres.

On the 10th July, 1917, the Division was again withdrawn from the line completely and proceeded to the Barastre Rest Area, the Company being encamped at Rocquigny, from which railhead supplies were drawn and delivered in detail to the 177th Infantry Brigade Group.

After about a month in this area the Division proceeded North to take part in the battle for Passchendaele, which was then raging near Ypres. On 20th September the

Division took over part of the line in the Ypres Sector to relieve the 55th Division in the St. Julien-Wieltze Area, the Company being situated at Vlamertinghe. Whilst in this area the Company ration convoys were working under great difficulties owing to the continuous shelling of roads by the enemy. Several casualties were sustained at this area through the activity of the enemy's bombing raids, the Company losing some of its best men. Owing to the severe casualties the Division was withdrawn into rest on the 28th September, and subsequently relieved a Canadian Division in the Lens Sector, the Company taking up camp at Carency, delivering supplies to the Brigade under fairly easy conditions.

After a month in this area the Company moved with the Division, which was withdrawn to take part in the Cambrai battle, relieving the Guards Division in Bourlon Wood after the successful advance on Cambrai.

The Division took part in the British retirement from Bourlon Wood, and also took part in repulsing the sudden German attack on Gouzeaucourt. When the enemy penetrated the line in this area the Company and S.R.P. was left on the ridge outside Metz-en-Conture, orders to retire having failed to reach them. The camp, horse lines and S.R.P. was subjected to a severe shelling, and orders were eventually received to retire to the outskirts of Havrincourt Wood. During this occasion Major V. D. R. Colan, R.A.S.C., S.S.O., 59th Division, who happened to be on the spot, fetched ammunition in his car, taking it up into the line and remaining there assisting the resisting party. For this he was awarded the D.S.O.

The Division remained in this sector until the end of December, 1917, when they were withdrawn into rest. The Company moved to Ambrines on the 24th and 25th December, 1917. During this trek severe climatic conditions had to be contended with.

After six weeks rest the Division went into the line again under the Sixth Corps, in the Bullecourt area, the Company being stationed at Gomiecourt. The Division was in the line in this sector when the great German offensive of March 21st, 1918, began. At 4.45 a.m. on the 21st March the Company came under shell fire, eventually being forced to abandon the camp and retire to Ayette. The following day it was again forced to retire, this time to Hannescamps. During this critical period there was desperate fighting round Bullecourt and Ecoust, the enemy only succeeding in driving the 176th and 178th Infantry Brigades back a few miles and failing entirely to cross the Arras-Bapaume Road, which was one of their objectives. In this defence these two Brigades were partly wiped out, but gallantly held on until relieved in the line on the morning of the 22nd March by the 177th Infantry Brigade Group, who remained in the line doing splendid work under the command of the 40th Division, whilst the remainder of the Division was withdrawn to be refitted. During the retirement and general confusion the Company Staff Sergeant-Major, with a convoy of supply wagons, was cut off from the Company and was unable to rejoin for a period of seven or eight days. After further fighting, the 177th Brigade, with Company, was withdrawn from the line, eventually rejoining the Division in the Houdain area, greatly to the relief of the Commanding Officer Divisional Train, as it had been persistently reported that the officers and half the Company had been captured by the enemy. During a short rest here, H.M. the King visited the 177th Infantry Brigade, personally thanking officers and men for their valuable services.

Shortly afterwards the Division again proceeded to the Ypres salient, relieving the 33rd Division in the line. Whilst holding this sector the second German offensive commenced, necessitating the withdrawal from Passchendaele. During this period the Company was encamped in the vicinity of Ypres, where they came under heavy shell fire from 10 p.m. to 4 a.m. on the night 10/11 April, 1918.

After this the Division was hurriedly withdrawn and put into the heavy fighting round Kemmel, sustaining casualties amounting to nearly 2,500. Great difficulty was experienced in delivering supplies in this area, the Company being situated behind Locre. On several days the convoys had to turn back three times owing to the intense hostile artillery fire on the roads. Several casualties were sustained by men and horses, but by proceeding in open order the supplies were eventually delivered. Here again the camp came under shell fire. The Division was ultimately withdrawn from the line, and on May 1st, 1918, proceeded to St. Omer, where orders were received for the Division to be reduced to training cadre establishment. On June 14th the Division was again made up with Category "B" men, the following units comprising the 177th Infantry Brigade Group:—15th Battalion The Essex Regiment, 2/6th Battalion Durham Light Infantry, and 11th Battalion Somerset Light Infantry.

From then the Company accompanied the new 177th Brigade when in the line in the Mercatel Sector in July and August, 1918, and again in the Merville Sector during September. Whilst in this area the Company sustained a severe loss by the death of Capt. F. J. G. Smith, S.O. 177th Infantry Brigade, which occurred on the 28th July. This officer had been with the Company since its formation, reporting for duty September 25th, 1914. About this time the enemy commenced their great retirement in this area, the Division closely following up, crossing the Rivers Lawe, Deule, Marq and L'Escault. The Company encountered considerable difficulties in negotiating the roads and bridges, which the enemy had destroyed during his retreat. These difficulties were, however, successfully overcome, contact with the Brigade Group being maintained throughout the whole advance, Lestrem to the River Scheldt. At this point the Division was squeezed out owing to the sudden shortening of the front, and the Brigade being part of the Fifth Army, it went into rest in the back areas, the Second and Fourth Armies only being chosen to go forward into Germany. On the 16th November, 1918, the Division proceeded to quarters in the Wattignies Area, the Company being stationed at Seclin.

A letter of recognition was received from the G.O.C. XI. Corps, expressing his appreciation of the very fine achievements accomplished during the above advance.

On December 3rd, 1918, the Company was inspected by the G.O.C. 59th Division, on the Square, Seclin, and was complimented by the Divisional General and Brigade General on the high state of efficiency it had maintained.

The Company was now in rest at Braquemont, Noeux-les-Mines, having finished its duties, and expecting to return to England as a cadre. Whilst in this area great attention was paid to education, sports and social events.

The Company, as a unit of the 177th Infantry Brigade Group, has taken its part in most of the big battles fought on the British front since February, 1917, and has gained for itself distinction by the efficient manner in which it always carried out its duties.

With the exception of the period January 29th, 1915, to March 15th, 1915, when appointed as Adjutant of the Train, and for two short periods O.C. Headquarter Company, I have always held the honour of Officer Commanding 515th Company Royal Army Service Corps.

Thanks are due to my chief clerk, Sergt. Jenkins, who gave me great help in getting these notes together.

Reminiscences by Capt. R. J. Green, 515th Company, R.A.S.C.

Lieut.-Col. A. E. Wright took over command of the 59th Train at Luton in January, 1915. This officer, who had considerable organizing abilities, was previously in command of the 46th Train, viz., the first line Train, but owing to a breakdown in health had relinquished that command on its departure overseas. He quickly got the four companies of the Train to an efficient state, and allocated to the various Brigade Groups for practical duties in supply and transport. The formation of the Train was:—

No. 1 or 513 Company—
O.C., Major Reading; S.O., Lieut. Sutton.
No. 2 or 515 Company—
O.C., Lieut. E. Pickard; S.O., Lieut. Peach.
No. 3 or 514 Company—
O.C., Capt. Clark; S.O., Lieut. Hartley.
No. 4 or 516 Company—
O.C., Capt. Fletcher; S.O., Lieut. Brownswood.

with Major Jones as Senior Supply Officer and Capt. R. J. Green as Adjutant.

Lieut.-Col. A. E. Wright left us in July, 1915, to form a third line Train, and Major Reading, promoted to Lieut.-Col., took over command. This officer handed over to Lieut.-Col. Hazlerigg in June, 1916, whilst stationed in Ireland.

The Divisional Train proceeded overseas from Fovant, Salisbury Plain, early in February, 1917, in the following formation:—

No. 1 or 513 Company—
O.C., Major A. T. Williams; S.O., Capt. A. N. Peach.
No. 2 or 515 Company—
O.C., Capt. R. J. Green; S.O., Capt. G. Smith.
No. 3 or 514 Company—
O.C., Capt. T. Hazlerigg; S.O., Capt. R. Hartley.
No. 4 or 516 Company—
O.C., Capt. Goddard; S.O., Capt. E. Ames.

with Major A. V. Conlon as Senior Supply Officer and Capt. S. R. Thornbury as Adjutant.

On proceeding overseas we had some splendid young, but restless, officers in the Train, several who had been out before, and on a call for officers to be attached to other units we lost the undermentioned :—

Killed :

Capt. Brayshay, A.S.C., attached R.A.F.
Lieut. F. Best, A.S.C., attached R.A.F.
Capt. Brownsword, A.S.C., attached Notts. and Derby.
Lieut. H. Fairall, M.C., A.S.C., attached 5th Leicester Regiment.
Lieut. W. Wood, A.S.C., attached London Regiment.

Wounded :

Lieut. R. D. Best, A.S.C., attached R.A.F.
Lieut. H. Wardill, A.S.C., attached R.A.F.
Lieut. J. Irvine, M.C., A.S.C., attached Royal Artillery.

Early in March, 1918, I well remember the C.O. giving all us Company Commanders a map plan for a retirement, if necessary, and that we had to rehearse it and report. How unnecessary we thought it was, that it was extra work ; but we did it under fire on March 21st, and then found how valuable the practice had been.

I also well remember sitting on our Brigade baggage and supplies with Capt. and Quartermaster J. Withers, of the 4th Leicesters, outside Hannescamps, watching the Artillery duel. We were both very fed up with retiring a few miles every few hours and hanging on for the two days and nights wondering how on earth we could keep in touch with Brigade. Joe Withers suddenly said: "I'll be dammed, Green, if I go back any further." And what's more, we didn't, as the end of the day saw us tacked on to the 40th Divisional Train, and we stuck on. I believe the rest of the Train had orders to move down the front towards Albert, and got entangled in the midst of a great retirement there.

Printed in Great Britain
by Amazon.co.uk, Ltd.,
Marston Gate.